1/23

THIRTY-THOUSAND STEPS

A Memoir of Sprinting toward Life after Loss

JESS KEEFE

Prometheus Books

Essex, Connecticut

Prometheus Books

An imprint of Globe Pequot, the trade division of
The Rowman & Littlefield Publishing Group, Inc.
4501 Forbes Blvd., Ste. 200
Lanham, MD 20706
www.rowman.com

Distributed by NATIONAL BOOK NETWORK

British Library Cataloguing in Publication Information Available

Library of Congress Cataloging-in-Publication Data

Names: Keefe, Jess, 1986– author.
Title: Thirty-thousand steps : a memoir of sprinting toward life after loss / Jess Keefe.
Description: Lanham, MD : Prometheus Books, [2022] | Summary: "This book is a powerful and transformative memoir that interweaves the author's training to becoming a distance runner, along with her singular, focused research into the science of addiction in the shadow of grief after the death of her brother"—Provided by publisher.
Identifiers: LCCN 2022018983 (print) | LCCN 2022018984 (ebook) | ISBN 9781633888425 (cloth) | ISBN 9781633888432 (epub)
Subjects: LCSH: Keefe, Jess, 1986– | Runners (Sports)—United States—Biography. | Long-distance runners—United States—Biography. | Running for women—United States. | Brothers and sisters—United States. | Addicts—Family relationships—United States.
Classification: LCC GV1061.15.K3944 A3 2022 (print) | LCC GV1061.15.K3944 (ebook) | DDC 796.42092 [B]—dc23/eng/20220509
LC record available at https://lccn.loc.gov/2022018983
LC ebook record available at https://lccn.loc.gov/2022018984

For my Matt and yours

The world is full of painful stories. Sometimes it seems as though there aren't any other kind and yet I found myself thinking how beautiful that glint of water was through the trees.
—LAUREN IN *PARABLE OF THE SOWER*
BY OCTAVIA E. BUTLER

CONTENTS

Author's Note

This is a true story.

I used to think the most important word in that sentence was "true." But that's a little on the nose. Now I see the most important word is "a."

This book contains my account and mine alone of real events, people, and places. Some names have been changed, and some time lines have been adjusted. Any events described during which I am not present are based upon stories told to me by my brother himself or by his friends. This book represents my memories, observations, emotions, research, and, when called for, imagination.

This is *a* true story.

PART I

Part 1

1

Larva

HUMAN BODIES ARE SO MUCH MESSIER THAN THEY SEEM. WHEN you imagine kidneys, livers, hearts, lungs, you might recall those tidy medical illustrations that often appear in science textbooks. They depict each organ as static and matte, with a well-defined color and shape, floating peacefully in the center of a white space. But bodies don't really look like that inside. If you've ever seen somebody cut open on an operating table, you know it's mostly a mess of mixed-up carnage in there. Slick, wet, pulsating. The organs have no clear shapes or colors, no surrounding white space. They look profane, animated, cartoonish even, like any one of them could spring to independent life, walk off and smoke a cigarette at any moment.

I tend to become hyperaware of my insides whenever I'm in motion but not adequately prepared for that motion—during a high school soccer practice the morning after a kegger, for example, or riding a roller coaster after eating oysters. This evening, as I jog along Boston's Southwest Corridor Park in the thick August air, I am very much feeling the heavy wetness of my lungs and liver.

I did not prepare for this motion. It's past 6 p.m. on a summer Friday. I can feel my insides—and my lunch—sloshing around as I run. A few hours ago, I was housing Swedish meatballs, mashed potatoes, and three beers at work. It's one of those hip, alcohol-centric workplaces where the combination of creative work and lowish salaries results in almost every non–department-head employee being hot, interesting, and under 30. (At 29 myself, I qualify just barely.) It's rare for me to get out of there for the week without first getting medium drunk in the chic on-site bar and insisting that my project manager or graphic design partner or, shudder, my boss watch inappropriate YouTube clips with me— maybe one of a monkey that screams like a person or a hip-hop remix of a Fox News talking head yelling at his producers. But about halfway through my Orange Line ride home from the office, my buzz wore off, and anxious dread took its place. Leaving my workplace behind for the weekend meant that it'd just be me and my own exploding personal life for the next 48 hours. And that made my guts tighten uncomfortably.

So now I'm running. It's a desperate attempt to quell the anxiety. This is my main motivation for running these days. I'm not on a training schedule; I don't meet up with friends or local track groups. I force myself into the occasional solitary jog only after all my internal angst has reached a fever pitch and I'm desperate for relief.

Because as much as I suffer through them, there's something irresistible about these runs. I know they will center me, but it's not because I achieve some sort of healthy Zen on my jogs—it's more a simple understanding of the physics of it all. Because I know that while I'm sweating out here, putting one foot in front of the other in this mindless but intentional way, I can beat my overactive brain into bloody submission. The panicky lights will dim, its sharp edges will smooth over. It will all feel much gooier, which is easier to handle. While I'm running, my brain can't obsess. Like rubbing your tummy and tapping your head at the same time, it's just too much to do it all at once.

It's hot as shit tonight. During northeastern summers, sunset doesn't bring any real relief. The discomfort just shape-shifts.

Instead of the sky roasting from above, the pavement sizzles from below. The air feels too full and on the verge of barfing, like perhaps it too had Swedish meatballs and three beers for lunch. I feel my insides churn. I quicken my pace.

I need this goo-brain time today because my little brother Matt is back in the hospital. He goes into a medical facility—an ER, a psych ward—about once a year at this point. This time, his hand has been swelling up again. About four years ago, Matt's heroin use resulted in some kind of infection that made the hand on his injecting arm balloon out like a Mickey Mouse glove. The swelling went down in the hospital, but the hand never quite returned to full working order. Nerve damage? Something I never knew drug use could do. I thought drugs just made you get so high you went crazy and threw yourself out of a window, like Helen Hunt in those after-school specials. But, turns out, problematic drug use doesn't always lead to a spontaneous combustion. It more often brings pernicious, lasting issues that contribute to a slow erosion.

Can't fixate on that right now though. Not while I'm running. It's too much for the goo to handle. As I approach Green Street station, a lean blond woman trots past me on my left. Her pony-tail swishes against the back of her hot pink New Balance singlet, and I catch a whiff of her elegant department store perfume as she breezes by. She's tricked out in all the gear: She's got her waist belt lined with little shot-glass-sized bottles of water, she's got the UV protective baseball cap, she's got the swishy shorts skimming her cellulite-free thighs. I watch her ponytail bob off into the distance in front of me, her perfection shrinking into the horizon, then dis-appearing around a bend.

As you can imagine, I'm wearing the Swedish-meatballs-and-three-beers equivalent of a running outfit. I've got on my knee-length bike shorts, which I require in an almost medical capacity in order to prevent bloody thigh chafing. I'm sporting a ratty old soccer camp t-shirt made of heavy-duty heathered gray cotton, and it's so soaked in sweat that it feels like one of those compression vests anxious dogs have to wear during thunderstorms. I know my face is beet red, as it always becomes during any period of exercise. This makes it look to others like I'm about to keel over any minute, so I try to smile a little, or at least wipe the pained look off my face, when confronted with concerned-looking passersby. I don't splurge on department store perfume, and even if I did, I'd never waste a precious spritz on a jog.

Now I'm coming up on English High School and its wide, empty football field. Behind the campus you've got the Midway Café, one of the best gay bars in the area, as well as Doyle's, a classic Boston Irish pub. The two spots look deceptively similar: crumbling exteriors, thick coke-bottle glass in the windows, creaking floors, a dim air of decay and alcoholism. It's only once you've spent some time in each, among the drag queens of Midway and the off-duty cops at Doyle's, that you understand the respective deals. I always pity the folks who wander into either spot clueless of its context, becoming more and more visibly uncomfortable as they begin to catch on to a vibe for which they were not briefed or prepared.

I was at Midway with Matt a few weeks ago, laughing and sip-ping Miller High Lifes beneath the bulbous year-round Christmas lights and the lacquered bust of Elvis Presley, which presides over the joint from a high shelf above the Wild Turkey. I was at Doyle's recently too, I realize. Just the other night with my parents. Over a basket of doughy onion rings and beneath the watchful gaze of framed photos of various Kennedys, I promised my parents Matt would be all right. I swore I was looking out for him and that they should not worry. This was before he called my mom in the middle of the day when he should have been at work, breathing choppily into the phone, and asked her to drive him to Beth Israel without providing any detail as to why.

My stomach does a gross little dip as I recall that phone call and those onion rings. The meatballs feel heavy. I halfway hope I do throw up. Maybe I'll feel better? But then of course I fear throwing up, always have. Who wants to lose control that way?

Almost at my turnaround spot now, up by Forest Hills and the Arnold Arboretum, a beautiful park maintained by Harvard University where you can look at bonsai trees and feel gently depressed over their smallness. My ex-boyfriend Elijah and I spent many an afternoon on a quilt outside the sweet little pavilion that houses the bonsais. We'd bring Eddie, a fluffy tan mutt with a black snout whom I impulsively adopted from a shelter in New Hampshire a few years prior. We'd bring a soccer ball, some shandies, and fresh fruit cut up meticulously. Jesus, the fruit. He'd always have to cut it himself because I never seemed to do it right. The long tapers of apple that I delivered, for example, made him cringe. He'd want it cut in these tidy little squares that I couldn't seem to replicate. I'd never seen anyone cut fruit that way before, but I'd end up feeling like the fool every time I tried and failed to square the edges just so. My stomach dips again.

Once I turn around, I feel a little pulse of satisfaction. Halfway done here, and I didn't even barf or die. It feels so good to be a winner. To be an athlete. A professional athlete winner! Take that, imagined hater masses. I'm clearly doing fine. Great, even! How could anyone say I'm not doing great when I just met the halfway point of my run and am now returning, triumphantly, to my home, where my ex-boyfriend no longer lives because we don't love each other anymore and where my brother is *supposed* to be living but where he is not currently because he is in the hospital once again as I mentioned and where I think even my dog is starting to feel bad for me? Can dogs feel pity, or is that too much of a B-side emotion? Anyway, right. Winning regardless.

I head back the way I came, with fewer mental distractions as I retrace my steps past sights that are no longer novel. There's the downed tree branch, there's the big pothole, there's English High School again.

Last quarter-ish mile here. With the immediate promise of a stopping point, I give myself permission to push. My breathing gets more labored as my elbows pump through the thick air. My feet slam the pavement, definitely landing too hard on my heels, but not focusing on that now. I want to bask in the too-hard pushing. My soaking t-shirt is heavy on my shoulders like fur. My teeth are catching the hot wind and smarting from the impact. My lungs scream and my heart slams and I halfway hope my ankles break and I collapse into the street. I don't have the energy to do what I know I have to do next, the sleeping alone and the hospital room and the furrowed brows on the parade of doctors who will tell us that Matt's on drugs and if he doesn't stop, he'll die—I just want to opt out. I want to skip back and ahead simultaneously. I want my boyfriend back but I also never want to see him again, I want my brother back but I never want to deal with his health again, I want to be happier than I was before but I also want it to be like none of this ever happened.

When I make it home, I barf.

2

Relapse

I'M STARING AT HIS HOSPITAL GOWN AGAIN. IT'S GOT THE SAME pattern that they always have: small blue shapes, almost like embroidery. The shapes are inscrutable. Round, but not dots. Embellished, but not flowers. Impressively subtle design for a glorified piece of paper in which you wrap a sick person. My brother's chest rises and falls. I look at the green charts on the machines. They are covered with numbers, spiking graphs, little ticks and tallies. They beep and hum but tell me nothing.

I hadn't spent much time in emergency rooms before Matt's drug problems began. I always imagined ERs to be echoing white spaces, clean and enormous, full of buffed marble surfaces like a museum. I imagined they were bustling with attractive medical professionals, their long glossy curls pulled back in loose ponytails, thick-rimmed glasses perched low on perfectly arched nose bridges, biceps bulging tastefully from beneath their short-sleeved scrubs. They'd be all around, I thought, walking briskly, quipping back and forth to each other, looking at charts with furrowed brows. Talking to patients with intensity, saying things like, "Hey. Look at me. You're not dying today, Danny. Not on my watch."

But the ER in Boston's Beth Israel feels more like a basement rec room. The ceilings are low, covered in flimsy tile and rattling vents. The beds are clustered together, forming something like a semicircle. No one talks. Most patients sleep, occasionally coughing or groaning, while family members stare at smartphone screens.

The medical professionals here wear color-coded uniforms: A green uniform means you're a tech, yellow means nurse, blue means doctor. There's a pathetic cardboard codex hanging on the wall, pocked with bubbles in the lamination, that outlines the whole system. The multicolored staffers shuffle around without much fanfare. I watch a green-uniformed young man surreptitiously pick his nose with a rubber-gloved index finger.

I'm impressed that Matt's sleeping. The fluorescent lighting in here is so bright, it creates a little halo reflection ring around the top of his dirty blond hair. His hair is coarse now, tougher than the silken locks he had when we were kids. His childhood bowl cut was so floppy and so soft, like a rabbit's ear. It smelled like straw. His hair was so blond then, too, practically platinum. But over the years the color has darkened, like it does for most people in our family, just as my formerly fire-engine-red hair has recently calmed down with a similar brown tinge.

It's late August 2015. Other patients and visitors in the ER have sunburnt noses, flip-flop-sheathed feet. In the city at this time of year, the summer always starts to sour into an itchy cloud of humid pollution. Despite this, I chose to ride my bike to the hospital from the apartment that Matt and I are sharing in Jamaica Plain, just a couple miles away. I thought the ride would help clear my head, but the filth heat took its toll—my cheap gauzy dress is ringed with sweat under the arms, around my chest and neck. I feel woozy from the humid ride, like I'll never get my body back to a normal temperature, even inside of the violently air-conditioned ER. My bike helmet has matted my hair to my forehead and scalp in weird wet wisps.

The doctors have asked Matt not to leave the ER until his medical triage team is able to find him a bed in a psych ward. Matt has agreed to this calmly. A change from last time. I'm relieved he's not being committed against his will. Not that it matters. Even with Matt's voluntary participation, his treatment plan won't be appropriate for what he really needs.

Matt's addicted to heroin. It should be the most obvious thing in the world. The constellation of pin pricks on his long arms, the clammy gray sallowness of his freckled skin. Several years ago, Oxy-Contin reached the apex of its popularity in Massachusetts as a recreational substance. Now, regulatory crackdowns and market forces have driven many users to the pill's stickier cousin. Heroin is chemically similar to Oxy: Both are opioids engineered to bind to the same receptors in the body, relieving pain and eliciting warm euphoria. Illegal heroin is cheaper and easier to find than the pills these days. It's the shrink-wrapped Canal Street handbag to Oxy's Louis Vuitton.

My phone vibrates. It's a text from my mom. "How is he?"

My parents have been supportive throughout Matt's struggles, and this time is no exception. They live nearby in Arlington, a suburb about nine miles from downtown, in the same house they bought when I was a baby and Matt was nonexistent. Mom is the one who brought Matt to the ER this time and she's been supervising his stay here with her trademark precision. Sometimes I get frustrated, even jealous watching her dote on Matt. But I know that I'll never understand her version of the pain of this situation, what it's like to have a child who's spent so much of his adult life teetering on the precipice of self-destruction. So I try to be a team player.

"He's sleeping," I type back.

"Did he eat?" She asks.

"They brought some food by, but he said he wasn't hungry."

"Did they leave tray?"

"No, they took it."

"OK. Next time ask them to leave tray."

I send back a thumbs-up emoji. I place my phone faceup on Matt's bedside table. I look over at my brother. He's still sleeping. A few minutes pass. Another vibration illuminates the phone screen.

"They really should have left tray."

I think about how to respond, but nothing comes. It makes sense to me that our mother is channeling the hissing, ambient stress of this situation into tinier things, the ones we can theoretically control, like the trays of plasticy hospital food. But I don't know how to react. The screen goes dark again.

Then another vibration. A bright new text bubble sits on top of the older one.

"Can you ring for someone and ask them to bring new tray?"

I feel a strain begin to form behind my eyes. Another vibration. And another. The texts stack high like flapjacks.

"Was it the right food for Matt? Should have been a VEG-ETARIAN tray. That must be why he didn't want it."

"Sorry, didn't mean to do all caps."

"I will call and ask them to bring over tray. VEGETARIAN."

"Why does it keep making VEGETARIAN all caps?"

Matt's addicted to heroin. And yet, the reality of that addiction is so easy to look away from, to make excuses for, to dance around the edges of. Matt's been trying to quit alone and cold turkey, but none of us understand that really. We don't know about the withdrawal symptoms he's experiencing, the small knives pricking upward from underneath his skin, the rubber bands wrapping his guts in heaving knots. We don't know that the exaggerated highs and lows of his drug use have scrambled up the signals in his brain, sapping his ability to enjoy things, to experience moods, even bad ones.

He is trying to quit cold turkey because in the late summer of 2015, legitimate medical treatment for drug addiction isn't really a thing. Matt has tried the church basement groups before. The earnestness of it all, the self-flagellation, the idea that a magic ghost would take away your cravings—it turned him off. He's tried jail, too. Not for long, thanks to our lawyer father's connections and our white Irish Catholic skin. But doing chain-gang community service, picking up cigarette butts and crumpled Burger King bags from the side of the interstate, it didn't quite have the corrective effect that we somehow expect from our prison system. Indeed, aside from a penitentiary, a 28-day stint in a Floridian detox resort, or the healing power of Jesus, there aren't many treatment options for people who want to stop using drugs but can't. Even in Boston, the premier hospital town in the United States. Even in Boston in the late summer of 2015, a hub of the germinating modern opioid epidemic.

And still, even as many towns throughout the United States sank into this crisis, opioids hadn't meaningfully entered the common national discourse as of summer 2015. The daily headlines, the political grandstanding, the long magazine profiles about Big Pharma's crimes and promising suburban quarterbacks getting addicted to pills—those will come a little later. There aren't any task forces or triages or code-athons dedicated to opioids just yet.

No, in late summer of 2015, the message for people with drug addiction was still mostly the same as it had always been. And that message was quite simple: Work hard and kick your habit. Step up and make good choices. Fix yourself. Grab a hold of your bootstraps and for the love of all that's holy, pull. But what happens when you try so hard to lift yourself up by your bootstraps that you rip the ropey tendrils clean off?

❦

That night in the ER, before I arrived, the young doctor on duty could tell that something urgent was wrong with my brother. As with all the doctors before him, he latched onto Matt's depression first. So, the doctor administered the usual introductory mental health evaluation, a Q & A intended to help assess a patient's risk and guide their treatment, which Matt told me about later.

"Do you ever feel restless, agitated, or frantic?" the young doctor asked.

"Oh, sure," Matt said with a breathy regality. Matt liked to take on this grandiose, flip tone when he was trying to annoy people. He let his words hang in the air and did not elaborate further, his wiry little mouth curling into a whiff of a smile at the edges.

"Do you ever feel down, lonely, or hopeless?" the young doctor pressed on.

"Of course," Matt said, cartoony inflection going strong.

"Do you ever contemplate suicide?" The young doctor asked, putting effort into maintaining a neutral and nonjudgmental tone, especially as he reached that last word.

Matt paused.

"Yes," he eventually said with a hot note of irritation, cartoon tone gone, a sense of "no *doy*" baked into his reply. He glanced down at his hospital bed, fussing over the blankets and smoothing out wrinkles.

The doctor swallowed his reaction and nodded without expression, then looked down to his clipboard and began scribbling onto his paperwork. As Matt watched this happen, the heft of what he'd just said must have caught up with my brother. He scoffed a little, like he'd just told a hilarious joke that everyone was taking way too personally. He flicked his arm around the room in a sweeping

Miss America gesture, drawing the doctor's eye back up from his clipboard.

"I mean," he clarified to the doctor with a flash of an eye roll, "doesn't everyone?"

Months later, I'm sitting on the edge of Matt's bed and trying to get him to look at me. He's upright with his head leaned against the wall, staring off into middle distance, fighting to keep his heavy eyelids open. His mouth, small and thin-lipped like mine, is ajar. Light glints off the edges of his slightly gapped teeth. His face is pale and ashen—usually Matt has acquired a golden tan by September, with a high-fashion smattering of freckles over the bridge of his wide nose, but not this year. His brown-blond hair is rumpled. He's wearing a thrift store t-shirt that features a little league logo from a town in Wisconsin. He got home from the psych ward a few weeks ago.

"I told them not to worry," Matt says slowly, referring to our parents. "I don't know why they get so worried."

"They get worried because they love you," I say, pulling my sweat-dampened hair into a loose bun.

Matt looks at me, chuckles once, and then shifts his heavy gaze to the open window. It's starting to rain outside, and fat droplets patter down on the sill. He absentmindedly lifts his right wrist and starts moving his hand in circles, stretching.

"No one thinks you need a babysitter," I say, "but I'm trying to help everybody sleep at night. You know? They need to know that you're breathing."

Matt takes an exaggerated inhale, and then blows it back out. He smiles. "See?"

"Yes, I can see," I say with sarcastic appreciation. "Thank you."

Matt looks down and fiddles with the blankets. "I'm just trying to relax until I can get this job stuff figured out," he says. "You don't remember what it's like to be job hunting. Cover letters. All those ghouls on LinkedIn. It's stressful. It's so dumb and so stressful and I need to be able to just relax without people getting, like, all on my butt about it."

I cock my head and squint at him. "I'm sorry, do you really think I'm being . . . what'd you just say? 'On your butt'?"

He thinks for a second. "You're butt-adjacent."

"Matt I'm not trying to be anywhere near your butt."

He leans to the side and mimics ripping a giant fart. We both laugh. He struggles to pull his body back into an upright position. We listen to the rain outside. I take the lightened mood as an opportunity to push forward.

"If you could call them more, you know? Check in. Then they won't sic me on you as often. I swear."

Matt rolls his eyes. "What will I even say to them, though? 'Hi, it's me, your hot mess spawn who can't even get his shit together'—"

Now I'm the one scoffing. "No, please. Come on, you're over-complicating this. They created you. They just want to hear your voice. Pick up the phone and talk to them about the weather and stuff. Tell them what you ate for lunch."

"I didn't eat lunch today . . ."

"It was a hypothetical."

The rain picks up outside. The warm scent of wet asphalt breezes through the window. It reminds me of school vacation, summer camp, pool decks. I think about Matt in his Power Rangers bathing suit, cannonballing into the deep end with a crazed laugh while the rest of his floaty-clad swim class looked on in terror.

"Sorry but this is boring," Matt complains, shrugging off my concern. "Can we, like, do something? Or something?"

"Sure," I say, giving up on the after-school special conversation. "What do you want to do?"

"Movie?"

"Okay," I say, getting up with a dramatic groan.

I cross the room to Matt's bookshelf. There's a stack of DVDs on the bottom shelf. I scan the titles. There are "Golden Girls" box sets, random made-for-Lifetime-movies with titles like *Fifteen and Pregnant*, the entire oeuvre of John Waters. I slide out a familiar-looking pink case, certain this one will cheer him up.

"When was the last time you watched *Drop Dead Gorgeous*?" I call over to him, smiling. "High school? Hah, remember when Mr. Rolston let us watch this in Drama Club because Lauren Tobin told him it was a Shakespeare remake—"

I turn around. Matt's asleep sitting up, eyes closed, mouth hanging open, head tipped back. This is my first glimpse of a heroin nod, I'll learn later. But here and now, I don't understand that that's what's happening.

"Matt!"

He rouses. Looks around, then to me. "Hm?"

I flap my hands a little in frustration. "Do you want to go to bed?"

"What?" He says slowly. It sounds like his voice is slurring. Is it slurring? "No, I'm fine."

"If you want to go to sleep, that's okay. I'll just sit here and read."

Matt raises his eyebrows and smiles a little. "You want to watch me sleep?"

"No, I want to read while you sleep."

"That's . . . creepy."

"Why is that creepy!"

"Whatever, fine," he says, still slowly. "I'm awake. I want to watch a movie. Let's watch the movie."

Should I stop the discussion here, I wonder? Or do I bring back the after-school special line of questioning? I decide to test the waters. "Why are you so tired though?" I ask with a calm tone, trying not to sound accusing, trying not to sound like I'm doing that very specific kind of insinuating that anyone with a drug history knows well and despises.

Matt breaks eye contact. He scans the posters on his walls: Andrew Bird, Bjork, a weird arty print that he bought in Barcelona, covered in Spanish phrases I don't understand. The print features an illustration of a pretty young woman wearing a bowl of fruit on her head, making saucy eye contact with a black cat. Matt fixes his stare on the cat.

"The antidepressants," he finally says. He looks back at me again, confident now, speaking faster. "They're positively weapons grade. They make me feel all wrung out."

"Well, that doesn't sound good," I say, hesitating, mind racing, trying to find the lie. Do antidepressants make you fall-asleep-sitting-up tired? I thought they mostly just made you constipated.

"It's not ideal, obviously," Matt cheers his tone a little. "But. I'm trying to do what the doctors say. I'm trying to do it for real. I guess that means trying to get used to the new pills. They say I will, eventually."

"How long has it been now?" I ask, soothed by his levity, by his clear intentions, by his once-in-a-blue-moon earnest self-expression.

"Just a few weeks, or something," he says.

I look back at the black cat. "Good. You'll get used to them, I know you will."

"Yeah, I think I will. I think it'll get better."

"Yes. And you'll call mom and dad and tell them."

"Ugh. Fine."

He smiles. His heavy lids have fully risen, and he looks a little more awake. I pop *Drop Dead Gorgeous* into the DVD slot on Matt's laptop. I sit down next to him, and we exhale together. He's here, he's safe. I'm here, I'm safe. The rain outside has picked up, coming down in a steady stream of smooth white noise. I ignore the hard pit of dread in my stomach and I focus on my feelings of relief.

I'll realize later that in this moment, I had him. I had him right there for a second. I held him in my loosely cupped palms, like a pile of wet sand. I kept him intact, protected, for a little while at least.

But wet sand taken away from water will always start to dry out eventually. The solid little chunks turn silky, and they slip through the crevices between my fingers. The more I try to reshape the mound, the quicker it all falls apart.

3

Overdose

AT ABOUT 4 P.M. ON OCTOBER 5, 2015, MY BROTHER AND I BOTH have needles in our arms at the same time.

I've got a 3:30 appointment at the tattoo shop. Yet here I am at 3:25, not having left my apartment yet, eating a string cheese over the kitchen sink and staring blankly at a crack in the backsplash tile. Suddenly I'm struck by the reality of my lateness, like Wile E. Coyote looking down and discovering that the road ended long ago, he's just been running on air this whole time. So I panic and grab my car keys because now I don't have time to walk there. Eddie follows me over to the door, wondering if he's coming. I give him a farewell scratch behind his pointy folded ear, a lousy consolation prize, before blowing out the front door. I inch my car out of its curbside parking spot then speed up Boylston Street a little recklessly, triple-decker homes whipping past my driver's-side window. Some are newly renovated and candy-colored, flying vibrant gay pride flags from their top decks, lawns manicured and adorned with the kind of overperforming bright flowers that you just know the owners refer to as "landscape art." Other homes are more dilapidated, crusted over with cracked shingles that curl up at the edges, chain link fences encasing the properties, patchy lawns peppered with rain-warped children's toys and garbage cans knocked over by man, beast, or wind. At this speed, the gentrification has a kaleidoscope effect.

This is my third tattoo in as many months. Elijah and I ended our years-long relationship for good in the spring, and since then I've been coping by becoming hyperfocused on transforming my appearance as quickly as possible. I had never dyed my long red hair before in my entire life, but now it's peppered with overdone blond highlights—a look which may have suited me at 15, nodding along to the screeching haze of some emo band at the local VFW hall, but now, as I push 30, projects an air of aging desperation. I've lost weight, but in that jaundiced way that comes from smoking cigarettes and eating candy for meals. And now, the tattoos.

My appointment is with Melanie, who also tattoos my brother. Last summer she gave Matt a beautiful spiraling arm piece: cranes and bamboo and a large, red sun right on his shoulder. He plans to turn it into a full sleeve eventually. But even on its own, the details of the bamboo, the folds of the crane's wings—it's mesmerizing. I often find myself staring at it during idle moments with my brother, while we watch TV or drink beers on the porch or prepare snacks side by side in the kitchen of the duplex apartment we share, the same place that I used to share with Elijah. My brother and I had both ended our relationships with our live-in boyfriends within a few months of each other, so one fringe benefit of all that simultaneous heartache was that we got to be housemates for the first time since childhood.

Melanie's done a few small pieces for me over the summer, but now on October 5 I'm sitting for a large tattoo on my left forearm. It's an illustration of a plant called spotted deadnettle, which I found in a 1920s-era botanical textbook. Reading about the deadnettle, I learned that it has two defining features: It can grow under even the most punishing and inhospitable conditions, and it is poisonous. Given my current state of mind, I'm quite drawn to this painfully literal meaning. Luckily for future-me, who will have to live with the consequences of my post-breakup whims, it's also a very beautiful plant.

Once I arrive, Melanie greets me at the front desk of the shop. She never minds that I'm always 10 minutes late. I start to apologize for it, but she just ignores the comments with a smile, like I'm not even talking.

She walks me back to her section of the shop. Her space is filled with framed illustrations and large textbooks about Japanese art, sailors, calligraphy. She's already made a stencil of the drawing that I emailed her. She positions the stencil on my arm and presses down lightly. It creates a purple, temporary outline of my soon-to-be-permanent body modification. I go look in the mirror and we're both happy with the size and positioning, so I return to my seat and prepare to be needled, stretching my arm out on the little leather-bound mini-table Melanie has set up. The bright blue veins underneath my pale skin catch my eye and make me gag a little, as they often do. Veins have always grossed me out, my own especially.

"Where's Matt been?" Melanie asks as she buzzes her needle in a small pot of bright fuchsia ink.

"Oh, he's around," I say, eyes scanning the art on the walls. "We're living together now, actually."

She presses the needle down into my forearm. I wince.

"Aw!" Melanie says into the crook of my elbow. "That's fun."

"Yeah, it's very, like, Brady Bunch. On bath salts."

Melanie moves the needle in a small circle, and hot pink ink floods out in a bloom of color.

"So, the boyfriend . . . he's all moved out then?" She's heard all about my heartache at my previous appointments.

"Yep," I say. "He's out."

Elijah and I met while we were both still in college and had lived together since 2011. But over the years, we slowly grew up and away from each other, like so many young couples do. It's the most commonplace breakup story there is, but since we're both dramatic and stubborn, we collaborated to turn this sad-but-understandable process into something much more painful and exaggerated. It was like we took a plate of fermented salmon heads and, not satisfied by the dish's inherent grotesqueness, poured motor oil all over it to taste. The past year and a half were filled with messy screaming fights that lasted for hours, cold-shoulder standoffs that dragged on for days. Ultimately, Elijah's elaborate, widespread cheating finally gave me the victim complex I needed to end it for good.

"Ding dong," Melanie sings, leaving the "witch is dead" part unsaid.

"He still has a few things in the basement," I say, "but for the most part, yeah. It's done. Finally."

"Weird feeling, huh," Melanie says, her eyes trained on the tattoo.

"I'm getting used to it," I say.

"It'll be the new normal faster than you think." Melanie buzzes the needle in a pot of green. "Anyway. Tell your new roommate he needs to book his next appointment. I still have his deposit for the rest of his sleeve."

I nod along to the hum of the tattoo needle.

To me, most tattooing feels like getting drawn on with a ball-point pen. It's like your elementary school best friend doodling your crush's initials on your hand, just with more pressure and occasional pings of sharp discomfort. Shading and curves come in small little spurts of buzzing activity. But the process is different for line work. With long straight lines, in order to achieve a clean and unbroken look, the needle needs to draw down your skin uninterrupted the whole way. It won't look right if you don't do it that way. So the long, unbroken outline of the deadnettle stem is the most painful part of this session. As the needle crawls down my arm in slow motion, I wince a little. No matter how many tattoos I get, I always find myself surprised to rediscover this particular pain of the long, long line. I draw in my breath in a thin spooling wisp, and then I hold it there, trying not to focus on the pain.

Around sunset I'm back home, forearm wrapped in gauze, unlocking my apartment door while Luke rubs my back a little. Luke is a guy I've been dating for the past month or so, a former Marine who grew up on the South Shore. He's got the type of low-key Boston accent that comes through hard only on certain words: "Sneakers," "New Hampshire," "Darling." Luke has an impressive beard and the sort of elegant, perfectly pointed nose that you'd see on a land baron in an old Flemish portrait.

Luke is also fresh off a breakup, wounded and dazed but aggressively interested in rebounding, just like me. We're perfect for each other right now. The trouble is that we like each other a little too much. We bonded quickly on our first date, an unstructured pizza-seeking mission that culminated on my back porch, sipping sweating Narragansett tall boys and listening to John Prine on my cheap Bluetooth speaker. We forged an immediate closeness that felt like home, and it only intensified the more we spent time together. So, hanging out has become tricky. Trying to engineer a casualness between us is like trying to play a game of musical chairs without stopping the record.

"Careful with that thing," Luke says as I jab my key around the edges of the deadbolt, failing to hitch it into the lock correctly.

"I know what I'm doing," I say with smarm.

"Doesn't look like it," Luke says.

"I'm a strong single woman, okay? They have a whole Netflix category dedicated to people like me."

Luke arches an eyebrow. "Isn't that category actually called 'strong female leads'?"

I flip my hair. "Same difference."

The key finally connects, and we tumble into the apartment, our laughter bouncing off of the still, dark walls. I flick on the kitchen light, turning the tint of the room from twilight blue to warm yellow. Eddie waddles over on his short legs to greet us, fluffy tail wagging. When he discovers we are foodless, he returns to his bed by the back door.

"Where is the whiskey in this strong single woman's house?" Luke asks.

"You seriously don't know where the whiskey is by now?" I ask. Luke smiles and flicks the correct cabinet open, revealing several half-empty bottles of varying brown liquors.

I fish a couple of mismatched tumblers out of a different cabinet. I twirl around to get ice from the fridge, but I stop as something catches my eye. It's the hallway light, shining eerily bright. I didn't turn the hallway light on. And it's not normally on when no one is home.

The next thing I think of is my brother that morning, loopy and disoriented. I had gone downstairs to his bedroom to make sure he was almost ready to leave for work, only to discover him still tucked into bed, fully asleep with his mouth open. I shook him awake, reminded him it was morning. He looked up at me like a stranger for a long moment before he finally started to sit up and pull off his covers.

I realize that I haven't heard from Matt all day. A knot starts to form in my stomach.

"I wonder if my brother's home," I say to Luke. I start to feel prickly and sharp, body buzzing with the beginnings of panic.

Matt's been weird lately. He tells me the same stories twice, sometimes within minutes. He wakes up in the middle of the night and gets in the shower, thinking he's late for work. His texts are increasingly riddled with slurry typos, the sort of super-obvious ones that you'd think someone would correct before hitting send. I sometimes catch him around the apartment, in the kitchen or by the front door, just standing and staring into space, his face vacant as a doll's. It's been like this for weeks.

The antidepressants, he keeps telling me. It's the new medication that's making him act this way. But I don't know. This behavior is such a particular flavor of strange—I feel like it can't possibly just be the medication causing it. Still, it's different enough from how he acted the last time he was on heroin, so I shoo away my worries that maybe he's injecting drugs again. Last time, he'd just sleep all day, I think to myself. This time, he's cooking breakfast in the middle of the night. Heroin doesn't make you cook breakfast in the middle of the night.

I shuffle toward the lit-up hallway, eyes wide, hypnotized. I crane my neck and look down the hallway stairs, which lead to the garden level of the duplex, where Matt's bedroom is. The stairs are all clear, normal, shining their lacquered shine beneath the yellow light. I listen for a second. For what, I'm not sure. But I hear nothing.

I leave Luke scrolling on his phone, and I head down the stairs. I get to the downstairs landing, and what I see next gives my animal panic a little spike: Matt's bedroom door is closed completely. Whenever Matt's home, his door is almost always open, at least a little crack. He usually only closes the door when he goes out.

But I don't feel like he's out right now. I can't explain why. I just know he's not out.

He's not out, and he's not upstairs.

I open the door. I open the door slowly.

And then, a shift in space and time. There he is: my baby brother, blue and unconscious, splayed across the floor. He'd been sitting in the wheeled office chair at the desk, and he must've passed out there and then fallen backwards. His right arm is stretched out to the side. His mouth is open a little, and the light glints off his teeth. His eyes are closed. It is silent. The air around us is still. The sound-less moment of realization feels like it goes on forever.

Then, this guttural scream is coming from my body, and I don't even realize it. The screaming is just there all of a sudden, all around me, sounding like it's raining down from the sky and not coming up from my throat. It's loud, loud, loud, and it's not helping anything.

I don't rush to Matt's body. I don't scoop up his head and cradle it lovingly, tell him to "just hang in there," like brave protagonists do in the movies. I contort my face in panic and yank my body around, jolting to the left and then to the right, before turning and rushing up the stairs to retrieve Luke.

He follows me back downstairs, and we pause at the doorway.

"What do we do," I'm saying to Luke, but he's not listening to me. He is rushing to my brother, beginning to pull Matt's long limbs from the desk chair.

"Call 911," Luke tells me, and so I do.

I hammer the numbers into my phone and press the green call button. It only rings a couple of times before a voice chimes, "911, what is your emergency." Oh my god they actually say that? Am I on SVU or something? Is this a Wednesday afternoon syndicated cable special, or is this my actual life? When's Ice-T coming out to tell me this is all fiction, that I've somehow wandered onto their set, and that the crew needs me to please leave so they can resume filming?

"My brother overdosed," I chuck the words forward like rocks. I'm surprised at how I don't stammer or dance around the issue. It's the first time in Matt's years of problematic drug use that I've ever said anything that straightforward about it out loud to anyone. I guess now that it's literally life or death right before my eyes, the importance of clarity occurs to me. I stammer out our address and the need for an ambulance.

"We need to get him out of the chair," Luke says. I rush over and we work together to get Matt untangled, to get him lying flat on the floor. Luke is driving the lower half of my brother's body, and I'm wrangling the top, shrugging my left shoulder up to hold my cell phone in the crook of my neck. I finally look down and notice my brother's face: gray. His lips: blue. His mouth is uselessly open, not drawing in air.

"Ma'am," the woman on the phone says flatly, "I need you to tell me if he's breathing."

I'm panicking. "You need to send an ambulance!"

The sharpness in my voice gets Luke's attention. He holds eye contact with me for a moment. "Move his arm please, Jess," he says, "we need to get it up further."

"Is your brother breathing, ma'am?" the woman asks.

"Get the arm up, Jess," Luke says, keeping his tone calm, looking at me, "it's getting caught on the side there."

"You need to send an ambulance," I say in a calmer tone as I lift my brother's heavy arm. "When is the ambulance coming—"

"An ambulance is already on its way, ma'am, don't worry. Now I just need you to tell me if he's breathing."

I look to Luke. My phone's volume is all the way up, so he heard the dispatcher's question, and I don't need to repeat it for him. We hold our gaze for another moment. I hope he'll tell me Matt's breathing. Luke knows I'm hoping he'll tell me Matt's breathing.

"Tell them he's not breathing," Luke says.

Panic again, panic again. "He's not breathing!"

"Okay," the dispatcher doesn't change her nothingness tone, "we need someone to begin CPR."

"Someone needs to begin CPR!" I repeat.

"Jess I'm going to do it," Luke says, "please keep breathing and give me a little space. I'm on it."

"Where is the ambulance!"

"It's just a few blocks away, ma'am, it's going to be there soon. I need you to tell me, is he warm?"

"He's not breathing!"

"I know, ma'am. Is he warm? Is someone administering CPR?"

"Yes, my . . . he's doing it!"

I look over at my not-boyfriend. His broad shoulders hovering purposefully over my lanky little brother. I finally get a glimpse of Luke in Marine mode, channeling the life he lived before he met me, which we often talk about in warm safe whisper tones while tangled up in bed. I never imagined I'd see it firsthand.

Luke breathes into my brother's mouth, sits up, and involuntarily gags. He catches my eye and forces the disgust from his face. He bends back down and attempts to breathe life back into a mouth full of unbreathing rot.

I look over at Matt's desk. All his drug-using equipment is meticulously spread out there. This desk used to be mine. I had imagined it'd be a great place to work on my writing. But instead, the desk quickly devolved into a junk repository, a surface upon which to accumulate stacks of unpaid bills and unread *New Yorker*s and unwashed dishes. It reflected a version of me that I hated. Matt hung onto it when I wanted to trash it, but clearly, just as it had for me, the desk had become Matt's receptacle of vice.

So, there it all is: a few vials, a couple baggies, a spoon, a syringe, a Cafe Bustelo can filled with needles, spiraling outward from the bottom like an asterisk. It's all arranged cleanly, geometrically, like a glossy magazine photo. This season's must-have drug paraphernalia, page 25. I've never seen it all laid out like this before. I've never considered the existence of a reality in which my darkest suspicions were true. I never thought it was this bad.

Finally, the buzzer sounds from upstairs. The EMTs are here. I lock Eddie safely in my bedroom, his little face still formed into the same serene expression that it's always making, and then I fling the front door open. For some reason I expect to be greeted by anguished faces that match mine. But the EMTs are expressionless. Levelheaded.

"Ma'am," one of them nods a greeting as he moves past me. I let the front door of the apartment hang open like a flesh wound as they all file in calmly behind the first guy, headed downstairs. Somehow, they know where to go.

There's a cop in this crowd of visitors, too. He comes inside last but stays by the front door. I shrink from his presence. After a decade of dealing with cops in relation to my brother's drug use, seeing one here now makes me feel worried, chastened.

Tall and broad-shouldered, the cop has tools, weapons and other shiny items hanging from his uniform. His eyes are round and sad, like a puppy on a greeting card. He has a sharp salt-and-pepper buzz cut and a leathery tan. He looks familiar—why? Oh, he sort of resembles the male lead from a fuzzy VHS tape porno I saw at a sleepover once. One of the girls found it in her older brother's room, and we pressed play after midnight, immediately laughing our heads off at the undulating music and the corny dialogue. Wait, why am I thinking about a porno I saw at a sleepover once? Your brother might die. Your brother might die! Stop thinking about the porno you saw at a sleepover once.

The cop with salt-and-pepper hair looks at me with those pitying eyes, stopping at the entryway to guard the front door of the house. Oh right, I realize, someone's got to "secure the perimeter." The walkie clipped to his chest fuzzes out unintelligible, bored chatter.

I turn to follow the EMTs, but Salt and Pepper stops me.

"We've got to let them do their work. Best to stay up here," he says to me.

I stop moving. I don't say anything. I just stare at him with my mouth a little open.

"What's your name?" he asks.

"Jess," I say.

"How do you know the young man down there?"

"He's my little brother," I say, out of breath even though I'm standing still.

Salt and Pepper's face falls a little. We stand together at the front door for a minute or two, looking out at the swirl of blue and red lights filling the concrete corners of my dead-end street.

The radio on the cop's shoulder fuzzes. Human voices say stuff, but I can't tell what the words are. I look at Salt and Pepper pleadingly.

"They're still working down there," he tells me. "That's a good sign. If it were going to . . . it's good that they're still working. There's a chance."

I feel my face inflate with hope. I look up at Salt and Pepper and smile a little, grateful.

"Say a little prayer," he says.

We keep looking out at the blue and red lights on the street. This sort of scene isn't particularly out of place on my block. The cops are a common fixture here, often showing up in reaction to break-ins and petty crimes, but this is the first time that it's me who's summoned the swirl. I feel embarrassed, suddenly overwhelmed by the imagined judgment of others. I think of my neighbors, peeking out their windows at the scene, wondering what's going on, whispering theories to each other with their faces all crumpled up.

A little prayer. What's a little prayer I know—Hail Mary? Blessed is the fruit of thy womb, Jesus. The sound of these words, the roundness of the words "thy womb," used to soothe me as a child. It's starting to soothe me now. Pray for us sinners, now and at the hour of our death—wait, is this the hour for Matt? Is he going to die? Is this when it finally happens? I've dreaded this moment for so long, but sitting on top of that dread like a mother hen didn't prepare me at all for what comes after it hatches into reality. I'm not ready. I'm jinxing it all with this prayer, I have to stop praying. I try to just concentrate on wishing really, really hard that everything will be okay.

The EMTs are administering naloxone to my brother right now. Naloxone is a simple, safe medication that can reverse the effects of an opioid overdose. When naloxone enters the body, either by injection or through a nasal spray, it heads straight for the brain receptors where the opioid is latched like a leech, and it yanks the opioid off of those receptors with a quickness. This process allows an overdosing person's body to remember to start breathing again, turning their blue edges warm and fleshy again, saving their life in just a few minutes. That is, when it's administered in time. Timing is everything.

You'd think everybody would know about naloxone. Especially the loved ones of drug users. But I didn't know.

Matt's drug use had dragged on for years, but the countless social workers and medical doctors and shrinks and court officials involved in Matt's situation only ever offered me and my family pitying hand pats and Narcotics Anonymous pamphlets. They encouraged Matt to find redemption, to recover, to kick his habits and create a substance-free life. They encouraged him to stay alive. They were short on practical details.

Five minutes go by. Maybe 10? 40?

An EMT emerges from downstairs. He must be in charge, I deduce, just based on his age and elder-statesman aura.

He scans the room, and our eyes meet. His brow furrows apologetically. My heart starts to slam. My mind starts making excuses: Maybe Matt's just brain dead, maybe he'll just need his arm sawed off, maybe anything other than what I already know.

It feels like our eyes have been locked for an hour. His face, apologetic. My face, pleading. Pleading. I'm pleading, pleading, pleading, over the invisible airwaves; I've never believed in spirits or angels, I forget how to believe in God, but right now I'm trying, oh my God I'm really trying to beg some invisible force to please let this EMT give me the news that my brother is alive.

The EMT walks closer to me, his work boots echoing on the bamboo flooring. He looks at me and says, with a regretful head shake, "No."

No. That's what it comes down to. It's just a no, after all that.

I fall down, my legs collapsing in segments onto the ground like a dropped heap of sticks. They thud and collect on the floor, one edge at a time, as Luke tries to pull me up on my feet. I feel like I did when I was a kid and having a full-body hissy fit, my parents trying to stand me on my feet while I willed my legs to be goo, Jell-O, formless and incapable of supporting my weight. Except now it's the opposite: I'm trying to stand, I'm trying to make my body behave, but it can't. It won't.

"I need you to think about standing up," Luke tells me.

I scream, I cry, barely noticing my own sounds. Screaming is the default now. I hang from Luke listlessly.

34

"I know," he replies calmly to my screams. "I just need you to try to stand up. Then we'll go and sit down."

I eventually manage to buckle my knees into place, and Luke takes me into the living room. I sit in there and scream some more for a while. The screams melt into wails, the wails into whimpers. The EMTs shuffle around in the background, zipping bags, rustling supplies.

A new man walks into the apartment through the open front door. He's got a little leather book. People on the scene, including Salt and Pepper, nod to him knowingly. I infer that he's a detective of some kind. Gelled black hair, floppy khaki trousers, shiny shoes. He is wearing a shirt that is so flowy, so lavender—it's a blouse, really. Where did he buy that fucking thing. Did he wander into the women's section at Kohl's by accident?

The detective comes into the living room, stands in front of me, and extends his arms in a little mini stretch. Then he flips open his notebook.

He does not greet me. He does not identify himself to me. He just says, without looking up from his notebook, "Name?"

"Jess. Jessica," I stammer.

"You the sistah?" His Boston accent sounds performative, swaggering, like that of so many thick-necked soccer coaches I've hated in my life. "You called 911?"

"Yes."

He nods a little. He scribbles on his pad. He scans me up and down.

"Yeah, so listen: Did yuh bruthah come into a lotta of money lately? I mean, there's *a-lawta* drugs down there," he says to me with what seems almost, I think, like a laugh.

"What? I . . . I don't know, really. No. No, I don't think so. I can't imagine, no."

"Right, right," he fills the air with these words as he writes his notes. "What about visitors? Anybody here with him today?"

"I don't know. I wasn't home. I don't know. I came home and I found him."

"Okay," he says, annoyed. He keeps writing in his notebook as he turns and walks away from me absentmindedly.

I'm waiting for someone, anyone, in this group of people to say something to me like, "I'm so sorry, how terrible." But it all feels like a business transaction at this point. People start to pack up, they have sidebar conversations about other things. No one's looking at me. The EMTs are fumbling with their gear. I wonder if someone's going to hand me some paperwork, but no one does.

I step out onto the back deck. I have to call my parents. It's weird to already be living in the reality where Matt's dead while they are not. I feel jealous for a split second. I dial their landline, the same phone number we've had since Matt and I were children.

"Hello," my mother answers.

I breathe into the receiver.

"Hello?"

"It's Jess," I eke out. She hears the strain, and her tone comes down several octaves.

"What . . ." she starts.

My voice twists thickly as I start to cry. I build my brother's name into the noises. I say, "Matt."

She understands immediately. We've all been waiting for this. She drops the phone and wails. My father's panicked yelling joins hers. I hear it all in booming echoes from their cordless phone's position on the floor.

Now all that's left for the emergency response team to do is the worst thing of all: bring my brother's lifeless body upstairs and out to their ambulance, full of its defibrillators and its bandages and its tools of hope. This task will be tough, logistically, because the front hallway of our apartment is narrow like a bowling lane. Bringing in furniture, wheeling out bicycles, it's all a pain with this little narrow hallway. It requires backing up and re-angling, strategizing. And it's the same thing with my brother's body bag. The EMTs are having a hard time getting Matt's six-foot-plus frame around the corners. It's like watching inelegant movers angle a mattress. I don't know why I'm seeing this, but I am seeing it. I had asked the crew of professionals to alert me when this moment would come so I could remove myself from the house and not have to watch, but it's business as usual for them. Someone forgets to liaise with the proper coworker. My request gets lost in the shuffle. I wonder if there's a feedback card I could fill out.

The bag crinkles on its way out. The twill ribbing of the body bag rubs against the nylon straps on the gurney, and the friction creates a sound that makes me feel like I'm going to throw up. I think about Matt's round red sun while the body bag goes. I'm not going to see it again, I realize.

One night when I was three years old, my parents came into the bedroom after my bedtime and flicked on the round too-yellow light. It was rarely a good sign when that light came on in the middle of the night. It usually meant that something bad had happened or someone was about to be in really big trouble.

My mother's eye makeup was smudged. My father seemed stiff, awkward. They sat down on my bed and told me that Nana, my mother's mother, had just died. I understood that they were sad and that I should be, too, but I didn't fully comprehend the details of what they were saying. They told me it was a heart attack, but I got this part muddled within a toddler dream. Because now whenever I think about my Nana dying, I don't think, "it was a heart attack." I think of an image I must have created later that night in my dreaming child-mind: My Nana is laying on her side on the couch, in the living room of my grandparents' split-level home. She's wearing the breezy, powder blue chiffon gown that I had seen her wearing in my favorite photo of her but had never actually seen her wear in reality. She then rolls herself off the couch, across the area rug, and into the television set. When she hits the set, it explodes. And then she dies.

That's how I honest to God thought she died for years. My brain told me it happened that way, and even as I started to grow up and learn it was illogical and unlikely, I still held onto it as true in some way.

I used to think this sort of self-delusion was a hallmark of childhood, of underdevelopment, of being small and stupid and not really knowing anything about anything. But now, even as an adult, my brain invents all sorts of weird circumstances to trick itself, to comfort and protect itself. For example, I know my brother died of a drug overdose on October 5, 2015. I know he was lying on the floor when I found him, having fallen backwards in that office chair. I know that the CPR and the naloxone did not work. I know rigorous efforts were made, and he was not saved. I know this to be true. But sometimes, my brain tells me that Matt just floated away, peacefully and all at once, his body wholly disappearing from planet Earth without a trace. Here one minute, gone the next. Never blue, never gray, never slack-jawed and unconscious and emanating a rotten cloud of air from his unbreathing mouth. Here one minute and then gone. Simple.

Those first several nights after Matt's death, I sleep on the living room couch at my parents' house, a heavy afghan on top of me like a straitjacket. Sometimes my mom joins me on the couch. Eddie keeps watch from the corner, occasionally licking his paws.

Each night, I wake up every few hours to my arm throbbing in pain. It feels like someone held my arm in an oven, like there should be strings of steam emanating from my skin. My new tattoo, this big ink-filled flesh wound, hurts so much more than usual.

I have many tattoos, and I consider myself proficient at healing them at this point. I know the drill. Wash it with soap, apply a little Aquaphor if you must, but mostly just leave it alone and resist the temptation to pull off the jagged, scabby flakes as the inked-up skin heals.

This time, though, for the first time ever, my tattoo doesn't heal right. When the scab flakes clear, about two weeks after October 5, the piece doesn't look great. The long brown stem of the plant has unnatural-looking striations, sections where the color didn't take correctly, didn't absorb low enough into my epidermis to render it permanent. It bailed on me.

A few months later, I'll go see Melanie for a new piece and to touch up my arm. I'll be sheepish about how poorly the arm art has healed. I'll stammer about how I really tried to leave it alone and keep it clean and go easy on the Aquaphor but it was always throbbing and always hot, extremely hot like a third-degree burn, and it stung, and I wondered what was wrong, wondered so much while I internally panicked and ran a million nightmare scenarios a minute through my stilted mind but didn't actually do anything. I can't believe I didn't do anything. How could a person be so stupid?

Melanie will look at me with soft eyes and wait for me to trail off, half-formed tears ringing the bottoms of my eyelids like moons.

"When your body is under duress, it can't heal itself," she will say.

And then, the relief will be immediate. I will find this concept so soothing that I'll want to hug her and cry into her chest forever, make her my mother and live with her, never go another minute without hearing her say a nice thing like that.

It's all okay, I'll think to myself, I didn't fuck it up. It's just all this duress.

4

Aftermath

MY DAD PULLS HIS ANCIENT TOYOTA CAMRY UP TO THE CURB
out front. I'm in the backseat. Since the overdose, I've been under
my parents' care. I'm staying in my old childhood bedroom, riding around in their cars, a 29-year-old teenager. I'm sullen and
slouching, my seat belt high on my neck, while I scroll on my
phone, taking in a social media stream of selfies and apple-picking
excursions from the people in my feed who are just having a nice
normal autumn. A sharp, tannic swell of envy rises up in my throat
like bile.

The funeral home looks like just that: a house, a homey house,
with curtains and a driveway and a nice lawn, a home where indeed
a family might live. I think this is supposed to comfort people, but
to me, the illusion just makes things worse. More menacing, less
trustworthy. The Victorian rooms with their overstuffed furniture,
gold-encased tissue boxes on every surface, heavily perfumed air
masking the smell of the embalming fluids used downstairs. It's
like when a dream about your old elementary school suddenly shifts
into a nightmare. Everything looks right, but it doesn't *feel* right.
Someone's tricking me. Something's wrong.

This particular funeral home is one I've spent time in since I
was small—many a grandparent and great uncle and family so-
and-so have had their services here. These services always followed

the traditional Catholic schedule of events. First, a long wake, 4 to 7 p.m. the night before the funeral, during which the surviving family stands in a long gloomy line, the formation awkwardly bending at the edges of the small room in order to accommodate everyone, shaking hands and accepting condolences next to the trussed-up body in its open casket. Then, bright and early the next morning, you do your funeral mass. You begin at the funeral home, and even though the church is right across the street, you still load the whole family up in the shiny black limousines, driving in a long square around the traffic-congested streets of the block, only to be dropped off with fanfare precisely 50 yards from where you started. After the funeral mass, it's back into the shiny black limousines, and this time you're carted maybe an eighth of a mile over to a cemetery that's visible from the church. After the cemetery portion, you're technically done, from the funeral home's point of view. Maybe the family goes on to congregate somewhere else, eat some cold cuts, but that's an independent event. Wake, funeral, cemetery. Bing bang boom.

I recall some not-great family experiences with this funeral home. When my grandmother died a few years earlier, my dad and his siblings selected a fine oak casket for her. It was matte, with a natural grain to the wood. The funeral director nodded along with their choices, validating them with a somber and respectful smile. A couple days later, we showed up at her wake, and there was Grandma, nestled among the flower arrangements, all laid up in a heavily lacquered, powder blue casket. It was so tackily shiny it almost looked plastic—surely it couldn't have been plastic? Do they lay people to rest inside plastic? It looked like we were burying Priscilla Presley. Luckily, they managed to get Grandma switched into the more tasteful casket my family had actually chosen in time for the funeral itself.

Walking into this sickly familiar building, this time with the funeral of a 26-year-old gay drug user on the agenda, I'm prepared for a whole new level of wriggling, dry-mouthed discomfort.

James is the funeral director. My dad has known his family for years. James is about 10 years younger than my dad, late 40s I'd guess. He greets us at the doorway, his round reddened face shining, his wet eyes orb-like. His crisp white shirt collar is too tight for his neck, but he's got it buttoned up to 11 regardless, creating an unflattering skin bubble at the top of the fabric.

James reaches out for solemn handshakes. He ushers us into one of the home's sitting rooms. We each take a perch on a large regal couch made of a stain-retardant woven fabric that feels like it's made of a million tiny zippers.

My parents are looking stricken. So as James opens up his leather folio and begins with some introductory questions, I jump in right away.

"We don't want anything too Catholic," I interject quickly and awkwardly. "But we want to, you know, *do* something. A funeral. A ceremony." It occurs to me that I'm still talking for some reason and should probably stop. "Like a funeral . . . ceremony."

James makes eye contact. His face strains for empathy. "Sure. There are, of course," he says, unsheathing paper after paper from his leather folio with an almost sultriness, "many options."

My dad jumps in, offering that the chapel in the Mount Auburn Cemetery would be a nice place to hold the service. James nods, with an "okay, sure" sort of expression on his face. Without the structure of the usual bing-bang-boom, he seems a little lost.

As talk turns to who will be presiding over the funeral ceremony, James casts his eyes down, consulting his papers with increasing concern, then excuses himself. He returns from his office a few moments later with a single fresh slice of paper. James hands it to me with a grimace.

The piece of paper features a head shot of a slick, blond, well-coiffed preacher man, dressed in a blue suit and shiny tie. He looks so different from the wrinkled faces and tight collars of the Catholic priests who are so familiar to me. I scan the paper, which is basically a large business card touting this man's fuzzy credentials and years of experience. I notice there's some small print at the bottom. It says, *Willing to do difficult/nontraditional ceremonies (murders, suicides, etc.).*

"Just someone to consider," James says.

My parents don't say anything. I think what I end up saying is, "Oh. Okay."

Murders, suicides, et cetera. The phrase rattles around in my head while James starts asking about Matt's remains. Cremation, we've all agreed.

"Great," James nods, shuffling his paperwork. "Do you intend to keep them, or to spread them?"

My parents and I exchange puzzled glances. We haven't really discussed it, but I feel like they want me to say something. "Spread them," I volunteer, after trying and failing to imagine an urn on my parents' mantle, a framed photo of Matt beside it, like he had been a beloved Golden Retriever. No.

"Okay," James continues. "So the ashes will be delivered to you in a, um," his eyes are scanning the wallpaper. "It's a bag. A green, plastic bag that's—"

"A . . . bag?" I repeat. I must've misheard. When you cremate a loved one, they are returned to you in a smooth silver canister or a filigreed bronze receptacle, and then you take that thing to the seaside and open it gently, and the ashes are whipped up by a single gust of glorious wind and carried off into the sea while a single tear streams down your face. I've seen movies, okay?

"Yes, it's standard," James says.

"Well, what about an urn or something?" Whether we're spreading the ashes or not, I would prefer to receive my brother of 26 years in a more dignified vessel than something designed to hold bologna sandwiches.

"Oh sure," James says, the manufactured empathy eyes resurfacing, "but if you're just going to *spread* them . . ."

"Yeah," I interrupt, making the upsell he didn't even try for, unless this approach is actually a masterpiece of reverse psychology. "We'll want the urn."

When we're finished with the planning and the clipboards and my parents have written the first deposit check, we make moves to leave. I stand up from the zipper couch, the seat cushions making a mechanical squeak as I stand.

"Oh! Almost forgot," James chirps, as my parents walk toward the front door. He roots around in his giant trouser pocket. James's hand emerges clutching a plastic bag covered in thick orange stripes and biohazard graphics. He hands the bag to me. Inside are the plug earrings my brother was wearing when he died. James grimaces at me one last time.

Murders, suicides, et cetera.

I turn and follow my parents.

The bill from the funeral home arrives at my parents' home by mail before we've even received notice that Matt's cremains are ready to be picked up. Matt's cremains will sit in the funeral home basement for months, among the formaldehyde and the stretched corpses and the tools and the trash, because no one bothered to let us know they were there and we were all too catatonic to call and ask. The bill is for $6,000.

45

I grew up Catholic on a pretty multiplatform level. I attended church most Sundays, plus Catholic high school and a regular schedule of baptisms, first communions, and funerals. So I've talked to a lot of priests—in classrooms ("Will you read on from verse 18, Jessica?"), after mass ("Did you enjoy our *Lord of the Rings* homily today, Jessica?"), in the confessional ("Are you sure there's nothing else you'd like to tell me, Jessica?"). But I never received a telephone call from a priest until a few nights before the funeral while eating pizza on my friend Colleen's couch. Colleen and her husband Tyler recently bought an apartment near Davis Square in Somerville, down a leafy bike path from the main thoroughfare, and I find myself spending more and more time in their perfectly executed world of adulthood as mine crumbles around me.

Davis Square used to be rougher. But these days, it's a gold standard neighborhood of Boston gentrification. Its storefronts are increasingly occupied by quirky gift shops, vegan burrito joints, hip bars whipping up mixed drinks that require proper tools to make rather than just a soda gun and a jaunty angle. Some old standards survive: Mike's Food & Spirits, the indie movie theater. Colleen and Tyler's is just a few blocks away from Sligo, one of my father's favorite sticky Irish dives.

Colleen and Tyler are my only married friends. Rather than renting some renovated old dump like the rest of us, they've recently purchased an apartment in a new building with finely sanded banisters and fresh blue paint. Even their couch has a distinctly adult feeling. The cushions are just a little bit plusher, the stitching just a little closer together, all those finer details that add up to a rare phenomenon for people our age: It wasn't manufactured by IKEA or purchased on Craigslist.

Just a few months ago I was crying on Colleen's grown-up couch about my breakup. I heaved snotty sobs, mourning the loss of my relationship even though it was the right time for it to finally dissolve. This time, my loss felt so much scarier. I couldn't even sob because I didn't know where to start. The breakup felt awful yet business-as-usual, a disappointment and a disruption— not a hole, like the loss of my brother. Not a dark void with no bottom or top.

Colleen wrangled our friends to come over and sit with me. It's like a party, but instead of being fun, it sucks. I ate my pizza in robotic bites, feeling the grease slide down my gullet and into my stomach, dripping down around the sides of the thick painful emptiness that had taken up permanent residency in my gut.

To distract from the emptiness, I'm performing a reenactment of my family's afternoon at the funeral home. The bit gets quite animated, and my friends humor me with laughs and gasps at all the right times. We talk about the funeral: what would be good for Matt, what he'd like. It's hard for me to imagine Matt wanting a funeral at all. He was always a fan of leaving parties with an Irish good-bye. Why lavish a bunch of attention on his departure now?

I felt stumped, especially about who'd be appropriate to emcee the event. Certainly not Mr. Murders, Suicides, Et Cetera. But who else?

"He's an old family friend," my friend Paul says about Father Flaherty as he airdrops contact information to my phone. "He's done weddings, funerals, all of it for us." Registering the skepticism on my face, he adds, "He's not a dick."

It's the closest I can get to a positive Yelp review, so I decide to give him a chance. Paul says he'll ask Father Flaherty to give me a call tomorrow.

Receiving a phone call from a priest on my iPhone feels wrong. It's like seeing the employees of Boston's historical tours, still dressed in their period garb, taking smoke breaks or waiting for the bus. An anachronism, a glitch in the matrix. To comfort myself, I imagine Father Flaherty within a bland stucco room, calling me from an old-fashioned telephone wired to the wall, sitting on an uncomfortable twin bed beneath a stark single wooden cross as he speaks to me.

"Hello, Jessica. Paul's told me all about you," Father Flaherty says warmly.

I steel myself against the kindness, suspicious. I start barking orders almost immediately. "We don't want anything too Catholic," I say, my new catchphrase.

"Okay," Father offers politely.

"Matt was gay. He used drugs. He didn't exactly feel welcome at church." I'm being a little mean, I'm surprised to realize, as the words come out of my mouth.

Father Flaherty inhales heavily on his end of the old-timey receiver I pictured in my mind. "This service . . . it's a chance to celebrate your brother's life, and the joy he brought to others. But it's also about your family, your parents—it's about you. We can make the service respectful to Matt's wishes and life, but you should also think about what would soothe your family to hear. What would help them. Because this is for them, too."

I had never thought about that, not even for a moment. I was so obsessed with making the service true to Matt, I wasn't exactly thinking of the fate of the survivors—my parents, his friends, myself. My guilty obsession with what Matt would have or would not have liked, from which Bob Dylan songs we'd play to what venue we'd book to what I would wear, what he'd think was cool and what he'd think was corny, had been fueling my fury-filled interactions with basically everyone this week besides inner-circle friends and family until right this moment. I feel a bit of pressure release.

With this perspective in mind, the priest inside my iPhone and I go on to review some finer run-of-show details (introductory prayer: yes; Eucharist: no), and I start to feel quite comfortable with Father Flaherty.

I used to like priests, after all. Church and church-adjacent events always felt safe to me as a child. But as a teenager, the fine print of Catholicism began to reveal itself. Premarital sex, depression, queer attraction, a curiosity about one's own body, so much of the stuff of coming of age—it was all hell-worthy, turns out. Priests stopped feeling like fathers and started feeling like Big Brothers, exacting agents of a surveilling God who was always watching, waiting for you to fuck up even just a little so that he might exact his punishment.

And then of course came that bright January day during my sophomore year when Ms. Meehan walked over to the heavy wooden classroom door that was typically kept wide open and pulled it closed, the large brass doorknob clicking into place with a foreign sound. "We need to talk about the news," she said in an uncharacteristically sensitive tone. I glanced around the room and noticed a few desks were empty. We'd later learned that some kids' parents had kept them at home once the story broke in the *Boston Globe*: the story of decades of sexual abuse perpetrated by priests at congregations all throughout our metro Boston neighborhoods. As the news rippled through school, it felt like September 11, a day we'd experienced just a few months earlier, all over again: eerie, uncertain, looming dread of unknown magnitudes, untallied trauma. Frantic whispers in the hallway, hollow speeches of reassurance from our teachers, a quiet sense of doom settling in. Ms. Meehan uttered all the words we'd seen in print, "priests" and "molested" and "cover up," the edges of her mouth tightening around each one. I scratched behind the band of my too-tight navy-blue knee socks as a few girls next to me started to cry in little whimpers.

"Text me if you think of anything else," Father Flaherty assures me as we wrap up our phone call. *Text!* I hoot in my head. *Text* the priest. So much for my mental image of the landline in a Spartan rectory bedroom. Technology is finally at such a level of cultural penetration that even the clergy are participating.

I did end up texting him. I wanted to thank him again for his humanity and kindness, something that felt rare lately.

"You're welcome, Jessica. See you tomorrow." His message pops up blue on my screen. Father's got an iPhone.

The sliver of light wakes me up before my alarm. It beams into my childhood bedroom from beneath the blackout blinds. The blinds are new, along with all the furniture—my mother has turned the room into a functional guest space instead of a graveyard of child-hood relics, even though my parents rarely host out-of-town visi-tors. The rickety metal bunk beds on which I used to do ill-advised gymnastic feats are long gone, replaced with an understated Pier 1 futon. The clear plastic inflatable chair, upon which I used to wist-fully browse Delia's catalogs and French kiss postcards of Leon-ardo DiCaprio, has also been removed, a solemn treadmill in its place. The bones of the room are familiar, but everything else is suspect.

I squint at the sliver, in that semi-lucid state between fully awake and still half-dreaming. In my mind, the sliver is some sort of alien intervention, a visitation, maybe even a welcome solution. They just might have the technology I need to fix this entire situa-tion—but how do I communicate with them?

My phone alarm goes off and snaps me back to earth. I then execute the morning routine I've become very familiar with the past few days. It is as follows:

- Wake up fully and aggressively at the alarm's first chime, body stiff yet flailing, not feeling rested at all despite my three whole hours of sleep, made possible by a probably-incorrect-but-likely-not-dangerous dosage of generic drugstore Unisom, which reliably drags me down into unconsciousness these days like cinder blocks sinking a mob-executed businessman
- Tap my iPhone alarm off with a single shaking finger (there's no more exaggerated alarm-clock-slamming in the age of ever-innovating tech conglomerates); then, enjoy several seconds of woozy brain-swirling before it morphs into a precise and pointed headache
- Feel nothing (duration: one to two seconds)
- Feel like I'm forgetting something (duration: three to seven seconds)
- Suddenly, violently, feel everything (continues in perpetuity)

As I begin to remember what has happened and what is real, the rock formation reassembles in my stomach, like a planet exploding but in reverse, creating a hard yet hollow heaviness that pulls my whole body floorward. I close my eyes again and attempt to forget, to re-blur everything, to sink through my mattress and into the hardwood. But I can't; not today. Today's the funeral.

My feet hit the floor quickly. The futon is only about a foot and a half above ground level, after all. Eddie trots over from his sleep spot near the door and licks my ankles, appreciating my alive-and-awake-ness. I look down at his sweet fluffy face and admire the side-tufts of his cheek fur, like stately, Civil War–era mutton chops.

He's so cute and calm it's hard to believe he was home, just up the stairs when my brother died and the body was gray and his lips were blue and Matt's arm was lying out to the side and his mouth was open and emitting noxious gas instead of processed carbon dioxide and—

"Jess?"

My mom's voice comes from behind my closed bedroom door, small and sweet. When me and Matt were growing up, our bedroom doors would just be flung open whenever my mother or father needed one of us. As if by supernatural vampire-ish breeze, the door would suddenly be ajar, and one of them would be standing before us, all at once, asking why we hadn't unloaded the dishwasher or fed the cat. None of the old-fashioned crystal doorknobs in our old colonial house had locks, and knocking first was too British a politeness for our home. Even the bathroom door didn't lock, and hearing someone noisily barge in looking for the toenail clippers while you stood in the shower behind a flimsy curtain lathering up your genitals was not uncommon.

But now I'm 29 years old, and Matt's age stopped tallying at 26. I'm an interloper in my childhood house, awkward and all elbows, groping for things where they once were, oafishly stepping on the decorative plastic flowers, knocking over newly arranged framed photos. My mother is offering some whiffs of polite privacy, and it makes the whole surreal feeling of our new reality without Matt that much more foreign.

"Yeah," I say, eyes squinted shut, face wincing, rubbing the arch of my nose like an overextended high school algebra teacher.

"Oh, just seeing if you were awake yet."

"I'm getting up now. What time do we have to leave?"

"Nine, I think."

"Okay."

I pad over to the closet. My mother has carefully hung the clothes I bought yesterday on the closet door, like she used to do with my outfits for band recitals and church events. I selected this shirt and skirt in a stupor at the mall, after the panicked realization that I didn't have the right kind of black clothes for the funeral. I had some black stuff, of course—I am a mopey urban 20-something, after all—but it was frequently embellished with unacceptable statement stripes or patterns or band names. And all my plain black clothing was made out of pilled old cotton or jersey, too casual or sheer to wear while delivering a eulogy. My one little black dress was overly formal, the neckline cut in such a swooping V that my breasts would occasionally start to spill out if I didn't check in on them scrupulously. I knew I couldn't be worrying about a nip slip on funeral day.

My mom, trying to be helpful, had held the cocktail dress out for my consideration as we searched the closet at my apartment for an appropriate outfit a few days earlier. "Just put a cardigan over it, that'll be fine!"

"A cardigan?" I spat the word back at her, as if she had suggested I cover my shoulders in warm runny dog shit. "I don't have any cardigans!"

"Come on Jess," she said as she looked over the contents of my closet, flicking the hangers, "you must have a cardigan somewhere."

"I really don't. Cardigans are frumpy," I whined. My mother offering helpful suggestions always launches me right back to contrary adolescent brat mode. "My boobs are too big," I told her. "Cardigans make me look like a frumpy Sunday school teacher."

My mother turned to glare at me with gently raised eyebrows. So off to the mall we went.

We went to Macy's first. As we browsed the formal-ish sections, I found myself suddenly raging at the clothes. These black evening gowns, these cubic-zirconia–festooned dresses, these drab heaps of fabric with inappropriate cutouts and long trains—Jesus, where do they expect people to even wear these things? What event on earth could possibly call for a floor-length matte jersey gown with the lower back hacked out, complete with a beaded bolero? These clothes looked appropriate only for an adult film awards show in a nursing home, for ballroom dances in a junkyard, for early bird buffets on Mars.

"Can I help you find anything?" The elderly Macy's employee called to me from over to my left. She had kind eyes, the glossy beginnings of glaucoma. Her brown hair was coiffed in that old lady hairstyle, you know the one, the one my Grandma had and yours probably did too, that short, fluffy look that somehow required hours at the hair salon.

Immediately, I felt self-righteous fury toward this woman. I whipped around to face her fully, the hangers of all the ugly dresses draped over my arm jumping up and then falling back down into formation as I moved. I looked her dead in the eye and imagined her being hit by a bus. I imagined she was personally responsible for all these hideously unacceptable garments, she probably ordered them herself, yeah she probably thinks these clothes are all just beautiful—or worse, she ordered them purposefully, knowing they're ugly and inappropriate, all part of her dastardly plan to ruin my life and rub it in, rub it in that my brother's dead and now we have to do all these horrible rituals that no one even likes or wants.

This all flashed before my eyes in seconds. I didn't actually react with anger toward this innocent old lady, luckily. I just nodded without smiling and walked away.

I dumped down the black garments without trying them on, tears welling up, and my mother wordlessly led me out into the main thoroughfare of the mall, which smelled like wet pennies and

Auntie Annie's pretzels. I calmed down as we walked in silence. Then I spotted a hip young women's clothing franchise on the horizon.

"Can we go in there?" I asked with relief.

Once we entered the meticulously maintained cool-girl store, I felt instantly soothed: the warmly lit small space, the edited selection of Breton-striped cotton blends, the gamine-chic mannequins immediately offering a salve from the fluorescent garishness of Macy's.

I found a silk shirt and a simple skirt, both in plain black, both on sale. I felt so grateful, holding the outfit in my hands waiting in line at the register, realizing I'd get to look like my actual self at Matt's funeral and not some overdressed, ill-fitted, business casual nightmare version. At checkout, the professionally styled salesgirl brushed her curtain bangs out of her face, her elegantly mismatched bracelets jangling against her pale bony wrist, and said, "Very chic! What's the occasion?"

I felt the heat rising again. I watched her go about the small, tidy business of processing the sale: swiping my mother's credit card (my mom has not allowed me to pay for anything, from iced coffees to silk clothing, since I found her son's dead body), tearing the receipt from its tiny printer, folding my new items up in that dramatic, flouncy salesperson way. My blood boiled. How could she possibly ask me that question? Was she born yesterday? Why do people buy plain black clothes, you absolute moron, you blockhead? Don't you know, some of us have dead brothers over here. How could you possibly not know it the way that I know it! Seriously, though, who wears all-black? At best, I've just landed a clutch new catering job serving bacon-wrapped figs off of faux-silver platters at suburban hotel weddings. At worst, well shit. Do you really want to hear about it?

"Oh—it's, yeah," is all I managed to stammer. Then I pretended to receive a text.

Despite the uncomfortable check-out experience, on funeral day, I feel grateful for our nation's chic chain retailers. The outfit looks good. It looks right. I pull on the silk blouse, and as the folds of the smooth fabric cascade down my love handles, I feel like myself. I weave my long, dirty hair into a messy fishtail braid. I rub deodorant into my stubbly armpits and in the sweat-prone crease underneath my breasts. I turn to the old wooden bureau, an heirloom, the one piece of my childhood furniture that persists in the Homegoods-ified space, and consider my makeup approach for the day.

I'm going to be crying a lot today, I think to myself clinically. Do I wear mascara? Is this mascara I have even waterproof? I feel like it's not, and I'll be entering a Tammy Faye Bakker situation relatively early in the day if I put it on. But if I don't, I'll be giving into the bare-faced grimness of grief. That doesn't feel right either. I don't wear a lot of makeup in my day-to-day life, but there are certain extras I'll add if it's an important day: mascara, blush, maybe a little lip color. I guess this is an important day.

And now I am weeping soundlessly as I squint at the smudged-bare fine print on my long-expired tube of mascara, trying to decipher if any of the chemicals in here are meant to prevent the ravages of moisture.

Eddie's getting impatient on the futon; every time I look over at him, he wags his tail with a little surge of anxious excitement. He needs a walk. I resolve to figure out my makeup situation later, and I hitch Eddie's leash onto the brass D-ring of his leather collar, leading him out the back door of my parents' house and over to the wide-open grassy park across the street, the park that Matt and I used to fly across to get to our elementary school, running hard down the small sloping hill, arms spread wide like turbojets, laughing like maniacs as our Adidas Sambas slammed against the baseball diamond, creating dust clouds in our wake.

On the same day I went shopping with my mom, I also went to scope out the funeral venue with my dad and the property manager. Mount Auburn Cemetery is a historical attraction in Cambridge, Massachusetts: Founded in 1831, it was one of the first "rural" cemeteries designed in the United States, inspired by a Parisian approach to burying the dead. Landscaped with lush trees and flowers, winding pathways, and quaint benches, it was designed to offer people a place of quiet reflection, maybe even provide a bit of enjoyment in the process of laying a loved one down in the earth. Notable burials include Henry Wadsworth Longfellow, Isabella Stewart Gardner, and plenty of abolitionists and heroes of the Underground Railroad, like Harriet Jacobs and Joshua Bowen Smith.

I felt grateful that my father had had the presence of mind to suggest such a perfect place for Matt's service. During the funeral parlor planning session, he had said "how about Mount Auburn?" with total certainty, clarity. I realized he had probably had the place picked out in the deeper cockles of his broken heart for years as Matt's problems intensified.

After a bend in the pathway, the chapel appeared before us, all at once and splendid. A feat of gothic architecture.

"The stained-glass windows were imported from Scotland," the property manager told us lightheartedly as we entered the chapel. The wooden seats, the soaring ceilings, the warm gray stone, the flying buttresses, are those flying buttresses? It was perfect. That imported Scottish stained glass was even more rich and luminous inside, glowing from all edges. One panel showed a young female angel with fire-red wings cradling a tiny blond baby boy, sleeping, his chin resting on her shoulder.

"So, who is the memorial for?" the property manager asked as he walked us out after the tour. I hadn't realized until that moment that he didn't know our whole horrible sob story. Everywhere I'd been around town that week—waiting in line at the liquor store, walking my dog around the block, shuffling along the sidewalk while picking up my mother's emergency Xanax prescription—I'd felt the burning stare of the local stranger who's not really a stranger because his cousin's kids play hockey with my uncle's brother-in-law's kids, who knew all of our family business through the timeless miracle of the gossip churn, who knew all about what happened to Matt, who looked at us as that sad, sad family. I was taken aback by the idea that this particular stranger didn't know what happened. I sort of relished it.

"My brother died," I jumped in before my father could reply, boxing him out protectively to corner the play, taking the lead on the latest uncomfortable expository conversation.

The property manager looked me over, sized up my age to assess the relative sadness of my brother having died and died young, obviously. "I'm so sorry," he said in an incredulous voice. "You know, my aunt lost a child. She never got over it. Never."

On funeral day, I set up the audio equipment and wonder if the property manager is around. I think of his aunt. As Bob Dylan's nasally tones fill the chapel, I start to panic that it's irredeemably cliché to be playing Bob Dylan at my brother's funeral, but no time to change it now. A big crowd starts to pour in. There's a fair amount of our extended family on both my mother's and father's sides. There are the family friends, Matt's and my friends, the friends of friends, the friends of friends of friends who are insinuating themselves into the situation because of its contagious tragedy.

Father Flaherty capably handles the service with unflashy professionalism. When prompted, I climb the few steps up to the podium and deliver the eulogy I had written on Colleen's couch at 2 a.m. As I talk about Matt's humor and gentleness and empathy, I look out at the lumpy faces before me: the puffy eyes and sniffling noses, the furrowed brows and pinched mouths, all that concern and pain communicated through human flesh. I turn and leave the podium, my steps echoing among the flying buttresses as my task is complete, my loss is made permanent. My ears start to ring and then terrified panic is all around me all at once, like wind.

Luckily Paul, a trained theater performer since childhood, is dutifully waiting for me in the wings. I melt into a big bear hug from him, letting him support my weight as I cry a few cracked animal sobs, my black suede pumps dangling on top of the floor like a hanged witch.

Outside the church after the service, we glad-hand to the tune of the bagpipes. Some people I greet like we're at a college reunion, weirdly cheery and "how've you been"-y. Some people make me angry to spot in the crowd, the randos drawn in by that unavoidable tractor beam of human curiosity that strikes anyone within six degrees of tragedy. I'm jealous of them, really. They get to leave here after the funeral and have their lives be normal, exactly as they left them. What the fuck do I do when I leave?

Well, first things first: I get drunk. I sip on a bottomless glass of Jameson back at my father's Knights of Columbus chapter, hovering by the cold cuts and nodding my way through dreamlike conversations. This whole portion of the day has disappeared into a part of my brain I can't access, like a nightmare you can't recall the details of. What did I say to people? What did they say to me? I've of course asked my friends to fill in the blanks, and whenever they recall snippets of the afternoon, it's like being told the details of your behavior from a drunk night out. "I did what? I peed where?"

Planning the funeral had taken up all the space in my mind since the day after Matt died. It was a simple and important chore that I could focus on. It felt good to plan the service down to the letter, to obsess over the flowers and the photos, to follow up and liaise and circle back and tick off the items on the morose to-do list. But now that source of focus had passed, and I didn't know where to direct my attention: what to do next, what to think about, how to use my brain and body to continue living. I'd feel that way for a while.

PART II

5

Reset

My employer at the time of Matt's death had a meticulously detailed bereavement leave policy. About three business days after finding my brother's gray-blue body in our apartment, an awkward phone call with my supervisor prompted me to log in to the Employee Portal and get the details on my "options."

The policy was presented in a tidy chart, like quarterly performance numbers. On the left, the relationship was identified. On the right, the corresponding amount of leave was indicated.

Parent, spouse: 8–16 days.

Grandparent, aunt, uncle: 5–7 days.

And so on like that, with the chart identifying increasingly extended relations alongside vanishingly small numbers. My stomach acids churned as my eyes scanned the chart for the word "sibling," like trying to find a familiar smiling head shot on an overstuffed Missing Persons bulletin board. I don't remember where exactly on the chart it fell—somewhere in the middle, I think. I didn't spend long engaging with the policy. I clicked out of the portal and opened Outlook, then wrote my boss an email letting him know I wouldn't be returning to the office and that they could just pay me out for whatever the corporation determined I was owed, that'd be just fine, thanks for your understanding and flexibility.

I had been planning to leave this job anyway, but now it felt more urgent. I had been wanting to leave Boston in general. Rocky breakup, aimless job prospects, the baggage and boredom—I had been feeling those preppy shiplap walls closing in on me for months now. After losing Matt, they crushed in at a faster clip.

My mom offered to come with me to look at apartments in New York. I dropped Eddie off at Colleen's for a long weekend, and we headed down Route 95 to a bigger city where I hoped to be freer and more anonymous, where I could have the space and stimuli to regrow the parts of my brain and heart that had been twisted around and snapped apart. I had friends in the city, a support system, but I was drawn to the harshness of the environment more than anything. I was looking forward to the subway delays, the fourth-floor walk-ups, the noise and the expense, the bodega snacks covered in dust and the garbage heaps piled so high they looked like modern art. I wanted life to be hard because I felt hard. New York didn't know my whole sob story. New York didn't care.

I found an apartment in a stately stone town house south of Prospect Park. It was far lovelier than I expected: a true one-bedroom featuring original hardwood floors with Art Deco patterned borders, soaring 12-foot ceilings, big closets, and a yard that was 90% dirt 10% weeds but 100% fenced in, perfectly adequate for fetch with Eddie. Two weeks later I found myself in the driver's seat of a U-Haul, sitting in traffic at Grand Army Plaza, listening to the ambient honking and curse words and four different genres of music blaring from various directions, all the noise mixing in the lightly humid air like half-digested stew.

"I'll get out! Don't think I won't!" the driver in the lane to my right screamed at the car behind him, his whole upper torso hanging out the driver's side window.

The other driver shook his head slowly and muttered, not intimidated in the least.

"You think I won't?" the first driver hollered. "I will!"

I had traded the hushed whispers and pitying glances of New Englanders I knew too well for the unfiltered, uncut emotion of New Yorkers who didn't give a fuck if I lived or died. As the driver next to me pantomimed opening his car door to further antagonize the driver behind him, I marveled at the cosmic bone that had been thrown in my hungry direction.

Once I got settled in Brooklyn, I started to freelance. I knew I was still too ruined to function acceptably inside one of those creative workplaces where I had built my career thus far, smiling and nodding at people with asymmetrical haircuts, chitchatting about French New Wave and Kafka in order to come up with a killer campaign to sell gladiator sandals, hashing out ideas on whiteboards, high-fiving and throwing Koosh balls and wearing expensive sneakers like everything's fine. So instead, I set up shop at my kitchen table.

I do mostly the same sort of work I'm used to, writing tag-lines to sell cashmere sweaters and quippy speeches for CEOs to deliver at fund-raising dinners, with the occasional news article or arty essay mixed in. I email these things out into the ether, and then the little numbers in my digital bank account click upwards. The money doesn't come in on any set schedule, but with my savings, it's enough to get by.

Today, I'm wrapped in a heavy blanket as I sit at the table, mind-lessly munching on bodega snacks and trying to muster the energy to check my emails. It's that awkward not-fall-but-not-yet-winter time of year, and my prewar building doesn't have the heating fully on yet. The old-fashioned radiators, like the ones in the house I grew up in, are just starting to emit that metallic robot-fart smell, the smell that lets you know they're getting around to it, rattling back to life after a long summer of hibernation—but the place is still cold. The kitchen window has wedges of cloudy condensation in each of its lower corners, a picturesque frame on my view of the dead leaves in the yard and the chain link fence that surrounds it. I'm browsing the internet mindlessly on my dead brother's laptop, which I have inherited.

I start Googling things I should have been Googling months, years ago. "What is drug addiction." "How does heroin affect body." "Mr. T, DARE, why." I find some recent reporting on the opioid epidemic, newly sympathetic stories about rural teens overdosing in their parents' basements. I find older, dog-whistlier reporting on the last big drug epidemic, stories about "crack babies" spending sleepless nights in urban NICUs, their mothers handcuffed to their hospital beds a ward away. I find studies and scientific papers on PubMed, decades' worth of research, information on how naloxone can reverse an overdose and how medications exist to treat heroin use disorders, so much of it peer reviewed and published before Matt was even born.

I also find rehabs. Page after page of search results promoting Rising Sun Valley and Shady Acres Community Center, expensive-looking facilities that seem to have harnessed the power of click bait-y page headers and undoubtedly massive spending on search terms to achieve high prominence on every page of results. If I think I've found a trustworthy informational article from some innocuous-sounding website like "addiction answers dot net," my heart falls when the "ARE YOU READY FOR RECOVERY? CALL US NOW FOR A FREE CONSULTATION" pop-up eventually appears, a fat fly in my informational Chardonnay, now tainting every previous sip that I thought I had enjoyed.

I spend time mainlining this stuff almost every day. Eventually, after sickening myself on the glut of digital junk food, I order some actual books. This new desire for information feels insatiable. The more I learn, the more I want to know. As I settle into the dull permanence of my loss, I find myself wondering, cornily, what went wrong. I know the short answer to that is "lots," but I feel an urge to know the answer's subgenres, its peaks and contours. Because my brother and I had so much in common. We'd shared so many experiences, growing up an arm's length away from each other, attending the same schools and church events and family vacations. Our temperaments and tastes were so similar. Our noses had the same shallow, fat base. We both had teeth too small for our mouths. When we spoke at the same time, it sounded like a prerecorded track of a singer harmonizing with himself.

So, given all this similarity, why'd my brother end up exiting this world via heroin overdose while I'm still sitting here, wrapped in a blanket, covered in Cheeto dust crumbs, enjoying a robustly active pulse?

My brother was born on June 30, 1989. I was almost three years old. I don't remember holding him in the hospital, but there are photos of it. My blunt copper bangs adorned with pastel plastic hair clips shaped like lambs, my pudgy doll body wrapped in one of those papery hospital gowns that looks like it's made of the same material that you find on the bottom of a mattress. My mom, so young, smiling but exhausted, by my side. Overseeing operations, making sure I don't squeeze him too hard or drop him like one of my Barbies.

Matt and I grew up in an old colonial house. My parents renovated the place over the years as they pulled our family's socioeconomic status into the upper middle class. The floral wallpaper in mustard, avocado, and other groovy food-based hues got replaced by smooth paint in modern Ethan Allen neutrals, the hardwood floors with dusty gaps in between the boards were redone and smoothed over, the furniture upgraded, the counters swapping uneven laminate for cool granite.

My dad was the first kid in his big Irish American family to graduate college and then to attend law school. My mom transcribed tapes for doctors at a local hospital before putting herself through nursing school, becoming an RN when I was in the second grade. Matt and I grew up in a densely settled Greater Boston neighborhood, a pale, homogeneous community in which Portuguese was considered ethnic, close to school friends and family members and grandparents. We attended Sunday mass in occasional bursts of commitment followed by lags of ambivalent absence. We'd ride our bikes to get ice cream cones, we'd play Kick the Can with the neighborhood kids, we'd get eaten alive by mosquitos while splayed out on a scratchy blanket at Robbins Farm, the big green park across the street from our house, watching the 4th of July fireworks over Boston Harbor, listening to the Pops on a white plastic radio with bent antennae.

Matt liked to run himself in circles at this park. He was this fountain of energy, always crazed and cackling. He had this shiny blond hair, his smattering of freckles sun-kissed and precise— unlike my freckles, which covered my ginger-flavored body head to toe like a pox. His eyes were big and round and blue, his pupils were almost always dilated. He was just so *riled up* all the time, like a housecat at midnight, scampering from one corner of a room to the next. He'd howl this craggy laugh and scream like a kazoo. He'd poke you and poke you and poke you till you either gave in and engaged in whatever game he was attempting to initiate, or you coldcocked him in the shoulder. Either outcome delighted him just the same.

Throughout childhood, my brother and I shared a particular flavor of neuroticism. Whenever we'd microwave something, we'd feel compelled to flick open the door just before the time ran out, crucially avoiding that screeching "time's up" beep we both couldn't stand. While our Easy Mac or Chef Boyardee spun around in the radiation, grandiose and regal beneath its yellow spotlight, we'd keep a rigorous watch, observing the digital numbers as they lessened, waiting for the exact moment to pull the door open and stop the process. The whole point of a timer seems to be that you set it and then go back to it when it loudly announces that the time has run out, but both my brother and I had the unique ability to take a thing that's supposed to make life easier and instead turn it into a big terrifying source of worry.

Being three years older than Matt gave me a nice sense of unjustified superiority. I'd get to act like he was an idiot for not knowing things that I myself hadn't known about until mere days prior. "You don't know what a *bastard* is?" I coughed at him incredulously one day, twirling my side-ponytail and sipping an EctoCooler juice box, "Double Dare" blaring in the background on our old wood-paneled TV. I was ten, he was seven, and I'd just returned from a particularly illuminating playdate. "A bastard is someone who's *older than their parents*."

He looked at me with thankful awe.

In the station wagon and at the kitchen table, on the playground and at family barbecues, we stayed tuned in to each other, sensitive to shifts in mood or need. I knew he looked up to me with that malleable brain of his, and I relished stuffing it full of things: my musical tastes, my book preferences, my latest knowledge of swear words and gossip. I got excited when he got the same teachers I had in school and would try to give him hints about their demeanor and demands, cheats on how to charm and succeed. On most days, I thought of him as a peer. On less generous days, I thought of him as more of a pet. I wanted to be proud of him for peeing on the newspaper I laid out. I wanted to bop his nose when he ate trash.

Most mornings we walked to school together along with a few other neighborhood kids. It was the 1990s, and all the scrapbook photos in my mom's sewing room make that painfully clear. Our outfits were ostentatious: fluorescent bike shorts, scrunchies, flannels tied around the waist, hoodies featuring irritable teenaged versions of Looney Tunes characters, scowling in their own backwards baseball caps and flannels, showcasing their 'tude with straightforwardly confrontational slogans like "Yeah, I've got an attitude problem." Other than the mean Looney Tunes apparel, there was probably one other style that was ubiquitous among kids our age and a bit older: the DARE t-shirt.

The classic iteration of this t-shirt was usually black with red and white writing, but I've also seen rainbow versions, unintentional queer relics going for $49.99 and up these days on eBay. "D.A.R.E.," the main slogan of the t-shirts read in a serial killer scrawl, with its subheadline, "to keep kids off drugs," nestled beneath in clear white lettering.

Short for the dystopian-sounding Drug Abuse Resistance Education program, DARE originated in Los Angeles public schools in 1983. The program involved a series of presentations and lessons structured around two purported goals: to highlight the negative effects of drugs and to give kids the self-esteem needed to just say no. To meet these goals, DARE sent uniformed cops clacking their heavy-heeled boots into the hollow hardwood of America's school gymnasia, once a week for several weeks in stints of 45 to 60 minutes, to lecture the wide-eyed children whose skulls had barely finished closing on the importance of being drug-free winners. Oh, and they'd also show videos.

"Your bad choices have consequences," the narrator on the DARE video might typically intone over B-roll of stereotypical bad kids wearing dark hoodies and sunglasses, sneering as they exhaled pot smoke and presumably skipped fourth period. Jump cut.

"Just say no. It'll be a slam dunk," some professional athlete might stammer while catching a pass on a gleaming basketball court. Cue the cornball smile. Then the mascot would come traipsing out, a nightmarish lion plushie in a DARE t-shirt and no pants, looking like a drunken discount Disney character. The mascot and the athlete would high-five, perhaps.

If this all doesn't sound particularly educational or self-esteem enhancing to you, you're not alone. But the two stated goals belied a true third. DARE wasn't just an education program. It was considered a crime prevention program, too, with equal heft and importance. After all, drug possession is a crime. And if having drugs is criminal, then using them certainly is, too. The children in the audience weren't individuals, per se. They were potential future deviants in need of corrective action before things got bad. Indeed, the DARE program taught my generation that being addicted to drugs is not just dangerous—it's against the law, even when the only person you're hurting is yourself.

At the height of its popularity, DARE was in place in 75% of American school districts. Everyone loved the program so much that for nearly a decade, they never really bothered to study it. There were no data measuring outcomes, no information to support the program's own claims. It just felt like it was working, and that was enough for a long time.

In 1994, when Matt was napping in kindergarten and I was memorizing times tables in the third grade, a study partially funded by the Justice Department discovered what other public health research had already begun to establish: DARE wasn't working. Study after study reached the same conclusion, that kids who received DARE outreach were no less likely to try drugs or become addicted to those drugs than kids who received zero drug education. In fact, some research suggested DARE kids were perhaps even more likely to experiment—which should come as no surprise to anyone who's ever met a kid.

"Petra, don't you dare do that," I heard an exhausted mother intone to her daughter in a coffee shop the other day while smug little Petra dangled a full juice box out the side of her stroller. "Don't," Mom warned again with severity. A few seconds later, splat: The box landed down hard on the deconstructed concrete floor, exploding non-GMO watermelon juice in all directions. Mom's brow furrowed and lips tightened. Petra laughed. It doesn't take a federally funded report to know that kids especially relish doing things they're explicitly told not to do.

Back in the 1990s, the Justice Department refused to release that first negative study to the public. DARE enthusiasts were gobsmacked and took the data personally. "I don't get it," DARE's Executive Director Glenn Levant said in the *Chicago Tribune*. "It's like kicking Santa Claus to me. We're as pure as the driven snow."

Eventually, the bright red writing on the wall could no longer be ignored. DARE lost its exorbitant funding. The videos featuring the Kirk Camerons of the world stopped production. That undulating lion turned in his plushie head.

But despite its clear and empirical failure, something about DARE always just felt right to people and continues to feel right to people today. It hits on some sort of squishy, false-logic spot that lives deep in the human brain. If we just *tell* people not to do something, if we just *show* them the terrifying consequences, then they won't do it. And if they choose to do it still, after we've gone to such trouble to carefully present them with all those terrifying facts, after we've created all these videos and printed all these t-shirts and coordinated all these bake sales, well then. That's their own problem, isn't it?

For us kids, the DARE program provided a tidy preview of adult life. The preview said this: Authority figures want badly to tell you what to do. They'll tell you this is for your own benefit, too. They'll say whatever they have to in order to sway you. If you listen to them, you'll be okay in a certain sense. And if you don't. Well.

6

Go

My grief is quite physical, and this takes me by surprise. I used to believe that I could take any heartache and box it up, squaring it away on a label-mastered mental shelf to be archived now, dealt with later. Not sure what gave me this impression. Perhaps it was that frosty New England attitude that seemed to prohibit expressing visible emotion about anything other than Tom Brady's successes or ballads on the Irish Hit Parade AM radio hour. Perhaps it was the expressionless faces of priests at funerals. Perhaps it was just some idea that my own unique constellation of trauma and mental illness came up with. Whatever gave me this coping mechanism, I had mostly been able to get away with deploying it up until now. But losing Matt was a different kind of thing. This time, the box isn't in my head at all. It sits in the center of my chest, and it is wide open all the time, wreaking havoc on my innards.

My skin is always prickling, like teeny centipedes are scattering just below on the surface of my bones. My mouth feels like I just finished eating a plate of sand, grimy particles lingering on my tongue and cheeks. My organs are trying to wring themselves out, it feels like—always tightening, loosening, then tightening again, like premenstrual cramps not just in my uterus but also my kidneys, my liver, my lungs. I ache. It's a dull discomfort most of the time. But sharp grief attacks come on occasionally and unpredictably.

They feel impossible to predict, and my body seems to plan them behind my brain's back, executing them at the most inconvenient and embarrassing times.

This becomes clear one cold, sunny afternoon when I decide to venture a few blocks up Flatbush Avenue to Erv's, a hip coffee shop tucked down a stubby dead-end street, surrounded by historic apartment buildings with tan bricks and charming Dutch details. As I wait in line behind an older lady in nursing scrubs and a young mom pushing a stroller, I rehearse the interaction in my head. I planned to order what every Bostonian craves in mid-December: an iced coffee. I rub the hem on my sweatshirt sleeve between my thumb and forefinger. I visualize the interaction: talk to barista, listen to her talk, then I perhaps talk again; put credit card in smooth white reader, tap screen, add tip; move to the side to wait. Smile. I try to harness the magic of positive thinking. *Ah yes, being normal. For me? It comes naturally.*

Three-fourths of the way through this visualization, I look up and realize suddenly that the customers in front of me have finished placing their orders. Now, the big gap between me and the counter yawns. I quickly shuffle up to the barista, a young woman wearing a slouchy open-knit beanie and thick gold hoop earrings. She smiles upward at me, finger hovering over her iPad.

"Can I please have an iced coffee," I ask in a bright tone. I always get a pang of sad nostalgia ordering things. It reminds me of being small and helpless and a little dumb. I imagine myself as a child, bony and freckly in a dripping purple one-piece swimsuit, clutching a damp $5 bill from my parents, nervously waiting to order a coconut popsicle from the YMCA snack bar. Whenever I place orders, I'm almost never standing in the right place, never have the exact lingo of the establishment down, always need a little gentle assistance from the clerk.

"Cold brew okay?" the barista asks.

"Yes. Yeah, that's great actually," I pepper in some unnecessary embellishment as an apology for my ignorance, trying to obscure the embarrassing needfulness I feel all the time, which I imagine broadcasts out of me like a spotlight.

She nods with a smile and taps her iPad. "$4.50."

I fish out my credit card and slide it into the reader. While I do this, I say to myself in a small singsong voice, "four . . . fif-tee." As I insert my card into the reader, I realize that this singsongy repeating is something Matt used to do. My brother Matt. My brother Matt who is dead.

This sudden realization lands upon me like an ACME anvil. My guts start doing their wringing thing with the quickness. The centipedes wake up, startled, and my skin gets prickly. My ears start to ring, and I feel my consciousness floating toward the ceiling. Moisture leaves my mouth and goes straight for my eyes.

I finally notice the barista is looking at me and waiting, a plastic cup of cold brew already slightly sweating on the counter while the credit card reader screams and the screen flashes "REMOVE YOUR CARD."

I smile sheepishly and yank the plastic back. I collect my coffee and burst back onto the street, the frigid air thwacking my cheeks, the sun bright and violent all around me like an atomic bomb. Great. Mission accomplished. Just the thing my raging heart needs: caffeine.

Even though my insides are a dervish of activity, I rarely move my body all that much. I walk my dog to Prospect Park. I go to Erv's. I putter to the Ideal Grocery for some sweet potatoes that I'll buy with a *New York Times* recipe in mind but that I'll end up cooking in my microwave after they've started to grow tentacles. Other than that, I'm mostly in a fetal position on my bed, my sofa, or, if I'm feeling particularly yogic, my living room floor.

This sort of stasis isn't normal for me. I've always been at least medium active. I played team sports for most of my childhood and thrived on the rigorous schedule of it all. I relished the daily practice, the weekly games, the need to structure your entire day around the stuff. It felt easier to keep the rest of my daily life spinning efficiently when I had sports at the center. In college and through my young adulthood, when the responsibility shifted entirely to myself to stay active, I started going for short jogs around the neighborhood, huffing and puffing through two to three miles, feeling bored and tired. Or I'd hit up my local budget gym in a clueless, lost way, shrinking away from the juiced-up lifter bros to get in my 30 minutes on the elliptical followed by some light flailing with the cable-oriented machines. Still, as pathetic as it all was, I maintained some semblance of a routine. Now, that felt so far away.

The lack of movement, the weird and rare eating, the grief—to be sure, I'm in the worst shape of my life. But when I look at my body in the mirror, I feel pleased that it has become so thin. I've always had a larger frame: tallish, broad shoulders, thick midfielder thighs, uncomfortably large breasts, a slight stomach paunch that I had loathed since middle school due to the brain damage I incurred growing up in the era of bedazzled low-rise jeans. But now, I see slightly more bulbous knees and shoulders, loosed from a bit of extra padding. I see a narrower waist, the dip in my hips gone. I see a thigh gap, and, I'm horrified to admit, it makes me feel a sick glee. I stare into any reflective surface I come across, poking at my flesh in awe. I take selfies. On the occasions when I do move, I sometimes catch myself in a bit of a strut. My body is disappearing. And somehow this feels like a lifelong pipe dream come true.

❀

Heroin addiction changed my brother's body. Not in that stereo-typical way you see on television crime dramas: rotted teeth, pock-marked skin, greasy hair. No, Matt's addiction never changed his fashion sense, his hygiene. And this is the case for a great many people with substance use disorders. The differences were more blink-and-you'd-miss-it subtle.

When Matt was healthy, he had the pale Irish skin all us Keefe kids had, but his took on a handsome golden hue in the summer-time. The sun never failed to give him a truly Grecian bronzing. Paired with his dusty blond hair, he would not have looked out of place in a PacSun advertisement. He effortlessly possessed the sort of cool surfer look that lesser tweens labored intensely to achieve and that girls in his middle school drooled over.

But when he was using, everything began to sink, sour. The filter changed. His skin turned sallow and then took on a gray tinge, like rocks in a river. He would sweat differently, soaking shirts in a briny damp that smelled foreign to me, not familial.

I often think about what it must've been like when Matt fell backward in that office chair the day he died. It must've made a loud thud. Had my dog heard, pricking his ears up? Did the neigh-bors hear? Did it hurt? It must've been painful. Was Matt even conscious when it happened? I hoped not.

When I found him, his skin was a more violent shade of gray, purple and veiny. It looked like he was about to begin some superhero-movie–style chemical transformation; after a few moments of shirt tearing and hair grabbing, he'd emerge The Hulk or Captain America or something. But no. He wasn't moving, he wasn't grabbing his hair. He was just lying there. Who knows how long he'd been lying there.

He was wearing his favorite outfit. A white t-shirt, skinny jeans, brown leather suspenders that he wore with more of a Duckie from *Pretty in Pink* sensibility than insufferable modern hipster. His nice wooden plug earrings, the ones the funeral home would hand me in a biohazard bag later. I wondered if he was planning on going out that night. The way people find themselves getting into bad car accidents when they were just running out quickly for a gallon of milk, I wondered if he fatally overdosed while trying to get a quick high before moving along with his evening.

One of my Grandpa's favorite phrases was "close, but no cigar." When one of my cousins or I would miss a free throw at the telephone pole basketball hoop on the block, he'd say it. When we'd whiff our little fingers around, trying to reach a snack on a high shelf, he'd say it. It'd come out mangled by his particular vocal pattern: a Boston accent, also influenced by the Irish accents of his off-the-boat parents, gravelly from a lifetime spent with a cigarette in his mouth. It gave this phrase a one-of-a-kind sound. "Clohhse, baht nohw cigah!"

He'd say this anytime we missed at anything, regardless of how "close" we actually were. It was lighthearted and kind. A small boost, a favor he did for us to preserve our gentle childish feelings.

That's what the "no" from the EMT felt like on October 5. Close, but no cigar.

I feel grateful that when I found Matt, his eyes were closed. I didn't have to see his face twisted in some wretched facsimile, some awful last gasp of pain. He looked like he was asleep, at least in the face. And that was a small favor the universe did for me.

People tell me I need a project. A hobby. A goal. They tell me something like this could give me a fixed point on the horizon to focus upon. They tell me this could "help," in that nebulous way everyone always invokes after you've been through something devastating.

The first few times this advice is dispensed, I roll my eyes and use the opportunity to make an excellent joke about, you know, taking up a life of crime as my hobby, achieving nothingness as being my goal. People do not laugh at these jokes.

By January, though, I'm starting to get bored of this. It's been months since Matt died, and the glamor of my self-pity is starting to strain. It no longer feels deserved and correct to waste my free time watching too much TV, sleeping during daylight hours, eating Sour Patch Kids instead of lean proteins. I'm loath to admit it, but it's starting to feel stifling. Instead of dedicating most of my mental energy to wallowing, I start to spend time wondering if I'll ever be capable of normal human activity again. The terror of my grief is occasionally replaced by this new terror: That I'm permanently broken. That I'll never emerge from this protective cocoon I've assembled around me.

One evening as I mindlessly scroll through Instagram, waiting for my sweet potatoes to overcook to a wrinkly softness in my microwave, I come across a post sponsored by the New York Road Runners. "Mark your calendars," the bright graphic reads. "Registration for the Brooklyn Half Marathon opens January 21!" There are many excited, emoji-heavy comments. Some ask logistical questions about the course—would it start outside the Brooklyn Museum on the Eastern Parkway again this year? Some post about how eager they are to triumphantly scarf several Nathan's Hot Dogs at the race's finish line on the Coney Island boardwalk. Some inquire about how quickly the race was likely to sell out, and others reply that the slots would likely fill within mere hours.

I sensed a community here, and my lonely little ears piqued right up to it. Look at these people, talking knowingly about something as impressive as a half marathon. They must really have their shit together. I'm intimidated, but I'm also intrigued. The child athlete in me thrills at the prospect of a finish line, a physical trial followed by a standard-issue reward. Could I do this? I hate running. But do I *really* hate running? I look at my phone's calendar and note today's date as January 7. I click on the 21st and put a little alarm in there. "Brooklyn Half Marathon registration opens," I type.

Some nights I dream that Matt is melting. It's always a slow-motion process. His hands reach out and touch mine. I regard our interlaced fingers with calm happiness. Then his skin takes on a rubbery sheen. Before my eyes, the air starts to seep out, like a flattening tire. I look up from our hands and discover that Matt's whole body is melting in this way, his sides drooping down as he loses his fullness. I try to tell him he's leaking. But he just looks at me expressionlessly as his face slims down to a slice.

Usually, I dream of Matt or I dream of nothing. But after learning about the race, I start to dream about running, too. Nothing too elaborate, plot-wise. It mostly just involves the act of running—but it's my own self that's interesting in the dream. While I'm running, I'm part woman, part robot, part mammalian creature. As my feet propel me forward, as my body bobs and dips, as my breath strings in and out, my form is changing. As the sinews of my thighs pulse, I notice there's a dry casing on the top of my skin, and it flakes off and takes flight like butterflies. Beneath, there's a wetter undercoat. I don't stop running, but I reach my hand down to my thigh and I scoop some of the sinew up with my index and middle finger. I lift it to my face and examine it closely, while my feet below keep propelling me forward. I rub the viscous shedding between my fingers, and then it dissolves into nothing.

I look back down at the thigh I had scooped this fleshiness up from. I see that now, it's smooth and sparkling. The new flesh that had been waiting underneath is now on glorious display. It's sparkling in the daylight like a newborn seal. This flesh is pristine—it hasn't ever been burned by the sun, plagued by a rash, bit by horse-fly, or cut by a razor; it doesn't know anything about why it's here or where it came from. It just goes, because that's what it's supposed to do.

7

Risk

ABOUT A MONTH LATER, ON A COLD AND CLEAR FEBRUARY MORN-
ing, it's time for my first official training run. I dutifully fish my
old soccer camp t-shirt out from the bottom of a Tupperware bin
in my big hallway closet. I have other shirts I could have worn on
this maiden training run, more appropriate sporty Lycra blends, but
this one feels like a talisman. I layer a long-sleeved heat-trapping
tee underneath, throw on some yoga tights, and top it all off with
an ugly knitted headband of unknown origins. I lace up my old
Asics, the logo peeling slightly off the sides, which I bought years
ago clearly, when Matt was alive and on the mend, when Elijah and
I were happy.

Without eating breakfast or warming up, I head out my apartment building's heavy front door and activate the tracker app on my
phone. My run starts now. I jog about four blocks, two short street
blocks followed by two longer avenue blocks, to the southeastern
entrance to Prospect Park. I feel lucky to live so close to such a fine
public space. It's one of the oldest and most splendid parks in New
York City, filling 500 urban acres with lush green beauty. Construction on this park began in the 1860s, about 30 years after Mount
Auburn Cemetery was built in Cambridge. The space gives me the
same calm feeling as the cemetery did on the day of Matt's funeral.
It's filled with curved pathways, intricately landscaped plant life,

open fields with gently rolling hills. It's a public space where you don't have to buy anything to justify your presence, where you don't have to pay admission or hold a membership, all intentionally and beautifully engineered to envelop weary city dwellers with peace and comfort. A real relic.

The park boasts a laundry list of attractions: a zoo, a band shell, a lake with a boathouse, a rink for ice skating in winter and roller skating in summer, picnic tables and gazebos, basketball courts, and playgrounds. There's a system of wide, well-paved paths that wind through the park. The main one forms a 3.5-mile loop, and this is the one I'll be following on today's run.

The lush majesty of the park is a bit dulled in winter, but the cold gives it a feeling all its own. The bright but weak sun washes the frosted fields in glittering light. Wintry trees loom above me, their bare tentacles forming a still yet wild thicket in the sky that reminds me of my own brain. The grass in the Long Meadow is trimmed tidily. It's impressively green, even during this deep winter freeze.

I am running, I think to myself smugly as I trot along. *Me, of all people, running. Training. Race training! Would a person who's a mess be capable of doing this? Of course not.*

My weird, knitted headband is a little too small, I'm realizing, as it keeps wandering upward on my head. I'm starting to remember where it came from—I think I received it as a Christmas gift when I was in the seventh grade. I tug it back down to cover my ears.

Registering for the race had been easier than I'd expected. Not long after I first saw that Instagram ad promoting the Brooklyn Half Marathon, I sat silently at my bare kitchen table on registration day, waiting for the clock to strike 12 p.m. The comments on Instagram let me know this was a very popular race, and the website had been known to crash on registration day. Luckily for me, I arrived at the confirmation screen with no hiccups. "You're in," the page stated, the words floating in the center of the screen among a sea of sponsor logos and inspiring photos from previous years' races, people hugging, high-fiving, pumping their fists toward the sky at the finish line. The important date I had dogeared in my mind shifted from January 21, registration day, to May 21, race day.

I didn't think much about the reality of the race at first. I just let myself bask in conceptual excitement. I texted my mom, my friends, announcing my intention to run this half marathon as if I were announcing a pregnancy. My texts informed my loved ones that my loneliness had a new friend, my trauma-addled brain had a new puzzle to fiddle with: this race. I now had a little project to focus on, and people seemed relieved.

After the thrill of being congratulated by others wore off, I started to look up training plans. It all seemed pretty straightforward. Most plans recommended four to five running days a week. Most of those runs would be under five miles, with one weekly long run that got longer each week as the race neared. I scanned the little calendar and took it all in at once. Rest days were marked "rest" on the square, which felt relaxing to behold. The little numbers on the run days grew larger as the calendar progressed. The last calendar square, day 84, colored in red, was marked "race day."

As my social media algorithms began to detect my new racing plans, I was increasingly served ads for gear, apps, nutritional goo to consume while running. The advertising for these products featured taut bodies in serious grayscale, beads of sweat running down their muscles, faces fixed with steely determination. Slogans abounded about hard work, patience, resilience, the importance of going big or, failing that, going home. No risk, no reward. I know these slogans are primarily sales tactics, but something inside me is motivated by them nonetheless. The child athlete in me is eager to please an invisible coach somewhere in my phone.

I think about these slogans during my training today. Just a few miles. Not even a full loop of the park. *You can do it*, I think, half believing it, trying to mimic the tone and authority of the slogans. My old-model iPhone jiggles heavily in the waist pocket of my yoga tights, like an AI gremlin trying to escape my pants. The park's cold air fills my lungs, then streams back out, warmed by my innards. Just do it. Go big and resist the temptation to go home. No risk, no reward.

There's good risk and there's bad risk. The surrounding words in the phrasing can clue you into which kind you're dealing with. "No risk, no reward"? This implies the risk will be good, worthwhile. "Take a risk"? Could be good if you're talking about a career move, could be bad if you're talking about sports betting. "At risk"? That one's pretty much always bad.

Like all health problems, some people are more at risk of developing an addiction than others. And to understand how something as destructive as addiction blossoms in a person, you need to first understand one seemingly contrary thing: The brain wants to survive above all else. And when it's addicted to something, it starts to associate the substance with survival.

Addiction is a clinical illness and as such has a clinical definition. That definition, though, seems to be ever evolving, always changing slightly over time, a good indicator of just how complicated and slippery attempts to understand it have been and continue to be. Trying to define addiction seems to be like trying to grip an eel with a greased glove.

One of the most widely accepted definitions comes from the fifth edition of the *Diagnostic and Statistical Manual of Mental Disorders* (*DSM*), the bible of the American Psychiatric Association.

It classifies addiction as a chronic, relapsing disorder characterized by compulsive drug seeking and use despite negative consequences. According to the *DSM*, addiction can range from mild to moderate to severe based on a list of specific symptoms.

When I first started taking in scientific information about addiction, I noticed a lot of talk about drugs "hijacking" brains. It always came up in that signature tone that scientist types take when they're trying to relate information to the general public. It reminded me of my high school biology teacher insisting that proteins are really just "building blocks," that the endoplasmic reticulum was more akin to a "fluffernutter sandwich" than anything else. This introductory scientific literature told me that drugs, especially opioids, impact dopamine production and rewire things problematically. According to the National Institute on Drug Abuse, the dramatic boost in dopamine that many substances provide can "'teach' the brain to seek drugs at the expense of other, healthier goals and activities."

This process begins in the most ancient, elementary part of the human brain, the one that's helped guide our survival since the Flintstones era: the nucleus accumbens. Scientists have a pet name for this one, too: the brain's "pleasure center," which to me sounds more like a grimy sex shop off of Route 1 in Revere, Massachusetts, but whatever gets the message across, I guess. Inside the nucleus accumbens, certain stimulation prompts the release of a neurotransmitter called dopamine, rewarding you for participating in behavior that is "goal-directed." That includes the basics like eating, drinking, having sex but also includes meaningful conversation, a warm hug. It's behaviors that either promote plain-old human survival or forge connection and community. These things earn you a nice boost of dopamine from your nucleus accumbens.

This neurotransmitter may sound familiar to you because its name is so similar to that horrible stuff you learned to say nope to in your DARE class: dope. It plays many roles in the body, including making you feel good, but the pleasure part is less important than the remembering part. Dopamine is the thing that presses ink to paper, making your brain remember to repeat certain behaviors that achieve certain results.

Opioids, when misused, affect this same system—and, once you're addicted to them, that's where the supposed hijacking comes in. For a person who's vulnerable, a drug-induced dopamine spike can feel like nothing they've ever been able to experience before. It can feel how they've imagined life was supposed to be feeling all along. But it's all a trick. A swizzle. Opioids let you live action role play (LARP) your own life. It can feel so good, so satisfying, so real in the moment. But once it's over and the drugs have worn off and your brain floats back down to its baseline, you may find yourself becoming acutely aware of the fact that you're just swinging a stick sword in the middle of a squat and limited forest area off of Route 1 in Revere, Massachusetts, right by the sex shop, wondering what the hell you're even faking it for.

When it comes to the chain reaction that leads to addiction, though, it's not just about pleasure. In fact, at a certain point, it kind of stops being about pleasure at all. Because dopamine itself is more complex and multifaceted than the tidbit I just described. It's not the only thing that makes you feel pleasure, and it's not the only important aspect of mammalian survival. As Maia Szalavitz explains in her seminal book on addiction, *Unbroken Brain*, "if dopamine is what creates the sense of pleasure, animals shouldn't be able to enjoy food without it. Yet they do." Further, as an addiction develops, pleasure becomes an even more elusive outcome, but many drug users keep pursuing it in ever-increasing vain. This is where addiction truly blooms. Szalavitz describes her own experiences with cocaine addiction, writing that even as she grew exhausted by her use and knew deep down that the drug would not provide her with the feelings she craved, "I couldn't learn to stop myself before I took it."

Dopamine overproduction alone isn't what creates addiction. If that were the case, every person who ever popped a Vicodin in a party bathroom would eventually overdose to death. I know plenty of lovely knuckleheads who used to use incredible amounts of drugs in their heyday but eventually just up and stopped, getting a job at UPS and having kids and posting niche memes about hard-core punk rock on social media. No harm, no foul, no permanent brain damage. Hell, I myself drank mammoth amounts of alcohol during college but never developed anything that could be approximated to an addiction. When alcohol caused negative consequences for me—a ripping hangover during an 8 a.m. lecture, a sloppy barroom make-out session with a man so old he had hard candy in his trouser pockets—my brain was able to learn from those situations and was mostly capable of helping me adjust my behavior accordingly. No more partying the night before my one early class of the week, no more tequila sunrises in general. In fact, the vast majority of people who use drugs, even scary-sounding ones like heroin, don't become addicted. Some people don't even like it. Just ask Dan Rather, who tried heroin in the 1950s for a story and discovered that all it did was give him "a hell of a headache." He put the stuff down and never reached for it again.

So if drugs hijack the brain, if they trigger a tsunami of dopamine that rewires things, why isn't every former party guest addicted to something? Why can some of us adjust, stop, and move on, while others get stuck in the mud of a harmful drug pattern?

Szalavitz's theory of addiction is that it's not so much about a rewired brain or misfiring pleasure centers—it's a learning disorder. She says addiction is often "a coping mechanism, a way to try to manage an environment that frequently feels threatening and overwhelming." It's "a search for safety rather than an attempt to rebel." The disorder does indeed change the brain and feed off our ancient human compulsion to survive, but it's not really a hijacking. It's more like an accidental rerouting, a plane bound for sunny St. Pete's in Florida somehow touching down upon the frozen tundra of St. Petersburg, Russia, instead. And critically, not all people are equally at risk of developing this learning disorder.

The factors that put some people at higher risk are often latent, hidden, unknowable to the naked eye. It's safe to say that every time a human being tries a drug, it's possible that this person will develop addiction issues. However, it's much more likely they'll put down the substance, capable of using only when the mood strikes or of never using again. Like doing a threesome or tasting octopus, there's no way to know if you'll emerge unscathed until the act has already been done.

Involuntary risk factors make all the difference. Some people have them, some people don't. Childhood trauma, mental illness, genetic predisposition, an uncertain home or community environment where survival is a struggle—these are the things that send a person's risk of developing addiction clicking ever upward. These factors can often lurk below the surface, well hidden by individuals who fear the social shame of admitting they have depression or were abused or bullied or misunderstood growing up.

And, crucially for secondhand witnesses like me, Szalavitz notes that it's not just the empirical data that calculates a person's addiction risk. An outsider can't take pen and paper and tick boxes of risk factors for you based on what's empirically knowable about your life and circumstances—"the way individuals perceive their own experience" is key as well. That makes the calculus even trickier, of course. Matt and I may have grown up an arm's length away from each other physically, but we could have been miles away in terms of our inner worlds and perceptions of our surroundings.

People who get addicted to drugs can often seem like anybody, anybody at all. But they're usually coming to drugs from a very specific biological, environmental, and developmental background. If your community is breathlessly wondering how Johnny Quarterback ended up dead of a heroin overdose, it sounds like the community didn't actually know Johnny very well.

"Addiction doesn't just appear," Szalavitz explains. "It unfolds."

Rounding the southeast corner of the park, Prospect Park Lake comes into view. The piercing sun reflects off the water like a laser and makes me squint. There are giant clusters of birds hanging out by the shore: ducks, geese, are those swans? I slow a bit to stare at them. A couple of Hasidic men on a walk have done the same— they talk to each other animatedly, gesturing toward the birds as if surprised. It does seem weird to me that this many birds are out in the cold weather, but I guess maybe this is normal? What would I know about it, anyway?

There'd be weird collections of birds at Robbins Farm sometimes, too. Just birds, but en masse, they'd freak me out. Not Matt though. Birds or no, he was so comfortable at the Farm he'd even sleep there sometimes. He liked to sneak out, which always cracked me up. We never had a strict curfew or anything like that; it felt like he did it just because he craved independence, the freedom to do as he wished without being perceived. Matt was always doing the type of things that teenagers in cheesy young adult novels do, and he did them without apologizing, like he invented it himself, like no one before him had smoked weed in the thick spongy dark of a quiet suburban field, and no one after him would either.

On a given Saturday night during high school, Matt would walk down the big hill from our parents' house to Mass Ave, a long main road running from downtown Boston through Cambridge, then slicing through Arlington and continuing on out into Lexington's manicured, quaint suburbia, all historic buildings and muffin shops and Revolutionary War battlefields. At the corner of Mount Vernon Street and Mass Ave he'd hop on the 77 bus, the same bus we'd ride to high school, but this time he'd ride it a couple of miles further, a straight shot, past the spooky nighttime Arlington dredge, the convenience store and the bizarrely situated BBQ restaurant, the closed Stop & Shop and the closed bagel shop, past one nail salon, past another nail salon, past yet a third fucking nail salon, riding from the more deteriorated Arlington street and sidewalks, all pothole-pocked and crumbling, up to the livelier evening bustle of the City of Cambridge. As the bus would lumber on into Porter Square, Mass Ave would begin filling up with more shops, brighter streetlights, better-maintained sidewalks with crisp edges, no weeds growing out of cracks in the concrete, and then there'd be more people, more different kinds of people, people still awake and out in the world and going to dinner and smoking cigarettes and tossing their heads back to laugh at a joke. Finally, the bus would pass the red brick of Harvard University and descend a yellowy-lit ramp into the heart of Harvard Square station. End of the line! Thank you for riding the MBTA!

He'd meet up with some friends by the benches outside the Dunkin Donuts. They'd already be smoking cigarettes, so Matt would shimmy the bent pack of Marlboros out of his back jean pocket and join them. They'd cackle, the air around them filling quickly with inside jokes and niche references to reality television stars and movies that are only available on VHS at the weird art rental place. Brooke Hogan, Divine, New York from "Flavor of Love." Impressions of these people would abound. The cackling would grow.

Then they'd walk down one of Harvard Square's twisting old streets to the Korean restaurant that everyone knew didn't card. They'd saunter up to the bar and order sake, and the elderly woman who ran the place would turn them down in a loud stately voice, before adding in a whisper, with a wink, that they should come back later. So they'd amble down the street to the Starbucks with the big bathroom and in there, beyond the stale croissants and the Elvis Costello CDs, they'd suit up: corsets, glitter, fishnets. They'd cackle and twirl and take pictures with one of those digital cameras that felt like the cutting edge of technology at the time but now looks like an ugly cheap hunk, delivering photographs that were grainy and red-eyed.

After a cigarette or seven they'd make their triumphant return to the restaurant all dragged up. At the sight of them, the restaurant owner would beam hugely, the corners of her mouth pushing the skin around her eyes into plump sacks, and she'd clap to show her delight. She'd seat them and serve them sake. She'd run a soft puckered palm over Matt's golden hair and compliment his makeup. They'd ask to take a picture with her, and her son who mans the host stand would oblige.

Full of sake and slippery noodles, they'd walk over to the Harvard Square Movie Theater for the midnight *Rocky Horror Picture Show*, joining up with hordes of strangers all dressed the same way. I know what you're probably thinking, here: Oh, your outsider brother would take the bus to the funky part of town for a Rocky Horror viewing? How very *Perks of Being a Wallflower*. But remember, Matt invented this for himself and his friends. He came up with it in a dream. He saw the future and reported back from it, and the future told them to go to the movies in drag.

With Pepsi-soaked popcorn stuck in his hair and a rip or two in his cheap fishnets, Matt would ride the 77 back to Arlington with his friends. Maybe he'd go home, sneaking back into the house exactly the way he came out, careful long-limbed maneuvers ensuring a completely undetected return. Or maybe he'd just sleep out in the middle of Robbins Farm, birds be damned. Just a stone's throw away from his own comfortable bedroom—with its Room & Board lofted bed, its miniature television, and its giant ceramic lamp in the shape of various sports balls emanating light from within their frosted glass centers—he'd still manage to feel like he was a world away as he made his bed in the cool, crabgrass-patched earth. And he was, for the most part.

My run is nearly done. I exit Prospect Park at the southeast entry and make my way down Flatbush Ave towards my apartment. The fire escapes hang over my head like guillotines. Inside an overstuffed bodega window, among the family-sized packages of Bounty and Dawn and Cheetos, an orange tabby naps in a beam of light. I run over a steel cellar door and it bounces under my weight.

8

Deviate

THERE'S THIS NEAT TRICK THAT COMES WITH RUNNING. ONCE I'VE soldiered through the first couple of miles and settled into my stride, my mind starts to automate. Sensing that my body is moving into autopilot mode, my brain starts to relax. The part that typically thinks about my feet, my breathing, my comfort level in relation to the weather—it switches off. And it takes a whole lot of other thinking parts with it. Matt's wilted arm, my loneliness, global warming. All the things my brain usually fixates on in a constant loping spiral of anxious thoughts first dims, then darkens completely. My brain transitions into this dream-like state, like it's suspended in a jar filled with liquid rather than in my own skull. It's still active and conscious in the immediate sense, still navigating me along my route, still taking note of when to yield to strollers or boxes blocking the sidewalk outside the bodega, still vaguely imagining what I'll eat when I get home. But it's gloriously free of any superfluous thought.

I knew about this running-induced goo-state before Matt died. I enjoyed accessing it then. But I was only scratching the surface of its powers, I realize now. Running before I had grief propelling me was a hobby, an obligation. Running during grieving has become more like medicine.

It's March by now, and my weekly mileage is starting to increase. My shorter runs have started to include intervals, hill repeats, form-related stuff that never occurred to me to pay attention to before formal race training. And my long runs are getting longer. Each is a new milestone, the longest amount of time I've ever spent in continuous motion.

Some are more pleasant than others. Sometimes I'm wilting under the blazing sun, regretting my long sleeves or the cocktails I consumed the night before. Sometimes I'm trotting along effortlessly as a show pony, legs feeling long, back sturdy, chin high.

Big picture, it feels like I'm getting away with something. And in many ways, I am. The disclaimers on every training plan I downloaded always featured the same spiel about a balanced diet, stretching, cross training, getting plenty of rest. They said it was critical to take a holistic approach to training in order to prevent injury and illness. I'd think to myself, *sure*, as I scrolled past these introductions and on to the meaty main course of the plan, the tidy chart featuring days of the week and their corresponding mileage and pacing suggestions, the part I could check-list-ify into satisfaction.

I'm looking for a shortcut, but I'm not aware of this. I just want the miles and the glory. I don't want the clamshell stretches and the yoga. Deep down, I feel like I'm a special exception. That I don't need to do the other stuff; I can muscle through the miles without it. Enough horrible things have already happened to me. What am I gonna do now—twist my ankle? Ho ho. He he. Besides, if I couldn't really pull it off, why does it all feel so good? Why do I feel so rapturously in control?

I've never struggled with addiction myself, but I have experience with the same sorts of mental illnesses that wracked Matt. Anxiety has thrummed inside me for as long as I can remember being conscious. As a young child I'd occasionally wake up in the middle of the night, crying deep sobs about worries I couldn't articulate while my mother rubbed my little back, compassionate but confused. Depression, I dealt with that too. I remember sitting on the floor of my bedroom in the middle of a hot summer day, all the yellowy lights switched on, blinds closed to keep out the natural sunlight. My boombox was tuned into WBCN, a local alternative rock station, and new metal music blared. I didn't really know what my musical tastes were yet, but this was loud and angry, and that felt correct in some way, so I dutifully listened to Staind and Disturbed, looking for emotional catharsis by way of Hot Topic. I had totems of my uncomplicated preteen existence splayed out on the rug in front of me: a few issues of *YM* magazine, a plastic box of yarn, a chipper illustrated guidebook on how to make friendship bracelets. I had been working diligently on a Chinese Staircase of purple, pink, and black yarn when the overpowering urge to harm myself appeared in my head. "Take a bunch of Tylenol," my brain said to me blithely. My ears started to tingle, and my heart started its anxious thrum. I stopped weaving my bracelet and stared at my hands like I'd never seen them before in my life. Pale, freckled, with squat little fingers. I turned them over to inspect my palms, then turned them back, again and again, backward and forward, feeling like I was seeing something I shouldn't be, like these were the hands of someone else, someone from the past or from a different plane of existence. I was thirteen years old.

In college I saw the school counselor in intermittent bursts. In my late twenties, spoiled with health insurance and disposable income, I saw therapists, psychiatrists. I tried Lexapro, but it wasn't for me. It felt like it accelerated my anxious heart into full-on arrhythmia. It gave me disturbing nightmares: scenes of medieval battles, heavy swords thudding into flesh with wet sounds, boots sinking into mud that ran red with blood. I'd wake up feeling scandalized by the stuff my brain was capable of creating.

When I told my psychiatrist I was having these nightmares, she told me in a honeyed voice that they weren't nightmares. Actually, she said, they were vivid dreams. "A common side effect of the medication," she said. Then she leaned in a little, smiled, and lifted her eyebrow playfully. "But, lots of my patients like them." I stopped taking the medication and never saw her again.

Running though. Running helps. Unlike prescriptions, unlike deep breathing and mindfulness exercises, unlike yoga and scented candles. Running gives me somewhere tangible to put all the extra anxious energy, a physical expulsion process. Once I release it, it feels like I can finally relax.

Running is helping, so I crave it in ever increasing portions. I want more and I want it now. I'll do anything to make sure I can run each day. Holding onto the thing that helps with two sweaty fists, desperate to keep it close.

When I lay awake at night, heart beating fast and head crammed with prickly thoughts, I root through my bedside table and dry swallow a Xanax. When I wake up at 4 or 5 a.m. and swear I can see my brother in the shadow of my closet, I take two. Get rest, the training plans said, after all. They didn't specify that it shouldn't be chemically induced. Running helps, and I need to be able to run. So this is what I do for a while.

Matt and I were in high school in the first years of the 2000s. OxyContin pills were everywhere—OCs, our classmates called them. The slim orange bottle of pills you'd receive from your dentist following wisdom teeth removal became a totem of early aughts teendom, a rite of passage up there with your first AIM screen name and your first open-mouth kiss behind a multiplex.

I never needed to have my wisdom teeth removed. I've got a couple molars permanently missing from the back of my mouth, so when my wisdom teeth showed up, there was plenty of room. Thanks to this genetic quirk, I never got the OCs. But lots and lots of kids did.

In the mornings before the first bell of the day, students would cluster in the cold stairwell by the back door of our high school. The door would swing open and shut as kids arrived, uniforms askew, sleeves rolled up, no coats on despite 20-degree winter weather, burning hot the way teenagers do. We'd eat the way teenagers eat, too, with stomachs of steel and an insatiable sugar tolerance. We'd fish handfuls of loose gummy worms out of a communal CVS bag, sipping Arizona Iced Tea from aluminum cans the size of our heads. In the morning hallway you could catch up on weekend gossip, frantically copy some math homework, or, if you'd been lucky enough to recently have your wisdom teeth removed, you could make clandestine arrangements to sell those extra pills.

Why did so many of us sell drugs to each other? Unclear. Most kids at this tuition-charging school came from families in healthy enough financial condition that we weren't desperate for cash to support our needs. But the wants, perhaps, were different. For example, there was a Wet Seal at the Cambridgeside Galleria. Those glittery halter tops and rhinestone thongs were cheap all right, but they weren't free.

Moreover, selling any pills you came across felt like a lark. It felt adult. The same way we'd enjoy entering chat rooms and purporting to be a sensuous older woman named Mitsy whose breasts were so large they gave her back problems, cosplaying adulthood by literally dealing drugs felt mostly like an ironical joke, the same way wearing our DARE t-shirts to keggers did.

I never tried the OCs. People told me it felt good, but I was too anxious, too afraid of losing control. Besides, I was more interested in the aesthetics of drug use, and I didn't get the appeal in this case. I used to think chic consumption methods were the main point of doing drugs. Chopping up cocaine on a mirror, slicing and reslicing into perfect little lines, and then delicately snorting it up—lightly touching your nose, rubbing remnants on your gums. Or crumbling marijuana leaves into a fine sawdust, arranging them inside a rolling paper, massaging it into a fat blunt. Licking the edges, flicking open your zippo on your jeans. The sneaky little rituals, the insider knowledge, it was all part of the appeal. That's why I didn't get OCs. What, I just take one, like I'm popping a Midol, and then that's it? I'm high? It sounded anticlimactic.

But we were stressed. We were bored. We had few options to entertain ourselves in our precious few hours of leisure time. Most American suburbs like the ones in Greater Boston have always been pretty bereft of places for young people to go and hang out. There weren't any cool coffee shops or arts spaces like you'd see on teen television dramas, just fluorescent-lit Dunkin Donuts franchises and haunted-seeming old theaters that played silent movies for local weirdos. Restaurants were hostile to big groups of teens with limited amounts of cash, and the nearest malls closed at 9.

So for kids at my high school, places like The Lot became go-to destinations. Although it sounds like it could have been a nightclub, The Lot was a painfully literal moniker. It was simply the parking lot behind our high school, right outside that back door. During the day, it was filled with the parked cars of townspeople running errands, teachers and school workers, and students whose parents were rich enough to enter them in the parking pass lottery. But at night, the meters were off, baby, and the teens roamed free. Kids would park their cars and pop the trunks, loaded up with indiscreet stocks of Natural Ice. They'd open the doors and let the JAMN 94.5 blare out, Tupac and T-Pain thumping into a crowd of mostly white private school kids who attempted to nod with swagger, awkwardly lining up with the 1 and 3 beats, never the 2 and 4.

This is where kids would competitively slurp their beers, toss back bottle-cap shots of Jim Beam, and pop pills like Tic Tacs. We'd do it till we were sick, then we'd do it again and again. Why? Maybe it really was that boredom, surrounded at night by shuttered pizzerias and darkened nail salons and circling cops in their menacingly silent cruisers. Maybe we were too desperate for against-the-rules entertainment at any cost, even if it involved huffing glue or crushing beer cans into your skull till it left a welt or spinning yourself around to the tune of Nelly's "Country Grammar" until you puked, whatever it took to get a good story out of the evening. Maybe it was because we were exhausted, in school from 7:30 a.m. till 3 p.m., then sports or part-time jobs, then hours of homework, then hours of SAT prep, then too much TV or America Online, then up at dawn to do it all again. Maybe it was because we were showing off to each other, peacocking around, grasping baldly at status and sexual attractiveness, seeking to reach the top of the teenage pecking order. Maybe it was because we were all a little sad, a little broken, a little more afraid and still craving the comfort of our mothers than anyone wanted to admit.

I don't know why it was what you did. But it was what you did.

All these years later, the disastrous impact of OxyContin has been well documented by news articles, books, movies, podcasts, even pop songs. The crimes of opioid manufacturers and distributors have been laid barer than ever for the public to see. The shortcomings of health care systems and government agencies have been illuminated and examined. The cultural reckoning feels simultaneously omnipresent and enigmatic.

The story goes like this: Over centuries, the medicinal use of opioids to treat pain has come into vogue and then fallen back out of popularity in waves. During the 1990s, the wave rose up once again with the added wind of booming capitalism at its back. Ruthless private businesses like Purdue Pharma, seeing an opportunity to make quite a lot of money, threw their hats into the magic pill race. Purdue created OxyContin, a new version of generic oxycodone that boasted over 12 hours of continuous pain relief, an irresistibly novel and groundbreaking claim. Purdue overhyped the benefits and downplayed the risks. They hired huge sales teams to take doctors to steak dinners and to conferences in Hawaii to tout the incredible healing powers of OxyContin, how it was good for postoperative pain, sure, but also for back trouble, headaches, and yeah, teen wisdom teeth removal. They sprinkled branded swag everywhere they went: OxyContin pens, stuffed monkeys wearing OxyContin t-shirts, even a CD of swing music entitled "Swing in the Right Direction with OxyContin."

Of course, the outstanding claims Purdue's salespeople made about their medication weren't precisely true. But by the time that all became clear, the train had long left the station. The FDA overlooked shortcomings in Purdue's research, private distributors seized the opportunity to ship OxyContin and other powerful opioids to pharmacies throughout the country, dentists wrote 30-day scripts for children. Communities teemed with the medication, prescribed and not. People took the medication in large quantities, prescribed and not. Pill mills popped up like modern-day roadside saloons.

And then came the prescribing crackdown. Problem solved, right? Not quite. Once the pills stopped flowing so freely, a whole bunch of newly addicted people still needed something. Once addiction unfolds, it changes your body and mind, and you can't just stop using when Walgreen's snaps their drive-thru window shut on your fingers. Enter heroin. Enter fentanyl. Cheap, powerful opioids made easily in labs to fill the void.

In *Empire of Pain*, journalist Patrick Radden Keefe (no relation, unfortunately) trains his focus on the hyperlitigious and shadowy family behind Purdue Pharma: the Sacklers. Tracing the family's roots back before Purdue, he shows how eldest brother Arthur Sackler rose up from humble beginnings to become a key founder of modern medical advertising. All those pharmaceutical ads you see on cable today, the ones showing a B-roll of families baking cookies and playing soccer while a voice-over lets you know that mild side effects such as nausea, mania, and limb loss may occur—you can in some ways thank Arthur Sackler for those. Radden Keefe understands that this history is important because spin becomes central to OxyContin's success. That's what made it different. When Arthur's nephew Richard introduced the medication, he followed his uncle's playbook. And many, many people on the payroll eventually came to understand what it was exactly that they were spinning. That's become clearer and clearer as more documents have emerged as part of the multistate opioid lawsuits that are currently ongoing.

In 1996, when Matt was seven years old and I was 10 and we were both learning from Mr. T how important it was for us to say no to dope, Richard Sackler presided over the official launch of Oxy-Contin, joyously evangelizing to his gathered sales team, calling for a "blizzard of prescriptions that will bury the competition."

In 2001, when the negative impact of that sales blizzard was only just beginning to become truly known, Richard Sackler wrote in an email, "We have to hammer on the abusers in every way possible. They are the culprits and the problem. They are reckless criminals."

In 2012, three years before Matt would die with a needle in his arm, an executive at AmerisourceBergen, one of the country's largest opioid distributors, sent around an email with a custom-made attachment, a photoshopped graphic of Kellogg's Honey Smacks cereal, edited to read "Killogg's Smack" and showing the frog mascot hungrily clutching a syringe along with his usual cereal spoon. "You're just a barrel of laughs today," a colleague replied.

The cruelty is exceptional in its straightforwardness. But it's not exceptionally cruel. They're simply saying the quiet part out loud.

It's easy to look at this story and vilify the pill itself. After all, that's what ends up pictured in so much of the reporting on the addiction crisis, a sort of unofficial stock art mascot. Little white circles with a clean line imprinted down the center, a pleasingly even, geometric form. Sometimes the pictures show a whole bottle of them, or sometimes it's a loose pile of them scattered across a countertop, pills raining from the sky or pills in stasis, pills arranged tidily or pills heaping chaotically. These images are meant to sum up all the suffering, to portray this crisis as a matter of one specific poison packaged as snake oil and sold en masse to a public who didn't need it. But that's not precisely what happened either, I don't think.

Because opioids do work for a lot of types of pain management. When their dosages and effects are properly noted, they're effective and safe for many patients. No one ever needed to be giving teenagers bottles of 30-day supplies, but that happens rarely these days. In fact, what happens much more often is that spooked doctors are afraid to offer patients pain relief because of the atmosphere of panic surrounding these little white pills. Prescribing has been declining for years, but overdoses are skyrocketing. The pill isn't a good mascot anymore. It probably never was.

Ultimately, OxyContin did us the service of showing us ourselves. It couldn't have grown so popular, kicking off an overdose crisis that's only continued to echo and intensify, if the soil hadn't been so fertile. Millions of patients throughout the United States suffer from intractable physical pain that doctors struggle to treat in 15-minute billable increments. Millions more suffer from depression, anxiety, PTSD, psychological conditions that can literally ache as deeply as a broken bone. Giant swaths of the country lack good jobs, schools, child care, housing, even adequate food and drinking water. Pharmaceutical greed and the brokenness of the American health care system across the board, not just in terms of opioid prescribing, have never been clearer. How can we look at all this and not see the sinewy connective tissues? How can what happened to my brother be chalked up to a few bad apples in one contained barrel when clearly the whole warehouse is rotten?

Addiction doesn't just happen. It unfolds.

It would be a little funny if I got addicted to these, I think to myself with dark amusement as I swallow my nightly Xanax. My run this morning was exhilarating, but now, my body is tired. My quads ache dully. My ankles feel creaky. I'm depleted, but it feels good to be so wrung out. I'm basking in my exhaustion, and the Xanax is giving me an extra boost of pleasant sleepiness. A heady brew indeed. If you could press this exact feeling into a pill and sell it, you'd be rich.

9

Medicate

MANY MONTHS AFTER OCTOBER 5, MY ENDURING FIXATION ON MY brother's corpse leaves me still unable to properly care for my own living, breathing, needy body.

I spend most waking hours obsessing over Matt's body as I had discovered it. I cling to the details of what I saw because I'm terrified to forget, because forgetting would mean that this whole thing becomes real in a way that I'm not ready for. So long as I'm fixated on the trauma and shock of it all, I can kick the can of dealing with the permanence a little further down the road.

Gray-blue and heavy, sack-like, sprawled. It's important to me that everyone knows how sprawled he was.

When my friends come around to check in, clutching bottles of cheap white wine and bouquets of bodega flowers, I often end up answering any inquiries about how I'm doing with more talk about Matt's body.

"And his arm? It was like *this*," I say, lifting mine aloft and wilting it to the side.

"Uh huh," they say, in pained voices, having heard versions of this before.

"But his torso, it was like, stuck. In the chair. We couldn't get it out of the chair."

"I know. Awful," they say.

I feel remarkably sane, even though I can hear myself acting not quite so. It occurs to me this is probably how most insane people feel.

As for my own body—well, I never realized how gastronomically oriented grieving can be. Franky, I can't poop. My whole body feels wrenched into a permanent fist, and my guts feel like they've been tied together in expert knots by a grizzled Nantucket fisherman. Any bowel movements I do eventually muster are truly pathetic. I stare down at them with scorn after what felt like hours of effort: wilted, ropey, and not anywhere near the mass I was expecting after all the strain.

My diet can't be helping things. I'm microwaving the sweet potatoes, sure. I guess that's technically healthy. But the idea of preparing meals, taking the pans out and using them and then cleaning them and then putting them away again—I can't fathom it. Cook a meal? Why don't I just solve the mystery of Stonehenge while I'm at it?

A lot of running and not a lot of eating. As I increase my mileage each week, I know I'm supposed to be "fueling" appropriately. Lean protein, packets of energy gels in sporty color schemes, carbohydrates. I read the nutrition tips online. But I never really feel hungry. It doesn't feel like there's any free space inside of me for the food to go. The fisherman sealed things up real tight, laughing with cool satisfaction, a cigarette dangling from the corner of his lipless mouth as he twisted my guts into a fine and mighty Blood Knot. So I continue to gravitate toward candy, snack items, small individually wrapped cakes that were doubtless created in some unholy midwestern plant on the same conveyor belt where they make crayons. If the item doesn't contain high-fructose corn syrup or feature a cartoon character mascot, I'm not interested in eating it.

Another rub for my dining schedule: Even with my Xanax to help things along, I'm awake most nights. At age 29, embracing the idea that it's never too late to try new things, I've become afraid of the dark. When I nap in the early morning or daytime, the warm orange glow beyond my closed eyelids provides a sort of buffer. It feels safer to sleep when I'm drenched in light. In the inky black of night, alone in my apartment, a horror version of Matt and the arm and the chair wait for me. I feel I deserve to be stuck with these images. But I do try to avoid them.

Most nights I stay up late watching television and swiping on dating apps. I've been enjoying this gamification of romance, a novelty to me after so many years in a relationship that began before Silicon Valley's cultural dominance. And I like spending time with strangers these days. I'm grateful for my friends, of course, but being so thoroughly perceived—so known—sometimes feels exhausting. They know what happened to me, and they know how I'm struggling. They look at my sunken eyes and greasy hair and they see trouble. A stranger, though, maybe just sees someone who parties too much. With them, on these dates, I can cosplay a happy person—maybe a scattered and wacky person but still a person whose brother didn't die in front of her nonetheless.

The rituals that go along with dating are soothing in their total ability to distract. Curling my eyelashes and moisturizing my knees, performing charm in those light getting-to-know-you conversations, grazing my finger over an unfamiliar wrist. It feels like nothing, and nothing feels like a wonderful little break.

But lately, it's all gotten a little loose, a little careless. In a rare flight of concern for my own well-being, I scheduled an appointment with a new gynecologist. I'm slightly overdue for my annual pap smear, true, but I'm mostly going because my Catholicism-rotted brain is convinced that I will be cosmically punished for my recent behavior with an HIV infection or a surprise 8.5-month-old fetus growing inside of me, somehow undetectable until right this moment.

So here I am at this doctor's office in Manhattan, inside a tall midtown skyscraper that's undergoing construction. In the pleasant office with a lime green statement wall, a kindly nurse in blue scrubs festooned with sleeping cartoon sheep is about to draw my blood. As I hear the wrappers containing the sterilized needle being yanked apart, I start to squirm. I extend my left arm for the nurse and wind my head so far to the right I worry I pulled a muscle in my neck.

"Sorry," I say to her with my eyes squinted shut. "I really don't do well with needles."

"Really?" the nurse asks, with a breathy chuckle. I assume she's amused because I'm a grown woman who should be able to handle blood work by now, but I realize later she's probably actually amused because there's a sizable full-color tattoo on my extended arm, the result of many hours with a needle in my skin.

I've always hated getting shots, but it's not the needle I have a problem with, really. It's the vein, the flesh where the needle enters my body, knowing that there's a foreign object spooling around inside me for a time. Feeling the needle plunge inside, getting deeper and deeper, makes me feel like I'm going to pass out.

"Don't worry, you have such good veins," the nurse dishes to me, as if she's complimenting my ankle boots.

Did Matt have good veins? I wonder.

I remember when Matt was in the emergency room for the second time, just months before his death. The staff were trying to find him a bed in a psych ward. I held his hand and talked to him gently while the machines bipped and patients around us groaned. I looked down at his arm. It was decently toned for a guy who never works out; Matt always miraculously maintained a lean athleticism, even well into his addiction. I looked at the crook behind his elbow, discolored with an astral array of purplish pinpoints. I looked and looked. So many of them. Panic crept in, but then, the record skipped. I remembered him as a baby: seven years old, his bowl haircut and boxy BUM Equipment shirts. How he'd stick one finger up, Poindexter style, and make declarations that he'd gleaned from strange prank-oriented books that relatives often gave us, with titles like *Shenanigans* and *SPLAT*.

"Did you know you can put a banana in the mail, as long as it's properly postmarked?"

"Did you know farts are mostly made of nitrogen?"

"Did you know there's no official name for the back of the elbow? Some people call it the 'elbow pit.'"

Did you know? Did you know?

In the ER, I pointed at Matt's elbow pit. "What are these?" I said, knowing the answer was "track marks."

His lie was instant, effortless, second nature. Like a supermodel selling cola, smiling, holding the logoed can up, telling the viewer through perfect white teeth, yes, I drink a cool glass of cola every day.

"I was on an IV earlier; it took a few tries," he said casually, throwing in an over-it sigh for flavor.

My mind sifted through the words like a game show host during the lightning round. Can we accept that as an answer? Judges say . . . yes!

It's good. It's safe. I'm back in control. I wanted to tell myself I was capable of asking the hard questions, and with this whiff of an attempt, I felt I had done it. The lies keep his real issues out of focus, blurred, not quite reality. But did I know? Really? Truly?

Yes, of course I fucking knew.

The first time Matt was hospitalized was December of 2011. Home from UMass for Christmas break, he'd been notably woozy one afternoon in the basement of my parents' house, in and out of consciousness, his hand red and swollen. Not quite knowing what was really going on but knowing enough to be worried, my parents brought him to the emergency room, and he was admitted to the ICU after that.

I drove over to visit on a cold afternoon, gliding my old white Corolla over the crackling salted pavement and into a free space in Parking Lot D. The hospital loomed large, wet and sparkling against the overcast sky. I got out of the car and stared the building down, eyes narrowed, taking clipped breaths.

A few yards to my right, there was an old woman wearing a silk headscarf, a full face of cakey makeup, and a floor-length authentic mink coat, cinched at the waist with a cheap elasticized fashion belt. She was watching a young boy sled down a browned pile of parking lot snow atop a Papa Gino's pizza box. The kid climbed to the top of the pile on all fours, then dragged himself down the makeshift hill at an anticlimactic snail's pace, then turned around and did it again. The woman watched without expression. She smoked a cigarette, milky plumes curling around her nose. I inhaled deeply to catch a whiff of the nicotine. I wished I had a cigarette.

Inside, Matt's hospital room was squat, stale. Yellow light filled the room, but it still seemed dark, obscured, like looking at undeveloped photo negatives. The walls at the front of the room were floor-to-ceiling glass, curtains drawn back, creating a dollhouse effect as we looked out at the busy hallway before us. Nurses dutifully walked this way and that, stopping to make phone calls or flip through charts.

Matt's machine's occasionally bipped. Didn't seem to be a rhyme or reason to it.

I sat next to his bed, in a chair so uniquely uncomfortable it felt like it was intentionally engineered to drive people insane. The rounded, lacquered-wood armrests were too thin to truly rest your arms upon yet too thick to work around. The plastic-glazed cushions felt like diapers behind my back and beneath my half-asleep ass. I shifted my position every few minutes in an attempt to awaken my buttocks, to no avail.

My MacBook sat on top of the woven hospital blanket covering Matt's bed. It was the sort of blanket that feels wet all the time—heavy and thick, even though it's of course bone dry, quadruple-sterilized. The MacBook played a comedy show off of Netflix. Matt had fallen asleep a while ago. His head was rolled over to the side, angled downward, facing me with his mouth and eyes peacefully closed. The papery fabric of his hospital gown stood tall, bunched up around his neck. He looked like a tranquilized puppy on his way home from surgery.

He sighed, sort of. The machine bipped.

The show mumbled on, and I shifted my weight again. My ass started to feel less like it had fallen asleep and more like it no longer existed. I coughed.

Matt and I were not alone. There was a man in the corner of the hospital room, focused on reading a yellowed paperback. He sat in the same sort of chair I'm sitting in, but he looked much more comfortable. He had on purple scrubs. His bald head shone under the fluorescent light. He looked up at me for a split second in reaction to the noise, then returned to his book.

Upon arrival earlier, I had asked Matt who this guy was. "I don't even know," he'd whispered with a dismissive eye roll. "Everyone here is ghastly. There's also this one woman who comes around, she smells like corn chips. I don't know what her job is, either. She pokes at the monitors and then she leaves."

"Is she perhaps a nurse?" I asked.

Matt stared at me with his eyebrows raised in faux-offense. "No doy. But like what is she doing? No one tells me anything. They don't even look at me! And it's like, excuse you, but what is your purpose? What is your reason? What is your *damage*, Heather?"

We giggled, and the conversation devolved into more movie quotes and catchphrases, while the mystery man watched stone-faced from the corner.

The mystery man hadn't left the room once in the hours I'd been by Matt's bed. I had my suspicions about his role. Has Matt been combative? Resistant to doctor's orders? Maybe he needed extra supervision because his usual contrariness has become a roadblock to his care? Later, I'd find out that the orderly was present because Matt was on suicide watch. My brother had tried to slit his wrists with the plastic butter knife on his dinner tray. He couldn't have thought that would actually work, but I guess I'll never know what his intent was.

Nestled in my diaper chair, I started to think I could hear my hair growing. The air in the hospital room buzzed like a mosquito trap. I wondered if my parents were having a nice dinner. Maybe they went to that Chinese food place around the corner, or perhaps they played it safe and stuck to the mall-esque food court on the corner of Longwood Avenue. They left to go get an actual meal for the first time in days rather than ordering up hospital food trays from the clunky room phone like some sort of miserable, purgatory version of hotel room service. I had pleaded with them to go out, get some air, eat some food with actual freshness to it. "I'll stay right here with him," I assured them.

Another bip. *What are these bips?* I wondered. It seemed impossible to know.

I looked up at Matt, and his shoulders started rocking. Slowly at first. Within a few seconds, his body began to jerk and sway, at first seeming like a sleep tremor, the kind you have when you dream you're falling off a ledge. I watched him as it escalated. *It's almost like he's having a seizure,* I thought. My childhood neighbor had epilepsy, and I remembered watching on a rainy Saturday afternoon as he transitioned from a fit of laughter on the floor into a full-on seizure, his sister calling out for their parents, his dad rushing down from upstairs to hold his head, whispering "I love you" into his quaking ear, following a number of calming fatherly steps that made me feel soothed by proxy.

Matt *is* having a seizure, my brain began to tell me. Oh, fuck. I rose from my diaper chair and looked at the orderly. He was still reading, unmoved. Matt's eyes were wide open and rolled back in his head. A trickle of blood leaked from the corner of his mouth. I was afraid to touch him, to do the wrong thing. *How do I soothe him? What is right?* I wanted to whisper in his ear but I couldn't bring myself to.

The machine blips were off the charts now. Furious, urgent.

"Help him!" I heard myself stammer out. The orderly's eyes darted up. He finally took in the scene and jumped up, flinging the paperback down. He darted toward the bed, then, thinking twice, ran out into the hallway. I followed him out, and he disappeared around a corner.

I stood in the middle of this hallway, the same hallway that earlier had felt narrow and claustrophobic, but which now felt immense and intimidating.

"My brother needs help," I said. I didn't yell it; I said it. Like I was afraid to make too much noise. Like I was unsure if what I was saying was even true.

A nurse at the station put her phone down and ran into Matt's room. I followed her in. Within a few moments more nurses rushed into the room, their printed pastel scrubs scattering across the laminate like multicolored marbles. They began the process of doing the board-certified Right Thing, but I can't remember the details of what that looked like anymore. I think they secured his arms, secured his head, began queuing up medication and calling his supervising physician.

"You need to go to the waiting room now," a short nurse with brown hair and boxy shoulders said to me. I looked at her, looked at Matt, not processing her words. She took my shoulders in her hands and shooed me out the door.

Dazed, I wandered down the hallway, shuffling along in loopy lines, like a Victorian ghost in a watchtower. I eventually found the waiting room, filled with rows of more diaper chairs, far as the eye can see. It seemed like a room you'd take your SATs in, not a room where you wait to find out if your brother is dead, if he's dead this time, if he finally did it to himself for good. I didn't like this room. I wanted to know what was going on. But I still lived in fear of rules, both real and perceived. So, terrified of getting into some sort of mystery trouble, I hobbled over to the first diaper chair in the line. I sat down. The too-blue television screen in the corner played a soap opera. The woman on the screen was crying desperately in the arms of her lover. She was howling about something. I wanted to howl.

After 30 minutes or so, outrage started to bloom in me as I focused on the kernel of the semi-rude nurse. Being angry felt easier, not as scary. So I zoomed in on that moment more and more, until I got myself so pissed I stormed back down the hallway toward Matt's room, furious they shooed me aside, that no one told me what was really going on and what was next. Shouldn't there be some sort of action plan? Don't doctors and nurses triage about these things? Aren't they obligated to keep family informed, goddamn it, instead of sweeping them off to SAT nightmare rooms?

As I rounded the corner back toward Matt's room, I saw my parents. The nurses must have called them back. They were probably mid bite, just starting to feel at ease, just starting to feel hungry and let that hunger be sated, when the call came. Their faces were tired. Their mouths were half open. Their eyebrows were weighed with the pain of a hundred years of worry.

I walked back to them with my head down, ashamed that this had happened on my watch. We hugged without embracing. No one cried.

By now, Matt was stabilized and sedated. A young man in green scrubs and a crisp white jacket came out of Matt's room to greet us, a stethoscope strung around his neck. His dark hair was crisply trimmed, his wrists and forearms were muscular. He was handsome and young. I imagined he biked to work, lived in a nice old Victorian in Brookline, watered his plants and read best sellers recommended by the *New York Review of Books*. Signed up for half marathons in other cities, traveled specifically for the race, posted Facebook photos of his medals next to his postrace brunch. He probably had an equally clean and attractive young wife. They probably rock climbed together. I was nearly lost in this warm fantasy when he started to speak.

"You guys are the family?" His voice was accusatory, brusque, like a cop's. We nodded.

He gestured for us to follow him to a small office. He pinned a few x-rays up on an illuminated wall. He spoke, but I was not paying attention fully, even though I wanted to. He said something about brain swelling.

"The swelling is consistent with what we usually see in heroin users," I finally manage to hear.

We looked at each other, baffled. We knew Matt was a stoner. We knew he was likely messing around with other stuff, prescriptions, stronger formulations of cough syrups. Silliness, we thought. But heroin? Needles and rubber hoses and Ewan McGregor in *Trainspotting*, all sweat and under-eye bags and gratuitous vomit? That seemed impossible, a bridge too far, too weird and truly wrong.

"I don't—this isn't—What can we do?" we stammered at the handsome young doctor, six blue eyes pleading.

"Well, drug use like this is very dangerous," he started out. His obtuse, chastising tone made my own brain swell with rage. The middle bit of his spiel sags in my memory. He certainly didn't talk about therapy or medication or any form of actual treatment for Matt's life-threatening health problem. He wraps it all up with the following helpful nugget of advice: "You've got to tell him, really, that he needs to stop."

What I did next felt like I invented it myself, but turns out, it's a fairly well-known coping mechanism. It's called disassociation. I took the whole previous 30 minutes and placed them gently in a box in my mind. I packaged it up with that really nice Scotch-brand packaging tape, the one that costs a little more but goes on smoother, seals so much better. Then I tucked the box away, high on a shelf, up there with the childhood Christmas memories and the old algebra and Magna Carta information. I kept it up there for a while.

The next few days after the seizure were long and blurry. There was talk of psych wards, but he didn't want to go, and after some evaluations, it turned out he wasn't out-of-it enough to be sent against his will. That's the thing about Matt's state of mind throughout all of this: Despite his obvious troubles, he always came across as ruthlessly sane.

It didn't occur to me at the time, but years later I'm left wondering one important question: Why were all of his diagnostics so focused on his mental health and not his obvious and worsening drug addiction? The hospital staff, the doctors and the social workers and the medical liaisons, they always focused on his mental state in a silo, his depression and suicidal ideation. But no one seemed to imagine that maybe this mental state was being exacerbated by the drug addiction that had taken up residence in Matt's brain, renovating his mind like a "House Hunters" couple from hell. Or that his drug use had been escalating as an effort to self-medicate, the two conditions making each other worse in real time, nightmarish twins dragging him closer and closer toward real danger.

I always thought addiction was this big fat mystery that eternally and presently confounded scientists, clergymen, and politicians alike. Surely that's why it was so deadly, so intractable, I thought. But it turns out, there is plenty of research, spanning decades, providing thorough and trustworthy guidance on what works to treat addiction and promote long-term recovery for people with opioid use disorders. We just don't use it.

Comedian John Mulaney does this great bit about noir detectives. He describes this old-timey gumshoe at the scene of a violent crime, trying to solve it before DNA evidence was widespread, at a time when the police confidently relied on their dated, limited methods. Mulaney takes on the persona of the detective. Walking around the scene, Mulaney's detective discovers a pool of the killer's blood. To the audience, that discovery sounds like a boon. The detective looks at the pool, considers it for a moment, and says "Hmm." Then after a beat, he walks away from the clear-as-day evidence right in front of his face. "Gross!" he exclaims dismissively. Next, Mulaney's detective raises his face to the sky with a smug look of satisfaction, knowing the true way to solve the case. "Now," he says, "back to my hunch."

The roots of our current addiction treatment model took hold in the mid-1800s. Anyone who's seen an episode of *Dr. Quinn* can tell you that medicine in general has come a long way since the 1800s: We no longer treat the flu with poultices, we no longer apply leeches to the cheekbones to bring down a fever. These days, we're far less concerned with one's humors, vapors, and tempers when it comes to treating classic medical conditions like pneumonia and cancers. We've got antibiotics, blood tests, reliable measures, and outcome-focused treatments. Overall, our medical practices now demand real science and proven results.

Addiction treatment missed this wave. It got left behind in the realm of humors, vapors, and tempers. There are two main reasons for this. The first is the pervasive, decades-spanning cultural perception of addiction as a moral failing, deserving of tough love and punishment, rather than a medical condition deserving of legitimate care. The second is the punishment itself: the illegality and criminal consequences associated with substance use. The connection to criminality perpetuates the idea of addiction as a moral failing, and the moral failing idea leads to criminal punishment, and so on. It's a vicious circle, a snake eating its own tail.

Even as we stand neck-deep in the worst overdose crisis in U.S. history, we have yet to outgrow the idea that addiction is a personality flaw. No matter how many new studies debunking this idea are released, it still makes sense to that squishy spot in our brains, the part that calls out for base things like vengeance, punishment, and retribution at any cost. To this spot, the idea of sending someone to their local doctor's office for drug addiction would be on par with the suggestion that someone be hospitalized for being a liar, a jerk, a flake. It doesn't make sense to lots of people. Instead, we prefer shipping people off to expensive rehab facilities where they can be discreetly saved from themselves, rebuilding their moral constitution by painting ceramics and petting horses.

Boston is a medical mecca within the United States, full of more state-of-the-art hospitals and medical schools than you can shake a syringe at. The city that managed to expertly triage and treat its way to preventing all but three deaths in the wake of a terrorist bombing at the finish line of the Boston Marathon in 2013. This is the place where we couldn't get Matt treatment for his heroin-swollen brain in 2011.

After Matt was released from the hospital and went home with my parents, I dragged myself back to Jamaica Plain. To my adult apartment. I didn't feel like an adult, though. I felt like a baby, knuckles fat and dimpled, skull not fully closed, motor skills underdeveloped.

I turned the deadbolt and greeted Eddie, shuffled through the foyer and into the kitchen. Elijah was waiting up at the table with just a small overhead lamp on, typing on his MacBook, his dark curls getting into his eyes, his elegant wrists poised carefully over the keyboard, his posture perfect, as always.

Elijah and I were still happy then. We enjoyed playing house in the newly renovated apartment we lucked into, a rare shining gem compared to the run-down, roommate-loaded, mouse-infested triple-deckers most of our friends rented. This place was all new renovation, granite countertops, stainless steel appliances, eco-friendly bamboo flooring. But we were still 20-somethings, and the decor hinted at that fact: the stove top covered in crappy IKEA pots with peeling Teflon, the sink perpetually full of dishes, the stacks of student loan bills in unopened envelopes that bulged with terms and conditions, and of course all the stray bottles of disgustingly saccharine liqueurs, stuff like Chambord and DiSaronno, the kind you buy with the intention of making grown-up cocktails but then end up just pouring into a basin of questionable vodka-based punch at your next house party.

I sat down sheepishly beside him at the table. I reached my right hand out to his face, to brush the stubble on his cheeks with my thumb, to wind a few longer tendrils around my index finger. He rubbed between my shoulder blades with his wide palm.

"How is he?"

I opened my mouth to speak calmly, but all of a sudden sobs emerged, unexpected and startling, like the endless knots of multi-colored scarves being pulled from the throat of a surprised-looking magician. The sobs came out like hacking coughs, the tears streamed down my instantly-red face like foamy spit. Elijah stood up and then stood me up too, guiding me by my shoulders. He walked me into the bedroom and laid me down. Eddie hopped up on the bed next to me, his hot breath on my neck.

"He's going to die," I stammered through the sobs.

"He's not going to die," Elijah said in a soothing tone.

"He is," I spat back, refusing the kind delusion. "He is going to die," I continued between cough sobs, speaking the harsh words without thought, as if drunk or possessed. "And I'll have to watch." I cried till I became unconscious, my body eventually shutting itself down without asking my brain's permission.

When Elijah brought this conversation up the next day, I pretended not to remember it.

10

Surrender

I'm jogging along 6th Avenue in Park Slope, taking the long way into Prospect Park for a change of scenery. The sidewalk is well cleared of the past week's snow, but some sharp brown mounds loiter in the gutter. The sky is dense with pregnant clouds, and the air is thick, wetter and warmer than usual. My arms are bare in my moisture-wicking t-shirt, but I still have on gloves and my crappy headband to keep my appendages from going numb.

This area of 6th Avenue is quiet and residential and lined with beautiful old brownstones. Their stoops are grand and wide, their wrought-iron gates adorned with decorative curly cues, their front gardens professionally landscaped and often dotted with gas-burning lanterns. It would be almost painfully quaint if it weren't for the occasional cues that remind you you're still in New York, like the heaps of black garbage bags dusted in gray snow, the occasional half-empty bottle of malt liquor (or half-full bottle of piss, depending on how you look at it) tucked into a leafy yard, or the crudely written notes duct-taped to stately old front doors, providing delivery-person instructions like "UPS/FEDEX DO NOT LEAVE PACKAGES ON STEPS, BUZZ #2!!!! SEAMLESS PLEASE CALL DO NOT BUZZ #2!!!!"

My training is going well so far. My stride's strengthening, my breathing is becoming less of a desperate wheeze and more of a cool, steady in-and-out. I don't feel like I'm getting faster when I'm out in the midst of my runs, but when I look at my progress on the tracker app, I see my pace quickening. Nothing major, just a few seconds here and there. But seconds count.

Today I have to do something called Fartleks, which sounds to me more like a gassy "Dr. Who" villain than a feat of athleticism, but here we are. Through internet searches, I've learned that Fartleks are basically a freestyle interval run during which you're encouraged to use the natural guideposts around you to mark starts and stops to periods of harder running followed by easy jogging. I decided to roughly follow a two-block push, one-block recovery approach, though I could easily have used the houses of worship all around me to mark my intervals.

Park Slope is home to many churches. There are more than 30 of them packed into this small area. Sixth Avenue features a couple of Catholic stunners, like St. Augustine and St. Francis Xavier, with all the gothic architecture, rich stained glass, and watchful gargoyles you'd expect. There are some more understated Protestant joints, still beautiful but less ostentatious, and there's a gorgeous Jewish temple up closer to the park, Beth Elohim, featuring enormous Ionic columns and a domed roof. There are also a few seemingly abandoned church buildings, their denominations unknown, their paint peeling, their old wooden doors rotting off the hinges.

I can't tell if I miss God. I forget what God's like. I remember how deep faith used to feel to me: dense and round like a pearl, sometimes even ecstatic and emotional. I can remember moments when I felt so held by the universe that I was sure that God was both real and good. These moments weren't particularly remarkable in any objective sense. They rarely occurred within the stiff wooden pews of my church; instead, they often washed over me when I found myself spending time outdoors alone, beholding a particularly beautiful tree, or feeling a warm August breeze on my neck, damp and familiar like human breath. Still, I was at my most religious when I was a young teenager, so it's difficult to parse the overwhelming feelings of joyful devotion from the hot thrum of hormones that likely turned those feelings up to 11. Puberty itself can be rapturous, unpredictable, emotionally charged, filled with extreme highs and lows. I feel grateful I got through that time without trying anything too damaging, like popping OCs in the Lot or joining a cult. But in a sense, I was already part of one.

Catholicism wore me down. It banged my innate faith from a fluffy pelt into a thin piece of leather. I couldn't separate the stuff I disliked about the church from the concept of faith in general, so I turned a hateful eye toward both. I thought condemning gay people and treating women like walking uteruses was a core tenet of all spiritual practice because it had been presented to me as a core tenet of Catholicism.

I guess Catholics who subscribe to these views wouldn't call it hate though. Maybe they'd call it tough love, the cold hand of shame on the bare backs of lost souls, guiding them toward the correct behavior through shocking discomfort. Churches of all variations open their doors to sinners, but indeed, there's often a catch. The sinner must present as adequately self-hating, asking for help with their head down, hat in hand, ready to admit their powerlessness and accept a new way of life.

Running down 6th Avenue with all these heavy thoughts rattling around in my consciousness, I start to wonder how many of these houses of worship host 12-step meetings.

Alcoholics Anonymous (AA) was created in 1935. Prohibition had just ended, but many of its moral tenets held strong. Alcoholism was considered something that weak-willed degenerates suffered from, and though alcohol itself was no longer illegal, reckless drinking was something at which people of high moral character (i.e., white Protestant nonimmigrants) looked down their noses. A stockbroker named Bill Wilson and a surgeon named Dr. Bob Smith came together to form a group that would eventually become a global phenomenon, with over 115,000 groups in 180 countries—60,000 groups in the United States alone.

The stated goal of AA membership is to "stay sober and help other alcoholics achieve sobriety." The approach is mostly what you've seen in movies: clandestine meetings in church basements or community rec centers, during which groups of people known to each other only by first names engage in a group dialogue. People take turns sharing as they are comfortable. Meetings are free, and all are welcomed. You're not asked intrusive questions or made to sign up for mailing lists or anything like that. At the end of the meeting, everybody prays. (You don't have to pray if you don't want to. But most people around you will pray.) Then everybody leaves.

The 12 steps guide AA and its sister programs like Narcotics Anonymous (NA), and most of these steps involve God: surrendering to Him, admitting wrongdoings to Him, praying to understand His will. Even in the softer, more modern wordings of the steps, which have replaced "God" with "a higher power," there's a sense that your addiction can truly be healed only by spirituality, something beyond your body, your logical mind, and the realms of earthly science. And it's not just the explicit higher-power talk (and the default identification of the higher power as a "He") that connects AA's approach to traditional Christianity. The group's interest in self-flagellation feels very biblical as well. Before you can achieve lasting sobriety, first you must don the hair shirt of your sins.

AA and NA programs have a reputation for being hostile toward people who use a prescription to support their recovery. Medications like methadone and buprenorphine are considered by most major health organizations to be the gold standard of treatment for opioid addiction. According to a meta-analysis published in *JAMA Psychiatry*, taking medications for addiction treatment is associated with half the risk of death compared with those not using medication. Someone who's dealing with addiction isn't getting "high" when they take these meds. Instead, the medications provide a long-acting, regulating effect that allows people to avoid withdrawal and fully participate in their lives. But within the walls of those church basements, medications are often dismissed as a crutch, as "replacing one drug with another." It's not real recovery to many sobriety hard-liners, and those resentments are thus codified: People who take addiction treatment medications are often not allowed to get up and share at meetings, to sponsor others, or to hold leadership positions. They're like ghosts.

But, of course, meetings vary wildly. A central tenet of AA is that it is not regulated by any governing body. Instead, the program is managed on a grassroots community level, and some meetings are more inclusive than others.

Indeed, AA and NA have helped many people get well. A recent study led by Massachusetts General Hospital's Recovery Research Institute has shown that for consenting participants, AA and 12-step programs can have a positive impact on achieving and maintaining recovery. But the word doing a lot of heavy lifting there is "consenting"—or, as the study identifies these participants, "noncoerced." To an extent, we can track the people who've been helped by AA. But it's harder to track the people who've been hurt by it. I would guess a large number of those people didn't live to tell the tale.

After Matt overdosed the first time, he was encouraged by his social worker to attend a 12-step-ish day treatment program. He did it. It's unclear how helpful he found that experience. For a few years after that first scare, he was okay. Whenever we'd joke around in the Jamaica Plain apartment kitchen about his treatment experiences, he'd roll his eyes as he took on various exaggerated accents to recite some of the self-help screeds and Jesus-loving tidbits he picked up in his program. We'd laugh about it.

A common adage in the world of addiction treatment policy is that care should not be "one size fits all." Yet the AA model is still the shoe we try to force onto every foot. It looms large in the cultural consciousness because it's all we know, really. And that alone makes it seem legitimate. To most civilians, it doesn't matter what goes on inside of those meetings. You could be required to stand on your head for an hour while reciting the alphabet backwards for all most people knew. It just feels like an answer. It's got tidy rules, a regular schedule, and a proper code to follow. When confronting such a confusing and frustrating illness, that feeling alone provides immense relief.

I can certainly understand the appeal of AA for people who are into it. I love to forget that I'm a human body. I like to think of myself as more of a floating brain instead, not just earthly muscle and bone but an inner vapor connected to the great big whatever-it-is. I like to be reminded that, big picture, my particular bullshit problems are nothing more than a fleck of a wet fart on the universe's anus. I aspire to hold myself accountable and be aware of my impact on my environment. Whether or not you have an issue with drug use, it's a wonderful life practice to attempt to regularly take stock of the people you've hurt and try to make things right with them. I can see how this could help people heal deep wounds in themselves, which may have eventually unfolded into a substance use disorder.

But AA itself isn't the problem, not really. The problem is that AA alone does not constitute addiction treatment. You'd never tell a cancer patient that their peer support group, as positive and nourishing as it may be, was an adequate substitute for chemotherapy. But we do exactly this for people with substance use disorders. It's the coercion, too. Again, while AA can be helpful for consenting participants, it can be deeply harmful for those who don't want it. Yet judges often mandate that people arrested for drug- or alcohol-related infractions attend these meetings as an aspect of their sentencing or as a condition of parole. Doctors hand out NA pamphlets to the families of people who'd recently survived an overdose, as they did to mine. It's a flyswatter. A deflection. "This is not my problem" made manifest. For the weak-willed degenerate who's addicted to something, you've got two choices: go here and lay prostrate before the power of the steps or die.

For the average person, there's something like 25,000 to 30,000 individual steps within a half marathon. By the time I complete my training, I'll have taken hundreds of thousands of steps in pursuit of this one finish line. Each one has felt essential, connecting the dashes along my winding little treasure map of progress, leading me toward the shining prize at the end. It wouldn't be possible to do it any faster or smoother than this, I know. I'm already cutting corners when it comes to supportive cross-training, smart fueling. But when it comes to the steps themselves, there is no shortcut. This is the amount of movement that the journey requires.

The steps are subjective, too. The total tally of how many steps a given mile contains depends on how fast you're moving. Each training session results in a unique tableau of ticks and tallies on my little tracker app—and someone who's a different height than me, who moves at a different speed than me, would see different results. The only thing all runs have in common is that all runs are different. Some runs feel good. Some runs suck ass. Sometimes I feel amazing. Sometimes I feel like crap. Sometimes I whip through a six-mile run barely breaking a sweat; sometimes it takes me just as many steps to slug through half that distance.

This is normal, mainstream running advice says. It's to be expected. In magazines and YouTube videos and social media posts, the running community is pretty great at screaming "do you" from the hilltops. And that's made it easier for me to accept that my progress won't be linear. That as long as I keep showing up and trying, I'm doing it right. It's a relief, frankly. It helps me stick with the whole scheme. Because if I'd been made to feel like I lost the thread all the way back in my wobbly starting steps, I probably would've kicked off my Asics in a rage and given up.

What would it be like if we gave this kind of grace to people pursuing addiction recovery? What if the advice was less laser-focused on abstaining, on the cleansing power of suffering, and more focused on things like: take your time. There's no fixed number of steps. Show up. Try. Do you. How many lives could be saved just by allowing people to exhale fully, feeling peace rather than prescriptiveness?

There are similar rigidities built into conceptions of grief in America, a place where the mystery of human death is viewed mainly as just another box to tick on a life's to-do list, right after rolling over your 401ks and choosing a cost-effective Medicare Part D supplementary plan. Grief comes in five stages, the thinking goes, and you're supposed to move through each linearly. But that hasn't been my experience. Sometimes I'm angry. Sometimes I'm depressed. Sometimes I'm depressingly angry, sometimes I'm angrily depressed. The entire concept of "bargaining" as a stage does nothing for me at all. I mean, it's not a flea market, it's death. I also feel like I never want to arrive at acceptance—the finality implied in it, the gold star achievement of having officially Moved On. Because my grief feels like a growth on my body, a new part of me, fleshy and throbbing, that I didn't ask for but nonetheless have. I know it's weird, I know it's ugly, but I don't want to have it removed yet. I probably never want it removed.

I feel lucky that I've avoided the platitudes of evangelizing religious types during my grief. You could make a bingo card out of the inappropriate catchphrases this type of person will often heave at the bereaved: *He's in a better place. God has a plan.* I don't really know anybody who'd say something like that to my face; one thing you've got to hand to the Catholics is that they tend to err on the side of silence. My hometown's religiousness has always felt more about duty than zeal, and most of my friends, especially my fellow Catholic-educated ones, are just as at sea with spiritual matters as I am.

I've at least mustered the will to finally start seeing a therapist to deal with my whole situation. Once a week in an office building around the corner from the Union Square McDonald's, I heave my wet sobs at her as I babble about Matt's heavy gray arm and my fears about where he is now and if he's okay and if I did enough to help him, how I should have done more to save him. She listens so well, her face still and accepting, illuminated gently by the warm glow of a stylish nearby table lamp. Once she offered me antidepressants. I declined, and she didn't bring it up again.

I've told her about my running, and she has been encouraging. She tells me it's a healthy coping mechanism. She tells me she is happy to see me invested in an activity that helps regulate my emotions and care for my body. Still, I think my grief would be easier to bear if I had even just a few wispy fumes of faith left to run on as well. Instead, I mostly just feel spiritually panicked, depleted.

But even in my lostness, when I look up at these churches on 6th Avenue, these moving works of stone and glass, I feel an impulse to do something old and strange, like get on my knees and weep.

A few months before Matt's death, I visited him in the psych ward. He'd gone voluntarily this time, on the recommendation of the ER doctor who gave him that mental health questionnaire. Waiting at the heavy mauve door to the unit, I flipped my old iPod Mini in the palm of my hand like a worry stone. The door has a small square window that I could see through from my nose up, but the hallway beyond was empty. There was no doorknob or handle. *Should I . . . knock?* I wondered. *Oh, there's a doorbell. An actual doorbell.* It was a fancy one, out of place in its domestic regality, the type that might look more at home on a Brooklyn brownstone. My finger lingered by the bell as I imagined ringing it and being greeted by an aproned 50s housewife holding a tray of brownies. "Yes? Oh, come in!" she might say as the psych patients milled around behind her. "Would you like some lemonade? It's so humid out there in that hall."

Eventually I caught a glint of a bald head and some shoulders covered in blue scrubs through the window. The head turned, and we made eye contact. I lifted my hand high and waved, gesturing toward the door with a little wrist swirl that started out as a pointing gesture and evolved, for some reason, into a thumbs up. The nurse put down his clipboard and approached me; after a loud, prison-y buzzing noise, he heaved the thick door open but did not invite me in.

"Name?" he asked.

"Jess. Jessica! Keefe," I stammered, intimidated as always.

"Who are you here to see?"

"Matthew Keefe."

"Relation?"

"I'm the sister."

He picked his clipboard back up and made a few scribbles. "Okay, right through here."

The nurse led me a few paces down the shiny hallway to another heavy, knobless mauve door. This one was propped open. Inside, a few scattered seats at particleboard tables and a couple of couches were occupied by patients and their visiting family members. The television was on, broadcasting the sweaty brows and bursting neck-veins of arguing talking heads on CNN, which felt like particularly cruel programming in a place where mentally ill people were trying to become less so. Some clusters of people played board games or picked at meals from trays. Some visitors looked comfortable and game, but others sat silent and tense, absorbing the fluorescent atmosphere, less able to ignore the weight of the fact that they were here visiting a loved one in an actual asylum.

I spotted Matt. He was seated at the far end of one of the corner tables, absentmindedly pulling at his fraying sweatshirt cuff, the edges all wavy from the unraveling threads. He looked up and spotted me back. He smiled feebly, did a little wave with his hand close to his chest.

I strolled over and slumped into the seat across from him.

"Hey!" I chirped, putting maximum effort into forcing a sunny tone.

"Hey," he said, his face showing a little embarrassment, a little fatigue. His skin was sallow. A few pearls of sweat hovered around his hairline, quivering but never breaking.

"Well," I spun around, taking it all in. I noticed what looked like flecks of orange Jell-O stuck to the far wall. "This is nice!"

Matt chuckled. "Yeah, it's a real palace." He wiped his runny nose. He was in heroin withdrawal, I realize now, and I'm not sure the psych ward staff were meaningfully addressing that.

I slid the smooth metal iPod across the table with the pads of my fingers. "Surprise!"

Matt picked it up curiously. He had complained at check-in that he wasn't allowed to use his iPhone (nothing with a cell signal allowed), but that's where all his music was. I remembered I had this ancient green iPod collecting dust on my desk downstairs, a gift from an unpaid media internship during my senior year of college. It had been on the cutting edge of technology at the time. The screen was in color and everything.

"I know The Man won't let you have your iPhone, so! Tunes and tunes alone. I loaded it up with some good stuff. *Blonde on Blonde*, Le Tigre, Elliott, Regina. I put the Neko Case album that has that half-hour of cricket noises on there." I mimed a meditative facial expression.

He smiled a bit and made eye contact for the first time. I felt that familiar rush of warmth that fixing something for someone always gave me. A safe little thrill, like going over the first baby bump on a log flume ride. Fluttery, with tingly edges. Perfect.

"Thanks," he said.

Across the room, a patient had started thumping his palm on the particleboard table. A broad-shouldered nurse's eyes flashed over to the patient and stayed there.

"This'll be good to have," Matt picked up the iPod and started worrying it in his hand like I had been doing on my way in here. We didn't say anything for a few moments.

"How is it going?" I asked, suddenly serious.

"It's . . . okay," he scanned the room a little, more embarrassment showing on his face when he registered the increasing thumping the other patient was causing. The nurse inched closer to the patient as his parents talked to him in gentle, hushed tones.

"This seems nicer than the last place," I said with genuine conviction, laser-focused on positivity. "There's a TV, that's good!"

"Yeah, it's a little better. The doctors are better." He was leaning into my bid for the upbeat.

"Are they getting you set up with medication?" Matt was never prescribed buprenorphine for his opioid addiction, but he was often offered antidepressants, antipsychotics.

A pause. "Yeah."

"Are you going to take it?"

Matt tapped the iPod on the table, matching the beat with the other patient's loudening table-pounding, a triangle to the other patient's bongo drum. "Yeah, it's worth a shot."

I became filled with a rush of pride that, coupled with my fixing-people feeling, bordered on illicit euphoria. Matt had been so resistant in previous treatment environments. Dragging him to that 12-step day program had been hard on my parents. I was convinced that his buy-in to the treatment approach this time was going to make all the difference.

"That's so great, Matt. That's really great." I brushed my bangs out of my face. "Great!"

I felt so relieved, I barely noticed the nurses now had the other patient on the ground in a headlock as he shouted slurred words. Matt glanced again at the other patient, watching the now trio of nurses forcibly remove him from the visiting room. The patient's parents looked on with defeated brows and sad open mouths, emanating an anxiety you could feel squiggling in the air.

Matt tapped the iPod onto the table one time like a grace note, then slid it into his hoodie pocket.

11

True Love

SUMMER'S COMING. THE AIR IS THICKENING, THE SUN FEELS closer, the sky is that shade of clear blinding blue that feels like it could suck you straight up into it. Grand Army Plaza is peppered with street performers and vendors selling handmade candles and plastic-wrapped pashminas. As I bob past the bustling mass, I catch the faces of a few little children watching a puppet show, their eyes wet and huge and delighted as the little wooden characters sway and smack each other.

This is a good running day. My stride lands evenly on the pavement, not too heavy, not too hard on my heels. I'm taking my time yet pushing consistently. Pacing: It finally feels like something I understand. Knowing and respecting the limit.

The park is crowded today; its daily mass always increases as the mercury rises. Little clusters of people dot the Longmeadow as far as the eye can see. The paved loop path is also dense with people. Intimidating Cyclists with a capital C whip around the inner bike lane while more mellow riders, milk crates affixed to their rear racks and boomboxes bungee-corded to their handlebars, cruise in the outer lane. Some people power walk in spandex and ankle weights, some stroll in cute brunch-ready outfits, some are alone and some are in groups, some are large families clustered around sets of double-wide strollers, moving together like a herd on a plain, calling jokes from the back of the group up to the front and from the front of the group toward the back. "What?" a tall woman in a gauzy hijab calls up to a shorter woman in their cluster. The short woman cranes her neck backward comically, eyebrow raised. Then they both burst out cackling.

Being one little flake in this community cake mix is quickly becoming one of my favorite parts of race training. I'm solitary in my activity, of course—but I'm not actually alone out here. I'm part of it. All of us out here together. Separate but together. Just doing what people do: moving, resting, eating, drinking, talking, telling little jokes to each other, occasionally reaching out for a nearby hand and drawing it inward, rubbing it like a fresh peach, maybe giving it a little kiss.

Eleven miles today. Another milestone. I complete it without incident, which fills me with puffy, overblown pride. I fling the heavy door of my apartment building open with one motion, feeling like Zeus, feeling like this door is a mere *play*thing. God, running is amazing, and *I'm* amazing for doing it. An image flashes in my mind of myself at the Coney Island finish line, having breezed through the race and finished under two hours. I can taste the beer. I can smell the ocean.

Inside my apartment, I take off my thick Red Sox cap and am bowled over by the smell. This brings me back to earth pretty quickly. My first long run in truly searing sunshine produced an incredible amount of sweat, and the hat has an eerie whitish halo of salt running around the edges, like the world's most disgusting margarita. I set it soaking in the kitchen sink and Google moisture-wicking running visors. *This is how it starts*, I think with a touch of dread. I suppose it's time to surrender to the gear.

No time to shop online now, though. I leave the tab open on my phone and take Eddie for a quick walk. I shower, dress, and hop on my bike, a fresh layer of sweaty brine brewing on my shoulders and chest within minutes of beginning my ride over to Kensington.

I'm going down to Jacob Riis Beach today with my friend Emily, her husband Alden, and a few of their pals. Another opportunity to be a part of a group, and in both my singleness and my grief, I'm grateful for it.

Emily and Alden have been together for years, and they just got married last summer. Bearing witness to their relationship always puts me at ease. The way they talk to each other, the way they talk *about* each other to the people around them—never terse, never strained, never "joking around" about each other's flaws in a way that feels strategically hurtful. No, they're calm and serene. They emanate respect and admiration. They feel like allies. Their devotion isn't this big dramatic thing. It's only clear as day.

I feel like an alien observing them. *Curious*, I think, when Alden places his hand lovingly on Emily's shoulder while she tells a muddled story, her mouth full of a toasted plain bagel with scallion cream cheese. *Intriguing*, I note when Emily pauses before reacting when Alden makes a wrong turn off of Flatbush Avenue. *These beings are truly evolved.*

Elijah was the first person I seriously dated in my 20s, and all my social cues from birth led me to believe that this meant we would probably get married and spend the rest of our lives together. With this immutable destiny in mind, I committed myself to weathering this relationship's low points. Through it all, I thought often of the adage that "relationships are work." I don't even remember who, if anyone, was explicitly saying this to me—maybe it was just something I absorbed from television sitcoms and cleaning product commercials. Nonetheless, it was always something I felt deep in my bones, this idea of relationships as work. But I misunderstood it. My comprehension was more like "relationships are war." I thought that constant conflict over the absolute stupidest things, freeze-outs and reconciliations, big gaping differences in personality, preferences, goals—I thought this all was the work.

But now, I'm learning from friends and my therapist and my own self-reflection, work can be pleasant. Work builds foundations. Work yields fruits. Tilling the soil, fertilizing it—but, critically, never personally shitting into it. This is the "work" I think everybody was already talking about, but it's all new to me.

When Elijah and I were in the process of breaking up, I felt sensitive to tiny omens. Cracking an egg and finding no yolk inside, only clear mucus. Seeing the same billboard all over town, the one advertising a local car dealership's junking services. Unusually bad cell phone reception. It made the back of my neck tingle, my pupils pinpoint. I'm not an especially superstitious person, but all the heft of months and months of unresolved tension with Elijah took its toll and made me feel animal, activated and alert in a way I'd never experienced before. Like a gopher spotting a raincloud, I'd read these little omens as prescient, predictive of darkness to come. But no single event felt more ominous than the night Mr. Porter's house burned down.

The screaming from the street woke us both up. Elijah and I were in the same bed, a king-sized West Elm number we bought several months ago, a triumphant gesture of adulthood that we relished at the time. More room for his long legs! For my decorative pillows! For the dog who refuses to sleep on his own hand-tufted corduroy bed! But, as is typical with any large impulse purchase, the acquisition of this bed was an attempted distraction from disaster-grade emotional anxiety.

Elijah and I were fighting so much, too much. Every small incident wounded deeply: the cast-off comments, the overflowing recycling bin, the forgotten text message. It all felt so heavy and complicated, but in objective reality, it was so painfully simple: We were growing up and away from each other, and we were starting to finally realize it.

As our love deteriorated, the giant bed just rubbed our faces in it. It took up almost the entire bedroom, cartoonishly out of place. You had to turn sideways to walk next to it. The bed's hulking presence served as a monument to the sex we were no longer having. It provided us a space where we could sleep together without even touching, coming to bed and waking up at vastly different times, at first because of an actual difference in our work schedules but pretty soon by design. Tonight when I woke up, Elijah was far removed, as has become usual, in the fetal position on the other side of the mattress.

The person screaming out on the street seemed to be saying words, but the noises were so guttural, soaked in naked fear, it was hard to make out.

Elijah got up and peered through the blinds. He adjusted the fraying waistband of his blue plaid PJ pants.

"Who's out there?" I slurred, groping for my glasses on the nightstand.

"I can't tell," he said. He looked out the window and to the left, toward the top of our dead-end street. "Oh, shit."

"What?" I asked, sitting up. Elijah didn't answer. He walked briskly to the kitchen, and I heard our kitchen drawers opening and closing, the various plastic crap in the junk drawer rustling around. He returned to the hallway outside our bedroom door and started putting his shoes on.

"There's a fire. I think Mr. Porter's house is on fire," Elijah said, sliding his feet into his Vans. He clutched a length of thick twine. "The dog's running around loose," he said, brandishing the twine.

He headed out into the freezing single-digit night, slamming the front door behind him.

Mr. Porter had lived in that clapboard house on the corner for most of his life, he'd told us when we first moved in down the block. We'd see him often, hanging out on his front deck in tube socks and Adidas slides, chuckling and chatting with family and friends who seemed to always be visiting. He'd wave and smile, and we'd wave and smile. If we had Eddie with us, we'd come over to the fence so Mr. Porter could give him big noogie-style pats on the head. He'd tell us about his own childhood dog while making deep, loving eye contact with Eddie. He'd chat with us about the neighborhood, the ways it had changed over the years.

Mr. Porter had brought home a Pitbull puppy about eight months prior to the fire. A proud papa, he came out into the street one day cradling the dog like a baby. The pup was black with white patches and had giant bat ears. I came down from our porch to zealously pet the puppy, kiss the puppy, tell the puppy what a good boy he was, while Eddie whined jealously from behind our little yard's fence. Mr. Porter chuckled. "Finally got myself a new buddy," he gushed, "we'll have to have some play dates!"

But shortly after the puppy came, Mr. Porter started to wilt. I was seeing a lot less of him, and when I did catch sight of him, he seemed ragged and on edge. His many visitors no longer seemed like familiar family or friends, and they matched his dour mood. The porch no longer hosted laughing and chilling, only solemn coming and going, whispered communications, cars idling outside late at night. At the same time, houses on the block were getting broken into, cash and randomly selected valuables stolen. Cars were being broken into, too, on a near nightly basis, leaving shattered rock-candy window glass glittering in piles on the sidewalk, waiting to be discovered by a crestfallen, coffee-clutching commuter at sunrise. The neighborhood chatter assigned vague responsibility for this to the dealings of Mr. Porter and his school of apprentices.

And the puppy, growing up in all this, got meaner. I'd never see Mr. Porter walking the dog. Instead, he'd let him out into the tiny slice of yard, leaving him there alone for hours at a time. The dog's fear and confusion and boredom eventually curdled into aggression. I'd dread walking Eddie past the yard, but our dead-end street provided no alternatives. Whenever we'd pass Mr. Porter's house, the dog would rush the fence, barking intensely at Eddie with strings of saliva flying out from his gnashing teeth. I'd have horrible visions of the flimsy fence snapping in one spot or folding over to the point where the dog could get out, chasing us down, sinking his teeth into Eddie's rear legs. What would I do if it happened? How are you supposed to break up a dogfight? Something about grabbing them by the back legs, not the neck, the neck just eggs on the fighting instinct, makes them lean in harder, chomp down tighter—

I felt badly for Mr. Porter's Pitbull. He clearly had a sad little life, pushed into fulfilling a stereotype of himself rather than growing into something beautiful. The moniker "Pitbull" is slang, you know. It's a term that applies to several breeds, including the American Staffordshire Terrier. I was surprised when I learned that—the true breed names sound so proper, so upper-crust. I was also surprised at the revelation that the Pitbull is a signature American breed, but then realized I shouldn't be. It is certainly very American to create something and then hate it for what it's become.

I put on my glasses and my bathrobe and looked out the bedroom window. I didn't have a great angle on Mr. Porter's house, but I could see the glowing orange mass reflected in the big windows of the apartment complex across the street.

I watched Elijah jog up the short distance to the intersection. He helped Mr. Porter knot the twine to the dog's collar, and

Mr. Porter held the makeshift leash taut, protectively close to his side. He was wearing basketball shorts and socks—no shoes, not even his flips flops, standing on the icy, salted pavement. Both their faces glowed orange and shadowy as they looked ahead, mouths slack, saying nothing. The giant fire reflected in Elijah's glasses, two rectangular boxes of flame.

Soon, red swirling lights of the arriving fire trucks mixed in with the orange glow as they pulled up to the house. I could hear the icy snow crunching under the heavy truck tires, even from down the block.

Once the trucks lurched to a stop, firefighters sprung out from all sides of the vehicles. They start to unfurl their heavy gray hoses, flopping the weight of them over the sides of the truck like a load of freshly caught halibut. A boss-looking guy, older than the others and wearing a snappy uniform, approached Mr. Porter.

Mr. Porter gestured wildly toward the house, and the captain nodded, looking at the blaze with a hint of queasiness. The fire was angrily bursting out of the top-floor windows, the smoke billowing skyward. I started to wonder if I should get Eddie and flee. We were just a few houses removed from the fire, and being at the base of the dead end, if we got stuck here, we'd be screwed.

Elijah came back. He grabbed a coat and some shoes and brought them back out to Mr. Porter. The fire captain was in the street speaking to the pajama-clad neighbors who'd gathered on the sidewalk. He said the blaze was bad but under control, he told them to relax, go home, no problem, this is what they do, they've got it handled. The firefighters proceeded through the motions of the firefight with the nonchalance of bored office workers circling a broken printer. They were at work, after all. Strategizing and coordinating the hoses, managing the growing crowd—it was all business as usual.

Mr. Porter stared up at his burning family home. Rather than putting his arms through the coat Elijah offered, he wrapped it around himself like a blanket. He looked like a child who just finished having a tantrum, blinking at the world, adjusting to his own new calmness. He clutched his dog's makeshift leash. Elijah stayed with him for a bit, but eventually some family members arrived and took over caring for Mr. Porter. I didn't know what else to do, so I just went back to bed. It was surprisingly easy for me to drift off to sleep while a fire raged three houses away. The mellow hollers of the firefighters, the mechanical sounds of the equipment, the beeps of trucks backing up soon sounded like nothing more than rushing and soothing white noise.

The next morning, I got up and threw a Frisbee around with Eddie in our tiny yard. Elijah was still sleeping—his work-from-home gig let him roll out of bed at the last possible second. I armed myself for my commute with layer upon layer, my hair getting static-y and stuck between fabrics as I swaddled myself. I opened the front door, heavy against the wind, and headed out into the shocking cold. As I approached the intersection I looked up and discovered something odd and eerie that immediately made me feel sick: The entire street was like an ice-skating rink. Turns out, shooting thick streams of water at a house for hours upon hours in eight-degree weather results in a Gaudí-ish winter wonderland. The cars, the sidewalks, everything had been covered in about an inch of ice that rippled and bulged like organic matter, like frozen intestines. The morning was silent and still all around it.

I shimmied down the ice-slick street in careful teensy steps, focusing on putting one foot in front of the other, when the smell of burned wood reminded me and I looked up at Mr. Porter's house. It was charred to oblivion beneath the bright white sky. The roof had caved in, there were violent holes on all sides. The sagging porch chairs looked like they had spontaneously combusted, with black explosive centers in the cushions. The brick foundation and all its hand-painted art were covered in grime. The block smelled like a barbecue for weeks.

Matt lived just a few blocks away at the time. He'd moved out of the small apartment he had shared with his boyfriend, now living in a spacious two-bedroom with a prim older gay guy who had in-unit laundry, many well-maintained houseplants, and a little terrier named Frank. Sometimes I'd go hang out with Matt at his place, but his roommate woke up early and had little patience for late-night giggling, so more often than not Matt would come to me. He'd sit on the back deck with me, smoking cigarettes while I foamed at the mouth complaining about Elijah. The more I worked myself up, the more I leaned into it, performing outrage perhaps more intensely than I actually felt it.

Matt's breakup had been finalized just a few months earlier. I had always loved his ex. He was warm, sweet, earnest—what you saw was what you got with him, and what you saw was always good. Matt had cried on my couch about that breakup plenty of times over lukewarm beers he'd bring from the mini-mart around the block. I always lobbied for the ex, for continuing the status quo, for going to therapy to "work on it." But even though he was unhappy about it, Matt was always certain. Their relationship was over. And that was all there was to it.

"Maybe he's just trying to spare you," Matt had said to me about Elijah, exhaling a stream of cigarette smoke. "Sounds like he has a lot of stuff he needs to figure out for himself. No one wants to be someone else's burden."

❀

"Ornacia! Ornaaaaaay-cia!" Matt scream-sang from the kitchen several months later, in our summer roommate era.

"Hold on," I shouted back from my bedroom. I was digging through my dresser, looking for my purple sequined tube top.

"Ornacia we're going to be laaaaate," Matt's singing skyrocketed up into a falsetto on the last syllable.

"Since when do *you* care about being late," I yelled back, jamming my breasts into the itchy fabric of the tube top.

"Okay truuuue," he sang out.

So, okay, about Ornacia. She was a character on season six of *RuPaul's Drag Race*, a television program that was often playing in the background when Matt and I were at home. Ornacia's not a queen in her own right but an unforgettable prop. A queen named Vivacious, one of the first contestants to be eliminated that season, enjoyed wearing a small Styrofoam head on top of her own head. This extra head was called Ornacia, and Ornacia was art, Vivacious told her skeptical cast mates. Vivacious took herself quite seriously, and as Ornacia's flimsy foam features wobbled atop Vivacious's head as she bellowed about her credentials as an original 80s club kid, you couldn't help but laugh. Matt, especially, couldn't help but laugh. He started calling people, animals, and objects Ornacia. Right now, he's calling me Ornacia. Sometimes he takes my dog's fuzzy face into his hands and lovingly calls Eddie Ornacia. Sometimes he sings Ornacia to the sky, directing the title at no one but maybe God him- or her- or themself.

We were getting ready to go to Jacques' Cabaret, one of Boston's most popular drag venues. We were very excited to see the performances. We were very excited in general. Whenever our manic good moods aligned, we would mind-meld into one screeching unit that was probably very annoying to others but incredibly funny to the two of us.

I was admiring my completed outfit in the mirror when I heard Matt clear his throat in my doorway. I looked over expecting to see him, but instead I saw a Styrofoam head, Matt's personal Ornacia, peeking in at me. Matt was out of sight, a committed puppeteer, angling this Ornacia's spooky face in the crevice of my open bedroom door. Matt had recently painted her silver, with jewels hot-glued to her eyebrows. Tonight, she was wearing Matt's giant, well-teased purple wig.

"Ornacia wants to know when Ornacia will be ready," Matt said in an affectation that was supposed to be some kind of girl voice but mostly just sounded like vocal fry.

"Why is Ornacia talking in the third person?" I asked.

Matt thought about it for a second. The Styrofoam head was still. Then suddenly it started shaking like Miss Piggy when she's angry: "Do not question Ornacia!"

I sauntered over to Ornacia and petted her purple wig. "Wow, this is a good color on you."

"Thank you, I—"

The wig fell off. It landed on the floor with a loud wet thud, like a pile of spaghetti. Ornacia was suddenly as profanely hairless as raw chicken.

Matt wrenched his head around the doorway, and we made startled eye contact. Our mouths were both frozen in an exaggerated cringe. Both sets of our eyebrows were yanked upward toward our hairlines in surprise. Both our heads were cocked sideways.

We started laughing at the same time. At first we were laughing about the wig, but then we were laughing about the laughing. Matt gestured at the wig on the floor, implying, Can you believe it? I shook my head and waved my hands in response, No!

The sound of an item that may or may not be food dropping onto the floor summoned Eddie from the living room, where he'd been napping on the couch. He sniffed the wig, licked it once, evaluating its edibility. Put off, he wandered away.

Matt and I wound down our chuckles, finishing with a few hearty, slow exhales. Matt stepped all the way into the doorway now and fully took in my outfit.

"Ooh-hoo-hoo-HOO!" He made his mouth really small and did a little golf clap. I think this is his impression of a British nobleman. "It's lovely, truly, you're looking smashing," he said with a lilt. Yes, he was a British nobleman.

"Do you want me to call a Lyft?" I asked.

"No," Matt said, pulling his cracked iPhone out of his pocket. "I'll do it now."

"I'm excited," I said.

"Me too!" He said, typing.

"This is going to be fun."

"I know!"

I looked at myself in the mirror again and felt a small but jolting current of self-consciousness. "You're sure it's okay for me to go?"

"What?" Matt was frowning at his phone, unable to get the finicky half-broken screen to respond.

"I don't want to, I don't know. Intrude," I said, smoothing my sequins. "It's not really *my* space."

He looked up and narrowed his eyes at me, pursed his lips quizzically. Matt knew I wasn't exactly straight, not really, but he never pushed me to identify any certain way. It was true that as I grew up and away from the Sunday homilies and 90s mass media that presented heterosexual relationships as the only option for romantic love, I began to realize I could be attracted to many types of human spirits inside many types of human skinsuits. This knowledge crystallized around me slowly but surely as I got older. Ironically, though, the magnanimousness of my preferences gave me an unexpected gift: the ability to pass. I could hide behind my male partners, enjoying the privilege and safety that the presentation of these relationships gave me in the world. I wanted to be that floating brain, free from labels or boxes, and Matt respected that. But he couldn't hide like I could. It often felt like Matt's capital G gayness was enough for both of us, and on nights like these I was lucky enough to mooch off it.

After staring me down for a long moment, Matt resumed pushing his thumbs into his phone screen with increasingly agitated violence. "You're right, it's not MySpace. Would you rather log on and DM Tom? Maybe, like, set a My Chemical Romance song to auto-play on your profile page?"

"Tell me it's okay to go!" I whined in a manipulative, needy nasal.

Matt looked up at me, eyebrow cocked. He raised his right hand and made the sign of the cross before me like a priest. "Jessica, I hereby give you my holy homo permission to go."

I curtsied a little to accept the blessing. Matt rolled his eyes and started poking at his frozen phone screen at increasingly weird angles, elbows akimbo, putting his whole body into the effort. "Ah! There we go. Eight minutes. Let's go have a cigarette," he said as he windmilled his arm toward the front door.

After the show, our Jack-and-Ginger–coated stomachs were craving grease. We tumbled out the narrow doorway of Jacques' and started to shuffle toward Tasty Burger in pursuit of steaming hot French fries.

It had rained while we were inside. The sidewalk sparkled like rock candy under the jaundiced glow of downtown Boston's weak old streetlamps. Little puddles had formed in the wrinkles of the trash bags that bulged out from rusty green dumpsters. It was quiet. Jacques' was the only bar for several blocks, and the street was mostly lined with locked-up law offices and darkened residential buildings.

"You want?" Matt asked with a cigarette dangling from his lips.

"Sure," I said after he had already begun to hand me one. He had started pulling it out of the package before I even answered, knowing what I'd say. "Special occasion."

Matt inhaled deeply, then exhaled smoke with a yogic "ahhh."

"My feet hurt," I whined as I shuffled along in my high-heeled boots.

"Amateur," Matt chided.

As we rounded the corner onto Columbus Avenue, a voice piped up from a darkened stoop.

"Spare a dollar?"

My first instinct was to recoil from this voice. You could say it's because I'm a woman and that the risk of gendered violence makes me vigilantly on guard and defensive when I'm out at night. But mostly, my recoiling was a result of my lifelong training to fear homeless people. The fear was embedded in stranger-danger ideology, very special episodes of Maury Povich, the nightly news, and, of course, the DARE videos that often featured a street urchin with missing teeth and matted hair trying to sell fresh-faced young white kids crack cocaine. I never noticed how much I had internalized all this until I lived on my own in cities and felt myself flinch whenever I passed someone sleeping on a stoop.

Matt didn't flinch, though. He stopped walking, and so I stopped too.

"Sure man, I got you." Matt rooted through his pockets and pulled out a five-dollar bill. He handed it to the guy.

"Thank you, brother, thank you," the man said in a gravelly voice. "Hey, any chance you could also spare one of—"

Matt cut the guy off, nodding. He reached for his back pocket and fished out his crumpled pack of Marlboros. Then he took out his lighter. He got down low, an inch from the guy's face maybe, and helped him light his cigarette. Once the tip bloomed orange and the guy took a satisfied puff, Matt stood up straight again.

The guy smiled. He waved the cigarette up to Matt in a salute. Matt saluted him back, turned, and walked on. I followed.

We walked a bit in silence, smoking our cigarettes down to the nubs and then tossing the filters into gutter puddles.

"That was nice of you," I finally said.

"Well, probably gonna be me someday," Matt chirped, "so I do always try to pay it forward."

I chuckled. I waited. He didn't elaborate. So I said, "That's not going to be you."

"Why not?"

"Because!" I scoffed, scanning through my gray matter looking for the best way to reply to this. "You're doing good, Matt. You are. You . . . you've got it." I sounded like an uninspired high school basketball coach.

Matt looked at me, then looked at the sparkling pavement. He pulled in a breath, and it hitched in his throat. He turned the noise into a scoff. He opened his mouth but didn't speak. Water droplets fell onto our heads from the fire escape above. He finally said, "Well."

I felt a little thump of panic. "That guy's probably got, like, *problems*—" I start to say without thinking. At least I left the adjective *drug* out, but that's clearly what I meant.

"And that's different from me, how?" he boomed with a sad laugh.

I knew why he was feeling this way. I knew it deep down. Matt had long struggled with drugs, but he'd struggled with his identity for much longer. He'd always known that he was gay, he told me in a coming-out Facebook message during his freshman year at UMass. He'd always known and he figured I always knew, but it was hard to tell anyone, so here he was, telling me, just for the record, haha. He said he had a boyfriend now. He sent me pictures of him: a lanky redhead with milky pale skin and full lips and a penchant for Grateful Dead t-shirts. He sent me pictures of them out and about, on hikes and at parties, with their arms around each other, smiling relaxed closed-mouth smiles. He said he didn't want me to tell anyone else yet.

I was so relieved to see him happy. It felt like he was different down to his core. Those decades of tense stiffness had floated out his nostrils like an old demon, it seemed. His whole body was freer with a different kind of ease in these pictures.

But all that time hiding himself must have taken a toll. We joked about it, but we never really discussed it. All those years of answering the house phone with an artificially deepened voice, going to lacrosse practice and laughing along with his teammates as they called each other homophobic slurs when they fucked up a play, declaring teachers and movies and bad weather and homework and certain kinds of snack foods to be "gay." His seventh-grade girlfriend, with her sweet blond bangs tucked back in glittery butterfly clips. The pained, faraway look on his face when people would tease him about her, asking if they'd kissed yet. His dresser drawer full of Abercrombie and Fitch shirts made to look like old-fashioned rugby jerseys, their mustard yellows and army greens washing my brother's shining features out, dulling him down to the single acceptable shade of hetero maleness that our middle school tolerated.

Addiction doesn't just happen; it unfolds. Our cultural obsession with portraying drugs themselves as the main culprit muddies this reality. We talk about drugs like villains using heavy-handed metaphors, but the pills, powders, and tinctures aren't evil. They're not cunning tricksters who suck people in, they're not wicked seductresses who set out to ruin lives. Drugs don't have brains or intentions or, it should go without saying, genitals. They're neutral. And for people who are hurting, they can become a conduit, a subway car that can rattle you along toward a better feeling, even if it's just temporary. Some people have to board this train because they aren't getting what they need from the Blue Cross Blue Shield-ification of American health care, the HMOs and the prior authorizations, the pharmaceuticals that need more pharmaceuticals to treat the side effects, or the total lack of access to the medicines that could really help because of costs or stigma. The thousand-dollar therapy bills and pitiful mindfulness apps. Or maybe they're not getting what they need from their spiritual communities, with so many leaders who wax in hexing tones about sin and guilt and shame, about the wailing and gnashing of teeth that awaits all who fail God by being themselves. Or it could be that they're not getting what they need from the post–Great Recession economic hellscape of gigs and girl bosses and side hustles, where there's little worker solidarity and few protections, where everyone's hired and fired at will and grateful for the opportunity, where there's no net to catch those who slip, where there's little hope for moving up the ladder because the ladder's been yanked up behind the last guy. Or maybe, just maybe, they're not getting what they need from their own families, who love them very much, who try to understand but can't seem to erase that final note of panic from their voices, who want them to be safe but by wanting that so blindly and recklessly put them at even greater risk.

"You *are* different," I said to Matt, stepping into the street to dodge a puddle on the sidewalk. "You're my roommate. You have a home."

Realizing he'd made me nervous, he backed off. "Yes, Ornacia. You're right. I'm okay."

"I know."

"I'm just saying." He pulled in a quivering breath. "You know."

"Okay."

Matt grabbed my shoulder and gave it a little squeeze. "Relax. It's just a guy who needed a dollar."

The edges of my mouth curled into a smile. "I know. Listen, it's nice! You're nice! Great job being nice. Thank you."

"Good," he said. "Because that was the last of my cash. Now, I am but a destitute peasant woman. So you're buying." He made a kissing noise as a thank-you.

Matt smiled back at me, then turned his focus forward again. We rounded a corner back onto the main drag and found ourselves face-to-face with a brilliantly lit convenience store. The intense light made us squint.

After the French fries, in the Lyft home, Matt rolled his window down. Rivulets of old raindrops rushed down the side of the car and into Matt's face. He leaned into it, laughing when they hit him in the eye, sticking his head out the window a little bit so the raindrops could make him an easier target.

I looked at him and felt joy bloom upward, fizzing in my skull. But the carbonation cleared, as it always does, evaporating up to the sky, and then I just felt a sense of impending loss. I'd been feeling like this more and more lately. Even though Matt was sitting right next to me, even though he was doing well. Even though he was taking his meds. Even though he was living with me and I was watching him real close and I wanted to believe that we were okay, that we were going to be okay. Still, I looked at him, and some marrow in me knew this wouldn't last. That he wouldn't make it to middle age. My marrow dreaded that he'd never meet my future spouse, that I'd never give a tipsy toast at his wedding, that we'd never rent a beach house together and share late-night spliffs, sitting at an old wooden kitchen table warped by the salty sea air, howling laughing over memories of nights like this one. My marrow could tell this was all too temporary, that some sad piece of our fate was written in cursive in wet cement a long time ago, and even though we can pile new stories on top of it, there's no un-writing what's been marked into the hard, formed rock at the base of it all.

I shooed the thoughts away and focused on the little spaces between Matt's teeth. I focused on the movement of his dirty blond hair in the breeze. I zoomed in on his face: for once, happy. Really.

12

Law & Order

THE DAY IT ALL GOES TO SHIT STARTS OUT AS THE SAME AS ALL the others. I suit up in my running clothes, amble through a few halfhearted stretches, and activate my tracker app. I head out the heavy front door of my apartment building and hit the ground running straight away. I bounce along Parkside Avenue, past the big grocery store with its enormous ads for $1.39-per-pound chicken thighs written in big red text, past the subway station entrance, past the clusters of people waiting at the bus stop, each person interpreting this confusing spring weather differently, some confident in cargo shorts and sandals while others shiver in puffer parkas and fur-trimmed boots.

Entering the park, I pass a big group of geese wandering across a soggy patch of grass; the once-towering piles of shoveled snow that sat on this spot have been reduced to little mounds, melting faster than the ground can absorb. I pass a pair of power-walking old ladies wearing tracksuits and ankle weights. My gait relaxes as I transition into the traffic-free, commotion-free setting of the park. I join up with the main loop, heading north and up the hill. I feel my brain melting into goo state. I feel a little burst of joy as my thoughts settle into nothingness. My breath quickens as I crest the top.

Then, pain.

Shocking, sharp pain. It shoots out from my left knee like an alarm, jolting the rest of my body in surprise. I slow down and then stop completely in the middle of the pathway. I pause my tracker app. I look at my knee. It looks the same as always. I rub it a little with my palm. *Oh God, what did I do?* My mind races for potential simple causes. Did I hit it on something? Did I sleep on it wrong? Can you even sleep on your knee wrong? Could it possibly be anything other than what it most likely is—a plain old running injury? Oh God, what did I do?

I move to the side of the paved path and stand on the mossy earth, clueless and stricken. I watch a blond mom push her designer stroller past. I watch a group of teenagers wander by, a couple of them walking squat BMX bicycles, music blasting from a Bluetooth speaker clipped to the handlebars.

My mind races as the sun beats down on my Lycra-clad shoulders. *Should I stretch? I guess I need to stretch more. You should have been stretching more this whole time, you idiot. How do you stretch your knee?*

I cross my left foot over my right and bend toward the ground, a standard hamstring stretch we used to do at soccer practices. Predictably, I feel nothing in my knee. I put my hands on my hips and swing my left leg around uselessly. My knee goes along for the ride but doesn't feel stimulated. I stare at the pavement while my heart beats with ever increasing panic.

After a few minutes of this and not really knowing what else to do, I attempt to resume my run. I hop on my right foot a few times to psych myself up. I take a deep breath and then strike out first with my right foot. Glorious. Milliseconds later, my left foot swings forward and strikes. Horrible. Very bad. Pain, pain, pain. Shooting pain again.

Fuck. Fuck! Fuck fuck fuck fuck.

It occurs to me that I cannot keep running. I have to go home, I guess. I'm a mile and a half-ish away. I look down the hill, the one that I had just conquered mere minutes prior, then feeling spry and endlessly capable. It's blanketed in beautiful, dappled shade, dotted with walkers and runners who crest the top and then pass me. I could cry. Maybe I will cry. My mouth opens in distress, forming a kidney-bean shape, but actual tears don't come. Just a couple little coughs and whimpers. I start walking down the hill with an uneven gait. Bending my knee doesn't necessarily hurt, but I'm so freaked out by the injury I walk like a pirate, barely using my left leg and foot out of a fear of making it all worse. I wince each time my left foot makes contact with the ground until I eventually settle into the predictable pattern of pain.

Down the hill I go. Back in the opposite direction around the Prospect Park loop. Going this way feels familiar but sinister, like seeing a beloved relative without their dentures in. I grimace at passersby, imagining that my failure is written on my forehead, visible from the sky. But they don't really look at me and certainly aren't registering the slight limp in my walk as anything other than what it is.

I limp past the bus stop, where different pairs of cargo shorts and puffer parkas wait for the B12. I waddle back past the red grocery store signs screaming about discounted cannellini beans.

About an hour after the pain began, I'm back at my apartment. I take a pathetic shower and then do some pathetic sitting on the couch. *A real runner would know what to do about this*, I think to myself, full to the brim with self-pity. I open my phone's web browser, intending to start googling my symptoms, but instead I get sucked back into a long newsmagazine article I'd been reading earlier about "drug-induced homicides."

In counties throughout the United States, prosecutors are charging people with murder if they give someone drugs and then those drugs lead to an overdose death. Often, the people charged with murder are friends, loved ones, even spouses of the deceased. Often, the two people were using drugs together—it's just that one woke up and the other didn't. The prosecutors say putting these people in prison is just and appropriate, that it's helping to "fight the opioid epidemic," talking about this homegrown social problem as if it were an overseas war, the villains easily identifiable and otherized, the victims only considered so once they're dead.

Already feeling dour and irritable, I sink right back into this news story, allowing the hot rage tingling in my ears to distract me from my big injury fuckup. Eddie watches me from across the room, head flat on the hardwood, suspicious of my mood.

Why are drugs like heroin and cocaine illegal? If you're a white woman like me, then it was ostensibly done for your protection.

The first law functionally outlawing a nonalcoholic substance in the United States didn't actually ban the drug itself. In 1875, the city of San Francisco passed an ordinance outlawing an environment instead: opium dens. The law was an extension of the xenophobia that many white Americans felt toward new Chinese immigrants coming to the United States to work on the railroads. These immigrants were stealing jobs and driving down wages, the racist mythmaking said. With that seed of mistrust planted, political systems turned a suspicious eye toward Chinese culture and pastimes. The opium den was quickly vilified as not just a place where immigrants partook in lasciviousness—it was damned as a place where innocent white women were sucked into the debauchery, too.

In his book *Chasing the Scream*, Johann Hari presents a heavily researched history of drug prohibition and how it connects to the bizarre patchwork of laws and regulations we have today. "The arguments we hear today for the drug war are that we must protect teenagers from drugs, and prevent addiction in general," Hari writes. "We assume, looking back, that these were the reasons this war was launched in the first place. But they were not. They crop up only occasionally, as asides."

It's true, I had long assumed there was a legitimate reason, even a bad one, for the way certain substances are so violently prohibited in this country. I figured there was some sort of clean, trustworthy chart summarizing all the research on substances, ranking and outlawing them on the basis of danger and public well-being. But the more I read about it, the more I realized how ridiculous that old idea of mine was. Indeed, the more I learned about American drug policy, the more it revealed itself to be primarily rooted in a classic combination of racism, panic, and inertia.

The roots of the drug war are a lot hornier than I had imagined, too. Even the word we use for illegal drugs—"illicit"—betrays the raunchy perversion of it all. In his book, Hari describes the pornographic detail into which drug prohibitionists would go when imagining and then condemning the fantastical sexual escapades of drugged-up white women and cocaine-using Black men or marijuana-smoking Latino men. It's got a certain *eau de Q-Anon* to it, reading it back today. Real Pizzagate: the Prequel type of energy. But this also tracks, I suppose. Queer love, interracial marriage, women wearing pants—powerful people huffing the fumes of imagined sexual deviance has often been responsible for lots of nonharmful things becoming outlawed.

San Francisco's opium den ordinance set the stage for the Harrison Act, a federal law passed in 1914. Again, the law didn't call for prohibition outright. It was meant to regulate and tax cocaine and opiates. But like most drug policies that would come after it, the law caused a ripple effect of unintended negative consequences that made matters worse. Law enforcement began cracking down on doctors who prescribed maintenance doses of opioids to patients who were addicted. Both doctor and patient become criminals more or less overnight. Then those patients, still addicted to opioids but now lacking the means to acquire them legitimately and safely, were driven to dark corners to find the substances that they desperately needed. (Sound familiar?) Resourceful criminals, like the Mafia, noticed the boon of this untapped market. Things followed from there into the situation we're in today: criminal enterprises controlling a clandestine and combustible underground drug trade, with addicted people getting swallowed up in the process.

Racism, panic, inertia.

Many studies and surveys over the past few decades have shown that white Americans use and sell drugs at just about the same rates as other racial groups. But according to the U.S. Department of Justice, more than 75% of the people in prison for a drug charge are Black or Latino. It's easier to make sense of this fact when you understand that our drug war is not rooted in scientific regulation or even good but misguided intentions but in eugenicist rants about skull shapes and lewd behavior. Racism.

Nixon officially cut the ribbon on the drug war, and Reagan armed it. Nancy started telling kids to just say no, and Mr. T and friends sang backup. Every presidential administration since has overseen their own crackdowns, their tough love, their nervous moral rhetoric around pills and powders. As overt racism fell out of fashion, people stopped publicly wringing their hands over the fates of white women and instead turned their anxieties toward the health of The Children. New punitive policies abounded, egged on by sensationalized media portrayals of crack users and bath salt maniacs. By the turn of the new millennium, drugs had become so inexorably woven into the fabric of American criminality that no one would bat an eye at the idea of people who use drugs being included under the same legislative umbrella as rapists and murderers. Panic.

And it turns out I was half right about the chart thing, too. There is indeed a chart that ranks drugs in some kind of order—it's just not an order that makes a whole lot of objective sense. The drug scheduling system we have today was introduced as part of the Controlled Substances Act of 1970, which purports to rank drugs from the most dangerous to the least. But it's not exactly the most up-to-date or scientifically sound measurement system. For example, this system classifies marijuana as a Schedule 1 substance, meaning it is deemed by the federal government to have no medical value and the most dangerous potential for misuse—even while it is simultaneously fully legal in many states and has a well-researched capacity to treat all sorts of illnesses. Meanwhile, alcohol and tobacco, substances which kill hundreds of thousands more Americans every year than drug overdoses and which serve no medical purpose beyond perhaps curing squareness, are not even included in this scheduling system at all. Inertia.

Prohibiting drugs is supposed to prevent addiction. To protect. So, is that happening? Well, no. Today illegal drugs are cheaper, more potent, and more widely available than ever. Overdoses are at record highs, pain management and drug treatment medications are prescribed at record lows, and prisons are filled with people of color serving decades-long sentences for simple possession or low-level dealing while white guys in fleece vests sell Schedule 1 drugs at little downtown shops that look like Apple stores.

There's a kicker to the opium dens story: You know who was actually the primary opium user in 1800s America? It wasn't Chinese immigrants. It was white women. And they weren't lured into the practice by foreigners and their uncouth pastimes. According to *Smithsonian* magazine, the stuff was often prescribed by doctors and easily acquired by unregulated pharmacies. It's hard to disentangle all the many layers of racism, panic, and inertia that have contributed to modern drug prohibition. It's like trying to turn a chocolate cake back into flour, eggs, and butter.

Protection means different things to different people. In the dictionary, the word contains this variant definition: "the practice of paying money to criminals so as to prevent them from attacking oneself or one's property." That feels closer to what has been done on behalf of white women and then children, the groups propped up as victims. The drug war stays bankrolled not in order to meaningfully prevent addiction but in order to prevent the property from being attacked. In this framework, kids and women are not so much individuals as commodities, barterable widgets, the reflections of a nearby man in power. They've historically wanted to protect us because they wanted to protect themselves and the vision of the world as they've created it. Racism, panic, inertia.

For too long, too many white women have gone along with this arrangement, willing to embrace an existence rooted in being a reflection, gladly donning the victim hat that's been crowned upon our heads by the patriarchy without noticing the bloody grip it has on our scalp. The proximity to power has been too intoxicating, the crusts we're thrown have been too delicious, the empty assurances of safety have been too comforting.

Lately, my victim hat has really begun to chafe.

I'm afraid I've done something serious and irreparable to my knee. I've heard of athletes developing knee problems, how it can be a persistent source of pain and stress and even requires surgery sometimes. But with the help of Doctor Google, I quickly self-diagnose myself with something much more commonplace: iliotibial (IT) band syndrome.

Web pages festooned with pink and red medical illustrations teach me that the IT band is a ribbon of tissue running from the hip all the way down the outside of your leg to your shinbone. It can become irritated through excessive use, like running too much too quickly, without adequate cross-training to engage and build the muscle. I think of all my training plan PDFs with their crisply indicated cross-train days, the cute icons of dumbbells and bicycles meant to denote mixing it up, and the quickness with which I ignored them. I cringe. IT band pain can also be worsened by bad shoes, I learn. I look over at the thinning gum sole of my ancient Asics and cringe some more.

The web pages urge me to "talk to my doctor" about treatment options. I laugh a little at the thought of a relationship so close with any health care professional as to justify the use of a possessive pronoun. *Do what now?* I think. *To my who?*

Luckily, Doctor Google has suggestions for generic treatment, and they're about what you'd expect. Rest, stretches, light physical therapy exercises involving resistance bands. Taking in this information, I'm guessing I'll be out of training commission for at least a week.

I'm relieved it's not something more serious but am annoyed I let this happen. Though in retrospect, it makes perfect sense. I did nothing to protect myself in earnest. I was too busy protecting my conception of myself as someone who can muscle through it alone, who doesn't need the supportive fluff so many training plans recommended. I ignored the warnings, I thought I knew better than the downloadable PDFs. And I was so wrong. Now, here it is. My cosmic punishment.

I hobble out to the backyard with Eddie. He still needs his exercise even if I can't get mine. I toss his ball toward the chain-link fence at the rear of the yard while sitting awkwardly on the cool concrete steps, still holding my left leg out like a disconnected peg. It's a lot warmer now than it was earlier in the day. If I had to pick an objective winner of the bus stop outfits, I'd say the cargo shorts people had it by a hair. I take out my phone and open my calendar app. The day marked "BK HALF MARATHON!" is only a few weeks away now.

All this time, I've been so obsessed with finishing the race in an impressive time, with an impressive look on my face. I've imagined what I'd do at the finish line, what I'd eat, whom I'd hug. Now the finish line itself feels like it could be out of reach.

A lump forms in my throat. Now, the only feeling more intense than the knee pain is the low throb of anxiety in my chest.

In 2012, Matt took me to my first protest. It was a racial justice rally and march, organized around the everyday American occurrence of a Black person's murder. The spring evening was cool but slightly humid—the cargo short folk would have felt right at home. We rode the Orange Line from Stony Brook station in Jamaica Plain to Downtown Crossing and walked over to the State House from there, its golden dome cresting on the horizon as we climbed the slight incline of Park Street.

People stood around on the lawn of the Boston Common in clusters, waiting for someone with a megaphone to rally the crowd. A few friends of Matt's waved over to us, smiling, relaxed, and we joined them. Once the leaders with the megaphones emerged, we gathered around them. I was so self-conscious. I didn't know where to stand, how fast to walk, how loudly to raise my voice during the call-and-repeats. I felt like a kindergartener thrust into the center of the show-and-tell circle with nothing to put on display.

But Matt knew what to do. And what he did was this: He just stood there. When people walked, he walked. When the group leader clapped, he clapped too. When the group leader hollered a chant, he hollered the refrain. He faded into the background appropriately while I was preoccupied with the delusion that this was all somehow about me in any way. He eyeballed people around us. He eyeballed the cops. He was tall and broad-shouldered and knew he could play a helpful bouncer role if needed to protect our fellow protesters. He was not precious about his body. He was not afraid.

I was. I was feeling really precious and really afraid. I had lived so much of my life from a place of worry up until this point, and the protest was no different. What if I got arrested? What if I needed to be bailed out? What if it all went on my permanent record? What if those little handcuff zip ties got wrapped around my wrists? What if they cut into my flesh, causing a moment of discomfort? What if the faceless amalgam of authority that I always imagined to be looming over me, like the Grim Reaper, became disappointed in me? What would I do then?

Matt would try to catch my eye every now and again. Sometimes he'd smile at me or give me a sly thumbs-up. Sometimes he'd bulge his eyes or raise his eyebrows at me in a joking way, and I'd laugh a little. As the group leader gave instructions into her megaphone on what to do if we were detained, Matt leaned into my ear and said "*Narf,*" which is a thing that the dumb sidekick character from the children's cartoon "Pinky and the Brain" often exclaims for no reason. I tried to erase the uneasy look from my face and said in return, "*narf.*"

His attempts to put me at ease worked. As the sunset streaked the sky with warm pinks, I felt more relaxed. My steps felt surer, my gaze felt stronger. *It's my constitutional right to protest,* I reminded myself each time a police officer leered at us the way a hungry Looney Tunes wolf looks at a pig, watching its sweet living body transform into the image of delicious, dead, roasted ham right before his eyes.

After we marched in a couple of loops around the cobbled streets circling the State House, we gathered around the quaint stone pavilion that houses the entrance to the Park Street T stop. Another group leader stood up on a milk crate and spoke to the crowd through his megaphone. The crowd cheered, hollered, and answered calls. The volume increased generally. The sun had gone down completely, and the sky had gone from pink to purple to ink.

What is it about that hot moment before a protest goes bad? It's like you can smell it. The line of cops stops looking like a formation of individuals and starts looking like an armed, mechanical wall. They shuffle forward, and forward, and the crowd shuffles back, and back. Maybe a loud crack rings out as a plastic water bottle makes contact with the ground, and then it's on. The bland menace of the cops as they unsheathe their tasers and batons. How can they simultaneously look so bored and so threatening?

The pavilion stood sturdy before us, long escalators unfurling to the Red Line and Green Line platforms below. Park Street Church loomed over us, its gleaming white steeple stretching toward the dark heavens. Up the hill, past the green of the Common, the gilded dome of the State House glittered condescendingly.

I looked behind us and saw twice as many cops as had been there before. The smell came on, and things suddenly started feeling dangerous. As the police presence increased, as they tapped their batons and set up a perimeter, I wanted to get on one of those long escalators and go home.

"Do you think it's time to go?" I said to Matt in a faux-breezy voice.

"Umm," he said. He scanned our surroundings calmly. He didn't appear menaced by the steeple, the dome, the cops. The crowd was electric, pulsing, and getting louder. He seemed a little amused, actually. "Well. I think you should go, if you want. But I think I'm going to . . ." he trailed off as a cloud of smoke plumed up from the crowd in the distance and some fresh, urgent shouting rang out.

He looked over at me and noticed my worried brow. He softened his expression, then smiled. He pulled me into a gentle hug, then stepped away from me and toward the horde. "*Narf.* I'll text you when I get home!"

"Okay," I said, trying to sound light. I couldn't muster a return narf. I edged backward toward the station entrance. He smiled again and offered a little wave with his hand down by his hips. Then he walked away, toward the floodlights and the smoke that now obscured most of the church, hiding the red brick and large windows of the main building, making it so that all you could really see of it was its piercing white steeple.

13

The Zebra

IT's ONLY BEEN A WEEK SINCE MY LAST RUN, AND YET ALREADY, the protective threads that my training routine had sewn around me are starting to unravel. I used to get up earlyish, so that I could get my run in before the sun got too intense and the day got too hot. But now, without a real reason to get out of bed in the morning, I'm staying up late again. I channel surf in that awful modern way, clicking endlessly through row after row of disappointing offerings on various television streaming apps, eventually resigning myself to inhaling entire seasons of reality series about log cabins or people who are afraid of buttons. I swipe on dating apps, intentionally matching with people I don't think I'll like so that I can have a confrontational conversation before unmatching them again.

One night, I have a long instant messenger chat with a Netflix customer service representative about a grotesque horror movie image. I tell him the image, which features a rotting grinning demon face with a pentagram carved into its forehead, triggers my PTSD. But it doesn't really; it just grosses me out, and I'd rather not see it. No, the things that trigger me—crinkling bags, closed doors in silent rooms—are much more insidious than obvious horror cheese. But my condition felt like a legitimate excuse to get what I wanted, so I figured I might as well use it to my advantage.

The customer service representative promises to block the movie from coming up on my feed, then we just kind of talk about our nights for a while.

Without regularly working up a sweat, my showering routine slips. I run my fingers through my greasy ponytail absentmindedly in front of the television. I scratch my itchy armpits, and little pills of dead skin come off. I settle into my sedentary misery with ease, and, mentally, it transports me right back to where I started.

When I was in the third grade, I got a concussion. Not in a cool sports-playing way but in a dumb falling-down way. It was the day of the Snowflake Festival, my elementary school's holiday recital. I was congregating on the playground with the other kids, awaiting the day's first bell, dressed up in thick navy tights, an itchy tartan skirt, and an even itchier cable-knit cardigan. I had started learning the violin that year and would be making my debut performance as part of the group of child-musicians that our school unironically referred to as "the orchestra," struggling along with the other eight-year-olds through the basic melody of something simple like "Twinkle, Twinkle, Little Star."

Outside the school entrance there was this big, rotting telephone pole that could give you a splinter just by looking at it wrong. Regardless of its treacherousness, it was the axis around which our morning spun, the spot where we'd dump our backpacks, our sports bags, our too-thick coats that our mothers always insisted upon, so that we could swing on the monkey bars or play flirtatious games of tag totally unencumbered. At the sound of the bell, kids would run—always running, and for no real reason—back over to the telephone pole, gather up belongings, and then shuffle indoors in one bobbing little mass.

When the morning bell rang on the day of the Snowflake Festival, I ran to the telephone pole as usual and scooped up my stuff, tossing my backpack over one shoulder and clutching the pebbled leather handle of my violin case in my fist. I turned to run toward the door with my usual yet unnecessary vigor, and just at that moment, two boys in my class escalated an argument into a physical shoving match. One of the boys fell to the ground in front of me, and I tripped over him mid-sprint. I sailed through the air for what felt like whole minutes before I crashed, headfirst, onto the pavement.

I don't remember how I got to the nurse's office, but I remember ending up there, smelling the band-aid plastic and cold metal, sitting atop a crinkling slice of parchment paper stretched over the examination table and holding an old-fashioned woven ice pack to my throbbing forehead. I swung my legs absentmindedly and noticed the big tears at the knees of my navy tights, skin pink and raw underneath. My mom arrived quickly, we lived just a few blocks away, and the sight of her made me cry in that way that kids do, after the physical pain has subsided but the drama of the situation still feels overwhelming and unsafe.

My violin case was crooked, the rental instrument inside mangled. My mom took me home and gave me a juice box and called my cousin to come babysit so she could return to see the rest of the family perform in the Snowflake Festival.

My mother propped my pillows up behind me to keep me upright in bed. She told me to be good and to try not to fall asleep because sleeping isn't good when you are concussed. I nodded solemnly, patting the stack of *American Girl* books on the bed to my left, the literary companions to the popular dolls. Surely the riveting tales of Revolutionary War–era American Girl Felicity, lacing her stays and baking Shrewsbury cakes and overhearing a lot of adult conversations about British Loyalism but none about the transatlantic slave trade, would keep me wide awake. But within minutes of my mother leaving the room, while my cousin watched *90210* reruns on the TV downstairs, the large serifed type on the pages of *Happy Birthday, Felicity!* began to fuzz over, and my eyes slipped shut.

I had dreams. Well, I guess they were more like hallucinations. With the Snowflake Festival fresh in my subconscious, my bed transformed into a gorgeous, gilded opera box, and my room melted into a theater. I looked down at the program on my lap, at the dressed-up people seated around me. There'd be a performance, it seemed.

On the stage below, the performers clambered out from the wings. But they weren't people. They were zebras. Two or four at first, then more and more. They stampeded the stage and arranged themselves in two clean lines, like I had during my own ballet recitals. Then, their dance began. At first it was careful and in sync. They went up en pointe on their glossy hooves, twirling in small circles with their front legs raised overhead in perfect arches. Their mohawk-looking manes trembled gently as they moved through the steps.

But then one zebra, one in the front, started to go a little too fast. The zebras around that one sped up in order to keep time. Soon, the whole group was moving through the dance too quickly. The zebras started clambering all together, like the kids in the playground, forming almost a single being, a zombie horde. They neighed and stomped their hooves. Their mohawk-looking manes shook like rows of wheat in the wind.

I saw them all around my opera box bed. I was awake now, eyes open, but the hallucination continued. I stared in front of me and saw my bedroom, but the opera hall was layered on top of it like a projector film. I watched the zebras now clamber around the velvet opera hall seats and bump into my bedroom's big wooden clothes bureau. I simultaneously perceived the dressed-up opera hall patrons and my bedroom's many stuffed animals.

I was afraid of these zebras but fascinated by them too. It felt like I could reach out and touch them, but I didn't dare. For some reason, I became afraid that they would take me with them. I didn't want them to—I clutched my fleece blankets in an attempt to anchor myself. They got closer. I could see the space between their individual furs, the hot skin underneath rising and falling with their rapid breath. I could see the milky white parts of their wide eyes. I could see their nostrils flaring.

I opened my mouth. In my dream logic, I was going to speak to them and tell them plainly to leave me be. But in reality, I was screaming. I kept screaming until my cousin came running in and shook me back to full consciousness and she asked me what was wrong, and I didn't know where to start.

The sort of psychedelia I achieved accidentally while concussed was the sort of thing Matt loved to intentionally chase down, arms open, ready to receive. In college at UMass Amherst, he read a lot of Tom Wolfe and William S. Burroughs and got into the more costume-centric Beatles albums. While his peers enjoyed binge drinking, Matt was more of a pot smoker. At a party, he'd rather get high and talk quietly about Brooke Hogan's reality TV show than do shots and keg stands. But he could occasionally be convinced to really rage.

After Matt died, I asked his friends if there were any particular memories of my brother that stuck with them. They shared many delightful glitter-doused anecdotes, many of them set in the frozen woods of Amherst. But the one with the zebra costume has always been my favorite.

One night around midterms during the fall semester, there was going to be a big Halloween party at an off-campus house, and the girls across the hall convinced him to attend.

"Suckin' on my titties like you wanted meeeee!" Matt screamed along with the Peaches album he had blasting from his crappy laptop speakers, door open for the whole floor to enjoy. The girls who lived across the cinder-block hall of the dormitory also had their door propped open, and they giggled in high-pitched trills at Matt's off-key belting. Once he put the finishing touches on his bright pink lipstick, Matt was ready to put on a little show. He kicked a leg out from behind the wall into the open doorframe, dramatically bringing his whole body into view in slow motion. First, his long dopey clown feet. Then his legs, stocky like mine, calves permanently sculpted thanks to an athletic childhood. His torso next, long and slippery-looking, both because he's relatively hairless and because he has a posture like someone sucked his spine out from the back of his neck. His bulbous shoulders came next, then his sturdy neck, his enormous Irish head, and his oval-shaped face. His squiggly little mouth twisted into a cackling smile, filled with teeth that had once been strenuously corrected through orthodontia but were now in the process of wandering back out to their original crooked formations. His eyes, huge and round and blue. His hair, golden.

His friends got a kick out of this, and so did he. They'd only returned from the dining hall about 20 minutes ago, and in that time, Matt had swapped his Levi's for Legg Avenue fishnets, the cheap kind. He had lots of variations of these dollar-store fishnets: classic black, of course, but also hot pink and lime green. This was on trend for the mid-aughts, when the look was all about shiny neon lamé, shellacked asymmetrical bangs, and a general sense of too-much-ness. It was easy to find these tacky fashions, even in hippie country Northampton, Massachusetts.

"*Fuck the pain away,*" he sang along to the Peaches song blasting from his tinny laptop speakers as he twirled out into the hallway, sashaying into the girls' room. He was doing a little hip gyration, and it was going over really well. The girls were whacking at him with faux-protesting soft arms as he mini-humped his way in their direction. On top of the fishnets he'd layered a pair of shiny hot shorts, and his large veiny feet had been slipped into pumps. On top he was wearing a Morrissey t-shirt and a blond wig, the hair parted and braided like Pippy Longstocking. On top of that, a Viking helmet.

"Serving sexy hipster Thor!" he said to the girls as their giggles sharpened into cackles. "Thor! On! Ec! Sta! CEE!" He punctuated each syllable with a hip thrust.

Matt always liked to dress up in costumes. Boas, hats, brightly colored Tina Turner–style wigs—he'd dig into our childhood dress-up bin more zealously than I. In middle school, Matt went inward, flying under the radar as a lacrosse playing, Abercrombie-cologne-soaked 13-year-old popular kid. But that center wouldn't hold. In high school, his clothes got tighter. His hair got longer. His cigarette smoking escalated into a full-blown aspect of his personality, and his sports participation ceased entirely.

Once he arrived at college, the huge class size and sprawling campus allowed Matt to fade into the crowd a little more. Get racier with his outfits, with the costumes, with the makeup. Even though he had some close friends at UMass, he also relished being an outlandish outlier, a clique shape-shifter, a wild supporting character in the lives of many.

"*Love* the costume. What time are you heading over there?" One of the girls asked Matt.

He looked at her blankly.

"The party?" she elaborated. "You're going, right?"

"Oh!" He said. "Yes, yes I am. But this isn't my costume."

The cackling began anew as Matt mimed a faux-serious expression, implying Sexy Hipster Thor was his usual garb.

"You'll see," he said in a singsong voice. He took a swig from the open bottle of discount vodka on the desk by the door and then went back to his own room.

Matt had made a special Halloween costume this year. A proficient self-taught tailor, he whipped himself up an entire ensemble: a striped jumpsuit, hoof hand covers, and an impressive headpiece with a mane. But, twist: The entire outfit was lovingly stitched with purple sequins, glitter, and shimmer not found in the Sahara. He'd be a zebra—but, like, a musical theater version of one.

The party was off campus, at a big house full of senior PoliSci majors. Matt didn't know any of them all too well, but he wasn't worried. It was sort of a perk, even. He hated spending parties talking about school with peers in his grade, standing around a deep kitchen sink discussing whether or not a weekend symposium would count for credit. It reminded him of the conversations he'd overhear parents having on the sidelines of his lacrosse games, weighing the pros and cons of different models of dishwashers or credit card rewards platforms. He didn't know it was possible for human beings to be that boring, and he dreaded achieving those levels himself. He feared it, that sputtering waterslide into mediocrity, more than anything. Matt wanted to talk about outer space and obscure internet animations and the latest movements of D-list VH1 celebrities. It was easier to achieve this with a rapt audience of relative strangers than actual acquaintances.

But he was striking out at this party.

People were nice enough, sure—the bros who lived in the house offered Matt windmill high-fives at the sight of his getup, the girls cooed over the details of the hot-glued stripes—but everyone was pretty distracted. Distracted by boners. Boners almost exclusively of the heterosexual variety. The late-fall weather was cold and unforgiving in western Massachusetts, and it'd only be getting colder. Students were looking for someone to get sweaty with tonight or someone to watch illegally downloaded sitcoms with for a few months while cuddled up on an extra-long twin dorm bed, or something in between.

"Have you ever looked up old Spanish television on YouTube?" Matt asked a drunk girl dressed as an angel. They were hanging around in the mostly abandoned kitchen while a dance party took over the living room, lights low, arms around waists and hands caressing necks, straight kids plucking their future sex partners from the pulsating mass. "It's ex-*treme*-ly entertaining."

"TV shows? Like, from Spain?" the angel asked, her obvious shit-faced-ness belying her cheerily attentive tone, grabbing Matt's forearm as she wobbled on her espadrilles.

"Yeah. They have all kinds. I like this weird late-night show from the 1950s the best. It has a whole segment devoted to contortionists."

A roar of approval emerged from the living room. Someone had turned the lights completely off, and now there were only laser machines pulsating green, red, and blue lines illuminating the space. The music got louder, the bass vibrating like a geological event.

"What's a confrantulist?" the angel asked, adjusting her hot pink bra straps.

"You know," he said, "someone who's really flexible."

The angel stared at Matt blankly.

"I like your head thing," she slurred, motioning to the zebra mane.

"*Thank* you," Matt says genuinely, petting the mane. "I skipped Modern American War Crimes to work on it all afternoon."

"You *made* that!" The angel inched her face closer to Matt's. "That's *so*. Cool." Her hand was still on his forearm, except now it wasn't grasping for safety. Now, she was tracing little circles with her chipped pink manicure.

Matt looked down at the pink manicure. What is that, Essie? No, too much sheen. Probably an OPI shade. He gently took her hand and moved it from his forearm to the countertop. He smiled warmly with his lips closed.

"My dear, I'm afraid I have to go. Thank you for the conversation." He readjusted his felt hooves, flipped the mane hair on his headpiece, and sauntered off toward the front door. The angel tilted her head after him, like a Cocker Spaniel trying to understand a new English word. She shrugged, steeled herself on the countertop, then shuffled into the dark loud living room to try again.

It had started to snow since Matt arrived at the party a couple hours ago. The overgrown grass in the front yard was covered with a thin layer of crisp white. Luckily Matt was all layered up underneath the zebra costume, and the getup itself was made of warm fuzzy felt. Besides, he liked a nice long walk in the cold, sharp air jolting his lungs like little needles in a pincushion, all the while knowing he's on his way somewhere warm and safe. And he had provisions, too—he reached inside his zebra jumpsuit and slipped a silver Urban Outfitters flask out of his jeans pocket, unscrewed the little top gingerly, and brought it to his lips for a sip.

He walked down the side street, which had neither sidewalks nor streetlights. It was pitch black, and the snow started coming down harder, an aggressive white blur. He couldn't see more than a foot in front of himself at this point, but he was sure he was on the right track. He found his way out to the main road, and it'd be a straight shot back to campus from here. But there was still no side-walk to speak of, so Matt lumbered down the center of the street, his zebra headpiece flopping from side to side.

Then, a quick beep of a car horn came from behind him. Matt was 30 minutes and ¾ of the flask into his walk now. His fingertips were cold and bluing, and he was feeling surly. He pretended not to hear the beep and continued walking in the dead center of the road.

Why should he have to move? He's the one out walking in the freaking elements, God dammit. That person in their comfortable, heated car can just fucking chill for a second till they get to the more well-lit part of the road.

The beep came again, this time slightly more sustained. Matt continued to ignore it, shaking his zebra mane in an over-the-top gesture, swigging the last few sips from his flask. There was actually plenty of room for this jackass to pass him, if he really wanted to, but he was being a dick, Matt decided. Energized by the conflict, his lunking gait turned more into a strut, a swagger, a show-offy prance.

Two more beeps now, in succession, like a voice saying "Move it!" Matt started to sashay like a ballerina, shifting his body from side to side, his Vans slipping through the freshly accumulated slush, creating little treads. Illuminated from behind by the car's headlights, Matt's shadow loomed large before him, stretching a million miles ahead, the zebra ears and mane looking fantastically defined, transforming Matt's figure from that of a regular human to a wild beast powering forward, proud and deliberate and absent of anxiety.

The driver leaned on the horn, and the long beep saturated every inch of air. Matt calmly slipped his now-empty flask back into his pocket. He began to raise both of his arms, stretched straight out at his sides, slowly lifting them toward the sky, cutting through the beep-filled atmosphere like hot knives. Once both arms were fully extended upward to the heavens, he flicked his fleece hooves backward to expose his hands fully. He wrenched each hand into a fist, and dramatically unfurled each middle finger until they were fully extended like radio antennae.

Matt heard the tires crunch in the snow behind him, twisting direction abruptly. The engine revved, and all of a sudden, the car was beside him. A mechanical sound clicked, and the passenger window glided downward. Matt snapped his neck to the left, looking in the window. The driver was a young guy, maybe late 30s, wearing the ugliest hat Matt had ever seen. It was super boxy and unflattering for his face shape. But maybe he was coming from a costume party too? Matt's eyes wandered to the body of the car, and he noticed the red stripes, the white serifed letters spelling out "Amherst Police." Oh.

The cop was still creeping the car forward to match Matt's marching. He gave Matt an expressionless stare. They lock eyes for a few seconds. Then the cop arched one eyebrow, a tell, a give. Matt stopped walking, stood up straight, and lit up his face with an ear-to-ear grin, his crooked little teeth glittering. He whipped one of his hands up and waved vigorously.

The cop rolled his eyes. "Be safe, okay?"

Matt nodded, his mane swaying along with his head. The cop rolled the window up and slowly drove away, disappearing into the blackness, the snowstorm curtain closing behind him.

14

Missing

"WALK/RUN." THAT'S ALWAYS BEEN AN OPTION ON MY TRAINING plan PDFs, letting you know it was okay to intermittently slow your pace to a stroll so long as you got your mileage in. But I never considered actually walking for any portion of my training runs. I only wanted to run, run like the *wind*, or at least run like a pushy breeze, barreling myself along with all the might I had, pounding my body on the pavement until my brain felt adequately tranquilized. Indeed, what could have possibly gone wrong with that approach?

I see my error now. And as I walk the last half mile home from today's quick two-miler, I don't feel discouraged. I feel grateful to be moving at all. My knee is feeling better, and I'm terrified of accidentally pushing too hard. This run is just my second after a week and a half off completely, and it has gone just fine. There's been some tightness in my knee, but nothing like the shooting pain I experienced before. I still got to enjoy the sun on my shoulders, the people in the park, the calm of my running goo brain.

I've been doing everything by the book, and that means a lot more intentional activity outside of my scheduled runs. Instead of taking Eddie into the yard for fetch, I take him on long leisurely walks each morning and evening, and instead of wearing crappy flip-flops on these walks, I lace up actual sneakers lined with foam inserts I bought at Duane Reade. Instead of laying around in my sweatpants in total stasis, I lay around in my sweatpants with my legs wrapped up in enormous rubber resistance bands I ordered online, performing clamshell stretches and other movements recommended by physical therapists I found on various websites.

It's May now. The hit-or-miss weather has turned into mostly hits. Each day's air is increasingly buttery, the sun more intent on shining, the snow all melted. On the 21st, for better or worse, I'll be running this race. My health feels precarious, precious, more fragile than ever. I'm no longer able to beat my body and brain into gory submission. If I want to compete, I simply must slow down. Be nice. There's no other way.

Pounding myself into oblivion isn't going to work anymore. It's not that I thought it was sustainable, necessarily. At the time, it just felt like the only solution.

In the months before he died, Matt used to wake up in the middle of the night confused. He'd start running the shower thinking it was time for work, or he'd come upstairs to the kitchen and crack a beer open, thinking he'd already been at work and just got home. I'd come out of my bedroom and talk him down, get him back into bed, help him make sure his alarm was set for the actual morning.

The quesadilla night in September was one of those. I remember slowly gaining consciousness when a sliver of hallway light flickered through the cracks around my closed bedroom door. I was lying on my side and felt the light on my face as soon as it came on. This door-facing sleeping position had become my go-to as I got used to sleeping alone most nights. I reasoned it'd be best to meet any potential murderers face-to-face before we began combat. I had recently taken a self-defense class at a local rec center and learned a bunch of moves. I learned that if the perp crouches on top of me,

I'm supposed to kick him upward with my knees, then use my upper torso to flip the asshole over and off. I mastered the move quickly along with my fellow students, a bunch of middle-aged women in long linen skirts carrying at least two NPR-related tote bags each. I think about their tote bags as I lay in half-sleep, waiting for the inevitable perp to come test my skills.

But there was no perp that night, there was just the kitchen light. The yellow seeping in around my door felt like it was getting brighter and brighter. I could hear Matt opening and closing kitchen cabinets as I lay on the other side of the wall. I pushed the home button on my iPhone. 3:26 a.m., September 24. The light of the phone screen flicked back off. My eyes adjusted, and the darkness started to feel a shade lighter. I could see the contours of my dresser, the fuzzy outline of Eddie sleeping in the corner.

A pot banged in the kitchen. Eddie lifted his head and cocked it to the side, considering barking, then just exhaled heavily and rolled over with a thud, probably catching a whiff of Matt's sweat and deciding there was nothing to worry about. The clanging was getting louder, and I heard the hollow pop of a soymilk carton landing on the granite countertop. I heard a burner click to ignite, then stop. Click to ignite, then stop. Silence. *Is he going to blow this fucking house up? Would it even matter?*

Then, there was a gentle rap at my bedroom door.

"What do you want on yours?" Matt said casually, as if we'd been in conversation for an hour, him just picking up where we left off.

"What?" I called groggily, pawing the floor around the bed looking for my sweatpants.

"What. Do you *want* on yours," he repeated, slower now, as if I just didn't understand which words he said, when in reality I didn't understand why he was saying any of these words.

"On my what?!" I found the sweats and was attempting to stuff my hot swollen legs into them, tripping over myself in the process.

He proclaimed, like a punch line, with exaggerated Spanish enunciation, "On your *quesadilla!*"

Then, he giggled. An actual little giggle.

I finished getting pants on and wandered out of the bedroom, Eddie lunking dutifully behind me. With my mouth slack and open, I took in the scene in the kitchen.

Matt was center stage with bowls and boxes and cartons all whirling around him. There were more food items out on the counter than I even realized we had in the house. He sprinkled pepper into a pan, then reached for a bag of shredded cheese, flicking his wrist to release about a half a cup of dairy into the pan. The tortilla was already in there, along with lots of chopped peppers—*oh my God he was out here using knives*—plus some vegetarian meat alternative, still twinkling at the edges with freezer burn, even in the scalding pan.

"Hm hm hm," he hummed as he tapped a wooden spoon on the side of the frying pan.

My half-open mouth twisted into the beginnings of an incredulous smile. *I shouldn't think this is funny*, I scolded myself internally. *Why is this funny?*

His right hand looked numb and limp. He was not even attempting to use it, keeping it close to his chest and out of the way as he used his left hand to poke the quesadilla with the wooden spoon.

He's high as a kite. It's sad. This is sad, right? Why is this funny?

He was doing a little dance now, tapping the spoon on the stove like a drumstick. Oh my God it was great, but it was also clearly textbook awful. The lilt in his voice was so happy. The corners of his mouth were flicked upward, a smile as small as a secret. His eyes were in that heavy half-lidded state, but the corners were cheerful, upturned to match his mouth.

I knew I should step in before he set himself on fire, but he was almost done cooking, anyway. I leaned on the granite counter and kept watch as he finished, slipping the spoon underneath the tortilla and sweeping it out of the pan, sliding it onto a plate with a little too much gusto—the food almost went sailing across the kitchen island directly into Eddie's eager, open mouth. Matt moved back to the fridge and rummaged through it. I watched as nearby glass jars of soy sauce and Ragu rattled perilously close to the edge of the shelf.

"I'll get it," I moved past him and dug into the back of the shelf. I knew what he was looking for. I grabbed the sour cream and popped the lid off, spooning a big heap onto his quesadilla first, then one onto mine. I glanced back at his face, and the warm fuzzy smile had faded. He looked content still but sleepy, like a toddler after a parade.

I started cleaning up: putting pans into the sink, putting lids back on ingredients and stowing them back in the fridge or the cabinet. I opened the freezer door to put back the frozen pizza Matt had inexplicably taken out, and then I spotted it: my Old Overholt. This bottle of rye whiskey had gone missing last week, and I had assumed Matt drank it all without asking. "Have you seen my rye?" I had asked him accusingly days ago. I made a big show of looking around, lifting up all the other bottles in the liquor corner of the counter, as if I would find it hidden underneath the crusty old triple sec or something. Matt, sober in the afternoon, told me he hadn't seen it, and I seethed at the perceived lie. God it was so annoying how he'd just *lie* about stuff, the stupidest stuff. I wouldn't even care if he drank it, I just wanted him to tell me, I reasoned with myself. And now, look. He didn't drink it, you idiot. He just got high and placed it gingerly in the freezer for no reason! I took it out and put it back in the liquor corner, ice crystals on the cap crackling in the room temperature warmth.

"Thanks for the snack, Matt," I said as I took a bite of mine. Cheese perfectly melted, tortilla perfectly crisped. It was, honestly, delicious. "Why don't you take yours with you and head back to bed?"

"Okay," he said brightly with his eyes shut, and I let him head down the stairs first. I followed after him with his plate. He got back into bed, and I set the plate down on the side table, knowing he was probably going to fall right back asleep and not eat this thing. Maybe he'd have it for breakfast.

"See you in a few hours, okay? Then it'll be time for work."

Matt appeared to do some math in his head, then nodded. "Right, okay."

I patted his comforter, switched off his bedside lamp, and closed his bedroom door behind me gingerly. I made my way back up the stairs, shut the rest of the lights off, and fumbled back into my own bed in the dark.

A long moment of silence passes. Longer than usual. I stop my clamshell stretching mid-thrust and hold my breath. The camera cuts back and forth between the contestants' faces. "Sharon Needles," RuPaul finally announces from behind the judge's bench. "Shantay, you stay."

Sharon collapses her pale shoulders in relief, rustling the fishnet-embellished epaulets she's wearing like a kinky, haunted sea captain. The underdog of *RuPaul's Drag Race* has narrowly survived this episode's lip sync battle and will advance to the next round. I too breathe a little sigh of relief, even though I've seen this episode many times before. I resume my little clamshell movements, opening my knees slowly and then bringing them back together while the resistance band applies challenging pressure. Once I've done 20 or so, I switch to lean on my right side and do some more.

Sharon and the losing queen exchange a warm embrace, rubbing each other's backs with their palms, fingers extended fully to protect their long acrylic fingernails from catching on the couture. Then, the losing contestant blows kisses gracefully at the panel. The panel nods solemnly, offering conciliatory half-smiles. The losing queen sashays down the runway one last time, her hourglass shadow lingering as she exits.

This program, a reality show slash cutthroat competition slash celebration of all things loud and gay and enhanced by foam padding, has been on television for more than 13 seasons now. Matt was alive for seven of them. His favorite was season four, the one with Sharon. Remembering Matt's devotion to Sharon Needles makes me feel a hot pang of pain, as if I just caught an elbow to my fleshy side, my mouth watering a little with acidic pre-puke saliva. He always treated his drug addiction like some flippant joke, a *Fear and Loathing*-style adventure through sweaty basement parties and accidental long weekends on the Cape. A charming quirk, like a nasal laugh or ambidextrousness. His love for Sharon felt like an extension of this.

The summer before Matt died, we'd spent lots of weekday evenings watching *Drag Race* in the Jamaica Plain apartment, eating take-out burritos and sipping Miller High Lifes. We'd watch it on his good days, when he'd cackle at the high-speed, innuendo-laden banter of the contestants, looking over at me wild-eyed, making sure I was laughing too (and explaining the niche references to me when I wasn't). We'd watch it on his bad days, when he'd nod off sitting up, mouth hanging open, then snap awake violently, panicked and forgetting what time it was, hauling himself off the sofa, muttering about needing to get dressed for work even as the glowing green slashes on the face of the cable box read "10:45 p.m." I'd try to talk him down, remind him of the date and time and where he is and what we're doing, tuck him into his bed. I'd casually make sure he was laying on his side so he wouldn't asphyxiate. *That's how Jimi Hendrix died*, I'd think to myself for a flash of a second, before shooing away the thought.

"You need to tell your psychiatrist everything you're putting in your body. *Everything*," I occasionally scolded Matt. I'd look him in the eye and insinuate. That was the closest I ever got to talking directly with him about his drug use. But what else was there? Stage a cable-ready intervention? Try to get him committed against his will? Drag him to a local basement meeting? I had no access to information about harm reduction: syringe exchanges, drug testing strips, naloxone, and, above all, a compassionate and respectful approach. That's the stuff that could have actually saved his life, helped him hop to the next lily pad of eventual health and happiness. Instead, my head was filled with 12-steps and psych wards and the judgmental doctors showing us the heroin-swollen brain scans. "Tell him to stop," they said.

Drag Race reminds me so viscerally of my brother that I trot it out whenever I want to wallow, which is ironic given its content. Even amid all the sex puns and the glitter and the silliness, I start to cry, slowly and silently at first, then with more steadiness. After about 20 minutes of that, the crying picks up velocity until I'm finally sobbing hard, so hard I think I'm going to throw up my intestines, coughing up my own organs until my body has fully flipped and I'm inside out and I have to sit my eyeglasses upon the sinewy red muscles of my sinuses.

I used to have these fantasies that I'd finally, effectively intervene for Matt. I'd imagine myself, chest full and proud, eyes clear, tearing through the inevitable mess of every bedroom Matt has ever occupied. "What are *these*!" I'd yell, holding up some inscrutable baggie of pills. "And what's . . . *this*!" I'd exaggeratedly discover a single syringe. Matt would watch me ferociously unveiling these many truths, and he'd be unable to look away. He'd be incapable of coming up with a cascade of fibs fast enough. I'd be too smart, too cunning, too *too*—I'd finally outwit him. He'd finally look me in my face and say, "I need help. I'm going to stop. Please help me. Please help me to stop."

But I didn't do anything like that. And he didn't say anything like that. We fumbled around it so much, did a horrible square dance around the edges of the idea, but we couldn't figure out how to have an open conversation about it all in earnest. The shame, the fear, the confusion, the fixation on how things should have been and not how they truly were. It all got in the way, sucking up all the air.

Matt, what happened to you? Something must have happened to you, and I want to know what it was. I know all about your mental health issues, the frayed areas of your wiring. I knew it since you were a kid and would cry, like me, over feeling big-picture alone and unloved as you shook in your ski boots on family vacations, as you ate flakes of Wise potato chips from greasy blue bags in front of pinball machines at birthday parties, as you laid your golden bowl cut to rest at night atop your Teenage Mutant Ninja Turtles sheets, faded from so many runs through the washing machine, Leonardo's red eye mask looking more like a Michelangelo orange. I knew it when you'd get so quiet at school dances in high school gymnasia, or in the backseat of my friends' cars during aimless high school drives blasting The Mars Volta while we circled the Route 60 roundabout in Medford over and over, or smoking cigarettes in the wide open and empty park at dusk where you should have felt good, where someone with the right chemical brain balance would feel good, but you couldn't, no.

I know the 1990s made it feel like a happy, healthy queer future was impossible, like being gay was a choice that would lead to inevitable suffering and alienation. I know that curse rode along in the backseat with you your whole life, its bony finger hovering an inch away from your shoulder, singing, "I'm not touching you! I'm not touching you!" I know even though you lived joyfully so much of the time, its shadow lingered.

What else? There must be more. Addiction doesn't just happen, it unfolds. How did it unfold in you?

Was it an event? An experience? An environmental factor? Someone must have done something to you, maybe it was multiple people. Multiple groups of people! They always say that, all those addiction science experts, PhDs in trustworthy earth-toned turtlenecks with crisp white jackets on top—they say that people who get addicted to drugs were most likely traumatized. Were you? Who did it? Was it a priest? Was it that shifty one, God what was his name, the young one, the "hip" one, with the too-clean 1950s serial killer haircut? The one that played Bone Thugs N Harmony on his boombox after CCD? Did he do something to you?

Or was it more about the trauma of living in the now? Was it the everyday mortification of trying to be your divine self within a modern experience that's quietly cruel, detached from real meaning, with a gaping open mouth dedicated exclusively and entirely to consumption? Getting home from long hours at the customer service cubicle jobs you got your bachelor's degree in order to perform, watching the police shootings and foreign bombings on the nightly news in between advertisements for Flamin' Hot Cheetos and Cialis and Ford F150s, wondering how this could possibly be considered a normal version of human reality? And the way people are deemed crazy, diseased, mentally ill, when they struggle to swim in this toxic water—did the drugs make it easier to swim?

If I collect all the information, if I can just get my arms around it, if I write everything down, and if I replay it over and over in my mind's eye—when will it start to make sense? It has to make sense at some point, right?

RuPaul would've never let Matt die. She would've known what to do, what to say to really help him. RuPaul is a self-made entrepreneur, an entertainer and a mogul, a Lady Liberty for outsider kids throughout the country, guiding them toward a new, better, prouder life. RuPaul has mentored queens by the hundreds, patented lacquers and lipsticks by the thousands, endorsed dating apps by the millions! RuPaul has been in a B-52s video! And not just any B-52s video, but the "Love Shack" video! RuPaul designed and sells a signature candy bar! RuPaul has released 11 studio albums—wait, or was it 12? Maybe I should do a quick Wikipedia search, just to get my facts straight—

On my way to grab my laptop off the kitchen table, I catch my reflection in the hallway mirror. I glimpse my sweat-stained flannel shirt. My stubbly kneecaps. My greasy strings of hair cascading down my braless chest. Jesus. Somehow, I've watched six forty-four-minute-long episodes of *RuPaul's Drag Race* in a single sitting. Now that I'm thinking about it, I don't even think I've urinated this whole time. *I should pee, I'm gonna get a UTI*, I think to myself catatonically as I continue to stand and stare uselessly. It's hard to accept what I know to be true. I just want to see Sharon Needles win season four again. I just want to see Sharon come out on top.

But then I realize: RuPaul would never have let *this* happen, either. This whole boob-sweat-stained situation right here. I can hear her feedback on my performance in surround sound in my mind. "In the self-pity challenge, you showed plenty of unhinged grief. But the judges were left wondering: Where's the beef? And this afternoon on the couch, your casual flannel look is more like a casual-*ty*—of fashion. I'm sorry my dear, but you are up for elimination."

I accept Ru's harsh criticisms. I steel myself to soldier on to the next round. I go to the bathroom. I splash water on my face and brush my hair back into a bun. I shuffle over to my kitchen window and look out at the winding half-dead trees in the scraggly yard.

I try to remember things that are nice, the things Matt and I shared that were certifiably good. Matt is dead now, but he wasn't always dead, I have the proof in my memories. Look, see, for example: There we are, eating coconut popsicles at the YMCA outdoor pool, banding together at our day camp even though we're technically in different age clusters and are supposed to be socializing with the peers in our own group. We run alongside the pool, playing an illogical game of tag, shrieking with joy, coconut popsicle melting down our forearms, our smooth, fresh little feet getting toughened up for summer by the rough, prickly concrete.

And oh look, here we are in the backseat of mom's station wagon—the way back, the cool spot. We're watching trees rush by, we're listening to the adult-contempo radio station my mom always tuned the car radio into, full of Don Henley and Whitney Houston, Annie Lennox. We're armed with one favorite toy each: his, the red Power Ranger, mine, my rare pink My Little Pony, the one that looks the most like my favorite character from the cartoon tape I watched so much that the plastic started to unspool from the tightly wound center. We make the toys run, run along the scenery flying by in the window, pink pony galloping while the red ranger does more of a hop, Matt occasionally bending the Ranger's legs into realistic running poses, both of us laughing, bopping our heads along to the music, waving the toys like they're batons and we're the conductors of the Boston Pops. *Desperado, why don't you come to your senses! How will I know if he really loves me! It feels just like I'm walking on broken glass!*

And look here: We are in the basement bar at the Knights of Columbus. We're bored while dad and Pa and the other regulars watch the Patriots game. Beer bottles clink, cigarettes rest on the edges of thick crystal ashtrays, smoke swirls in the yellow light around us. We've already played several rounds of pool, using our greasy hands to send the balls flying, instead of the wooden sticks that measured longer than our small bodies. We giggled beneath the yellow light of the old-school Budweiser lamp, its glass as multicolored and intricately designed as a Tiffany piece, brandishing that cheap beer logo as if it were a royal insignia. We're being loud, as usual, but our cackles blend in with the bellows and hollers of all the men reacting to the highs and lows of the football game, and all the madness blends together. We pull back the handles of the cigarette machines and then let them go, pretending to play pinball. We ooh and ahh in reaction to the pulls, even though the faces of the cigarette boxes remain unchanged and no prizes are distributed. We flick the knobs of the scratch card machines, we ask for more fountain sodas, which are slung down the bar to us, past the bottles of Bud Light, little red straws bobbing cheerfully among the bubbles.

We devise a new game. We press our faces to the cold red metal door, the main entrance to the downstairs bar. We turn our ears to listen. This door is now a dungeon door to us. It keeps out dragons, fire, aliens, spaceships, Bigfoot, *all* of it. We're so quiet listening, listening for imaginary noises, and then we're screaming laughing, and then we're so quiet again, and then we're screaming again.

Pa rolls his eyes and extinguishes his cigarette and walks over to tell us to ree-*lax*, will you? Before he gets to us though we take off running up the cool concrete steps, using our hands and feet like little animals. We're screaming, screaming laughing.

I treasure these memories, the classical movie montages of the happiness we shared. But the memories from our adult lives are less cut and dry. Sometimes they're warm and soft, sometimes they're stale and brittle. Sometimes they're both.

December 31, 2014, was Matt's last New Year's Eve. We didn't know that at the time, of course. Around 11 a.m. that day, I went to a strip mall liquor expo and loaded a grocery cart up with the works: several bottles of champagne, a few cases of Narragansett, cheap bourbon, fancy bourbon, cheap blended scotch, fancy single malt. Feeling magnanimous, I cruised past the baggies of red solo cups and instead reached for the fancy plastic cocktail cups with reinforced edges, the disposable champagne flutes. I was working a schmancy copy chief job at a big corporation at the time, and it came with a salary that felt exorbitant. But the downsides were plentiful: hours of round-trip daily car commuting to work in a beige particleboard office off of an enormous, ever-congested highway, lined with squat mall plazas of various sizes. I spent my days wandering the gray carpets of the corporate campus, smiling at the SEO managers and product directors and chief innovation officers. At lunch I'd take long walks around the enormous, shadeless, midsized-Lexus–filled parking lot for my daily exercise. It was all starting to take a toll on my nerves, and wasting money on stuff became my Valium.

So I loaded hundreds of dollars' worth of booze and party supplies into the trunk of my car, wheeled my shopping cart back to the front entrance of the Liquor Emporium, and drove home to start getting the house ready.

Elijah and I had created a tradition of hosting this New Year's Eve party at the Jamaica Plain apartment. We called it "Champagne Death Ray" because we were in that part of mid-20s adulthood where everything feels like it needs to be a customized joke all the time. We started the party to serve as an oasis from the high-stakes planning of New Year's Eve, a guaranteed way for us and our friends to enjoy the holiday without having to buy $200 tickets to a mediocre bar party full of bros in topsiders engaging in light date rape. This year was the fourth edition of Champagne Death Ray, and we had a solid cast of regulars who always attended.

The night of the party, music thumped out of Elijah's cat-scratched amplifiers. Clumps of people socialized in sections. Some hung out around the kitchen island, mixing up drinks or flicking the tops off pony-neck beer bottles. Some danced in the darkened living room. Some stood out on the deck to smoke weed and cigarettes, illuminated by the string of warm Christmas lights rigged all around the banisters, making each tableau of action out there look like a regal painting: Two Men in Beanies Ignite Bong, Young Woman in Weather-Inappropriate Tube Top Pets Feral Cat.

I stepped out and joined the tableau. I liked being on the deck in the cold; it gave me a nice safe feeling, chilled and buzzed with my coat not-all-the-way on, feeling the sharp air crackle in my lungs while I huddled into myself on the creaky wood, knowing that comfort and warmth was just a few feet away behind the sliding glass door.

"You wanna hit this?" our buddy John asked, extending his thick rugby-playing arm toward me to offer a purple pipe shaped like an alien character from *The Simpsons*.

"No thanks," I said as I sipped my drink, "pot makes me too sleepy to socialize."

"Oh. Sucks," John says, smoke unfurling from his half-open mouth like a gauzy scroll.

"I know. Better just stick with," I rattled my rocks glass around a little. "I don't want to end up pulling an Irish exit at my own party."

"Solid plan," John nodded.

I settled into one of our IKEA deck chairs, pulling my faux-fur coat closer around my shoulders. I wasn't ready to go back inside yet and needed something to do with my hands. So I grabbed the bright yellow pack of American Spirits from the middle of the deck table and dabbed one onto my damp lower lip. I groped around the miscellany on the table in search of a lighter but came up short.

"John, how'd you light that thing?"

"Kid with the lighter just left to go get a pizza. I think I have, though . . ." He patted his jean pockets, his face morphing from a strained ponder to a smug smile as he produced an immaculate book of matches. He flicked it over to me and I clapped my palms together to catch it.

A fresh book of matches is one of the most wonderful things. You know eventually it'll rot down into nothing after being toted around in purses and pockets, well-used and lovingly fondled. It'll be all frayed edges and ripped stubs, its strike strip worn down, an ashy ode to former explosions. But in its newness, it's immaculate. Elegantly folded up like a precious gift. Ready to eventually serve its purpose but still beautifully intact.

I slipped the cover out from under its little lip enclosure and gently pushed it back, revealing the stately rows of matches underneath. I carefully slid the outermost match between my thumb and forefinger and gently tore it from the pack. I planted the match head on the striking strip, pressed down with my thumb, and let 'er rip. Yanking the match across the strip, feeling it ignite under my thick finger pad skin, flashing too-warm on my thumb for just a split second, bordering on pain but not quite, and then watching the match flare up with a roar. Perfect. A blissful moment of starting something fresh, before you have to deal with all the rest of it.

A few hours of party went by and I was back inside, telling an elaborate story outside the bathroom, when I heard people exclaim greetings and my brother's name toward the front of the apartment. I made my way to the front door, and yes there he was, coming in from the cold, smiling and hugging people in the dim light.

As I got closer, I saw his eyelids were heavy, purplish, and half drawn down, shoulders slightly slumped, wavy smile exposing his little teeth. He was encircled by a few people I didn't recognize; must be the friends he had asked about bringing along. I made my way over to him, but got waylaid around the oven—"Jess, I think the mini-quiches are burning, unless, are they supposed to be bubbling on top?"—and I lost eyes on him, getting sucked back into the swirl of the party.

I've spotted Matt out at parties looking this way before. It looked different from the average person's fucked-up-ness, a little unsafe, distorted. It's like his buzz had gone brown while everyone else's blossomed, like his had been overwatered and allowed to fester, like a soggy succulent on a shadowy sill. At parties, Matt's face would appear either stone sober or way too fucked up—there was rarely an in between.

A few years ago, he talked me into tagging along to this college kegger in Allston, in the top-floor apartment of a sagging old triple decker down a Boston University party street. The sort of house that looked equal parts condemned and haunted yet still fetched unbelievable rents due to housing shortages and proximity to the Green Line and a general overabundance of fat-cheeked freshman rubes from out of state, their starter checking accounts flush with their parents' money to spend on housing.

I was supposed to meet him there, so I arrived alone, and the first thing I noticed was the couch. The reason I noticed it first was because the couch was not inside the house. It sat proudly on the lawn, where you'd expect a swing set or maybe a stone Catholic Madonna figurine to be. It was weather-warped and an ugly 1970s orange, covered in fresh clumps of glitter. Kids were actually sitting on this thing, pulling from their Parliaments and sipping from their Sam Lights and chatting as the bass from the party fuzzed through behind them. *Aren't they worried about bed bugs?* I thought. *This is how you get bed bugs.* At 24, I felt 100 years older than everyone else.

There's no feeling of ancientness quite like having just barely aged out of college parties.

I passed the outdoor living room scene and entered the party, which was raging in every single room of the house's first floor. An iguana in a fluorescent-lit glass terrarium looked out upon the room with bored disdain as the college students raved around him. I accepted a glow stick from a sweet girl in a pink halter top, smiling gratefully as she bopped away. Only after she left did it occur to me that I didn't know what I was supposed to do with the glow stick. Wear it around my neck like a choker? Wear it on my head like a crown? Weave it through my fingers and dance with it like I was in a Prodigy music video?

Finally, Matt appeared, all heavy lids and slumped limbs. He was wearing a t-shirt my mom gave him a few years ago that says "Galway" across the chest in collegiate-style letters. His arms weren't covered in tattooed cranes and the red sun just yet. He hair was still long and moppish, and I watched his head bob along with someone's story, quaking with a little laugh here and there. He was smiling and chuckling and making the movements a human body typically makes when it's nice and buzzed and having a good time, but it was like there was a shadow over him.

I made my way over and grabbed his shoulder. "Hey!" he shouted at me with genuine excitement, pulling me in for a hug.

"I'm so glad you're here," he slurred, hiccupping the last few syllables. "Did you see the iguana? His name is Hank."

Matt's eyes looked glazed like melty doughnuts. He seemed fucked up in a way I didn't understand. The shadow over him perked my ears up, like an animal, but I didn't know why. I told myself I was overreacting, and we spent the rest of the party sipping beers and laughing. I gave him a ride home later. By then, he seemed back to normal.

At the New Year's Eve party, I wondered what Matt was on. I got distracted by the mini quiches, which, it turned out, were indeed burning. But I still offered up the too-tough bits of cheese and bread on a nice West Elm platter my mom had given Elijah and me for Christmas, and my drunken guests gnawed on them absentmindedly, unmoved by the charring.

I finally got back to Matt and his pals. It was almost midnight at this point, and we were getting ready for the most high-stakes part of New Year's Eve. A few random guests still streamed in, while some streamed out, everyone clutching their phones, carefully calculating where they'll be spending the moments surrounding 12:00 a.m. I handed out little party hats and these vintage noisemakers my friend Kate brought. Elijah had printed out the words to "Auld Lang Syne" on little slips of paper and circulated those.

"Matt!" I called out to my brother, ushering over a handful of sparkly green party hats. "Here, you have to put one on, it's almost midnight."

"What?" He said, half looking at me, half looking at a guy I didn't know in a red and black flannel.

"The hat!" I insisted, situating it on his head, stretching the skinny elastic band around his chin and releasing, letting it snap into place maybe a little too hard. Matt closed one eye and winced.

"There you go. Now you're ready for midnight."

Ol' Red Flannel was still blabbing directly to Matt, like I wasn't even there. He leaned into Matt, his words turning into whispers. Matt chuckled once, breathily, and then looked back at me, visibly annoyed by my lingering.

"Come in the living room!" I was tired of being ignored but couldn't resist making one final attempt to influence my brother's behavior. I turned on a heel and left them in the now sparsely populated kitchen, entering the mosh pit of people in the other room, the TV at the center broadcasting a pixelated livestream of the ball drop. I was handed a full and fizzing champagne flute from one direction, and from the other a festive headband was perched atop my dome, and I could feel the plastic "2015" baubles on the top of the thing swinging from their springs. Everyone's faces were near and warm, excited. At 11:59 someone started jokingly counting down—FIFTY-NINE, FIFTY-EIGHT, FIFTY-SEVEN—but it actually caught on, and now the whole drunk room was doing it. I looked around at happy couples with their arms draped around each other, faces so close, maybe even touching, little roaming fingers on each other's waists and arms and necks, loving glances, loving smiles, but the confident kind that doesn't need much fanfare. I wondered where my boyfriend was, then decided finding him now and putting my arms around him would just annoy him, make him bristle and sigh heavily, looking at me placating with a tight, closed-lip smile. I looked to my friends instead and caught their eyes, and we counted down together, screaming "Happy New Year" to each other at the final moment. Hugging and kissing, toasting and dancing, doing little loops with our fingers in the confetti-filled air around us, Eddie wagging his tail, approving of the cheer and silly champagne-dampened movements, expecting that any second now, scraps of food would start falling from the square hors d'oeuvres plates held at an angle by intoxicated, slackened wrists.

I stopped and looked for Matt in the madness, scanning the faces, but didn't see him. I went back to the kitchen, and sure enough he'd gone, his heavy peacoat having tidily disappeared from the hook where it once hung, like he'd never been here at all, like I dreamed the whole thing up.

PART III

15

Persistence

ABOUT 6:30 A.M. ON MAY 21, BROOKLYN'S EASTERN PARKWAY IS divided up into pens as far as the eye can see. Each is marked with numbers and letters and is filled with runners who mill about like farm chickens, performing little tics, checking their shoelaces and adjusting their waist belts, swinging their arms around. Race day. It's here.

I barely slept last night—nerves about the race, sure, but mainly I was anxious about oversleeping. I positioned my iPhone an inch away from my ear, my finger close to its screen, awaiting the dinging that would not wake me up necessarily but more remind me that I was currently awake and should get out of bed.

Following my brush with injury, I'd been clinging to the advice in my training PDFs like gospel. Luckily, a couple of them featured race day tips. They said to get in bed early the night before even if you're not tired, so I got in bed early last night, even though I wasn't tired. They said to wake up early and try to go to the bathroom, so I woke up early and tried to go to the bathroom. They said to eat a light but filling breakfast like a bagel with peanut butter, so I choked down a bagel with peanut butter, the bread feeling like sand in my bone-dry early morning mouth, the hunks hitching in my throat with each swallow.

After the bathroom and the bagel, I suited up in the actual running gear I'd acquired over the past few months. No cotton soccer camp t-shirt or middle school headband for me today. I put on a pair of nice black running tights and a sleeveless singlet. I laced up my fresh running shoes, a pair that I'd purchased a couple of weeks ago when I realized my old ones had likely contributed to my injury. I pulled my hair, smooth and washed just yesterday, into a ponytail. Onto my singlet I pinned my race number, a waxy rectangle of paper with a tracker chip embedded inside, taking me a few tries to get it on evenly, fumbling with the safety pins like a nervous prom date.

I took Eddie for a rushed walk around the block. Sensing my nervous energy, he stole upward glances at me, almost looking sarcastic, as we ambled past the neighborhood brownstones and big apartment complexes and trash heaps. I got him set up with a big scoop of kibble and a fresh bowl of water before rushing out the front door toward my destiny or my doom.

The race would begin up at the top of Prospect Park, an easy jog from my apartment, but to save my energy I rode the 2 train a couple of stops. Emerging from Grand Army Plaza station felt like stepping into Disneyland: the corrals, the crowds, the distant fuzz of music and announcements, the excitement hanging in the air like humidity. The Brooklyn Museum presides over the sprawling starting-line scene, its Beaux-Arts facade a mass of smooth gray stone with clusters of finely carved details.

I've spent so much time lately obsessing over the opioid crisis—something the country seems to have become more aware of over the past several months, or perhaps that's just my myopic grief, finally seeing the signs that were probably there before Matt died. In early 2016, there'd been a story about it in the *New York Times* at least every couple of weeks, and just days before the race, the Editorial Board of the paper put out a column called "Congress

Wakes Up to the Opioid Epidemic." In the column, they called for increased treatment funding and addiction medication prescribing, two obvious solutions that will continue to be overlooked for years. And just a few weeks after race day, Prince would die from a fentanyl overdose at his home in Minnesota, raising a new level of awareness around overdose and opioid potency. Either way, it's become impossible for me to move through the world without noticing the crisis' tentacles, and even race day is no exception. I recall that inside the Brooklyn Museum, on the fourth floor, sits the Elizabeth A. Sackler Center for Feminist Art. Elizabeth is the daughter of Arthur, the eldest and most visionary of the Sackler brothers, who purchased Purdue for his siblings to run. Her collection includes plenty of political art, including posters created by ACT UP, an outrage-fueled grassroots organization who protested the government's inaction on the AIDS crisis in the 1980s. One of ACT UP's most famous slogans: "Stop killing us."

I visited that wing of the museum countless times before my brother died, before the OxyContin discourse, before the Sackler name had become so widely condemned. As I walk past today, bare arms shivering in my singlet, I look to the upper floors of the museum building and wonder if any OxyContin protest art will ever make its way into the Elizabeth A. Sackler wing.

Need to warm up now. I accelerate my walk into a trot, passing the starting line and the rows of temporary bleachers that have been erected around it. I've got to get to my preassigned corral, way down at the back of Wave 2. The paper number pinned to my shirt rustles in the breeze. My heart thumps with anticipation.

The Brooklyn Half Marathon is one of the largest in America. More than 27,000 runners will be on the course today. All the elite athletes are in the pens at the front; mine is full of normal people like me. Inside the corral, I'm surrounded by runners big and small, taller and shorter, thinner and fatter, older and younger, darker and lighter, freckled and smooth. Some bodies are boney, some bodies are muscled, some bodies are fleshy and dimpled—but most bodies are a combination of it all. All of us are here with the same goal in mind. All of us have trained for months, experiencing the elation and the boredom and the frustration and the joy, all of us have endured our little stretches and foam rolled our tight quads and bruised our toenails and now, this. Together. All of us. Every time I accidentally make eye contact with someone as we stand around waiting, we give each other an eye-widening "wowie" kind of look, like children.

The race begins with a loud horn to send off the elites, but for the regular runners it's more anticlimactic. As pens are unleashed onto the course one by one, we shuffle forward slowly, sometimes beginning a jog that then slows back down to a walk each time the large mass of people bottlenecks again. We shuffle up and shuffle up, poking at our GPS watches and smartphone apps. The Brooklyn Museum gets closer and closer; the sound of the race emcee on the PA gets clearer and crisper. My senses feel heightened. I hear ambient cheering from the spectators gathered on the bleachers. I smell rubber, Vaseline, and the artificial fruit flavoring of sports gels mixing in with the scent of warm pavement and blossoming tree flowers. The starting line inches closer and closer until finally it's underfoot and we're off.

A swarm of us stampedes forward onto the official course. Ahead of us, masses of runners. Behind us, masses of runners. Oh my God, here we all go. First we coast down Washington Avenue, a pleasant initial downhill, before turning around and heading right back up Flatbush Avenue, a gradual uphill that turns my coast into more of a crawl. We run alongside the stone enclosures of the Brooklyn Botanical Garden, and I can see the purple blossoms of eastern redbuds and the creamy fluff of crabapple trees just beyond the walls. At the top of Flatbush, we do a lap around Grand Army Plaza, and there's a big crowd here with signs and noisemakers, clapping and cheering and offering high fives. There are no pashmina or candle sellers today, but there are snow cone stands and soft pretzel vendors, and they ring their little bells and triumphantly wave bottles of condiments as we pass.

Back down Flatbush now, then onward to Ocean Avenue until we reach the southeastern corner of Prospect Park, my usual territory, near my subway station and bus stop and the bodega I passed countless times during my training. We all file into the park for one lap around, following the very same loop I've stomped upon and sailed over and suffered through these past few months, up the hill that almost broke me, this time with no issues. Grateful to be pain-free, I focus on shortening my stride and leaning into the hill like the experts tell you to, adding in some extra bounce to steadily work my way to the top.

There are lots of spectators in the park. I feel so grateful for them too, and my gratitude mixes with my adrenalized general emotion, and I feel my eyes start to water. Cowbells clamor, small kids bounce on their parents' shoulders. There's one guy waving a handmade sign that just says HOLY SHIT! In giant black lettering. *Holy shit!* I think to myself.

We pop out at the bottom of Prospect Park on the southwestern side, in the sleepy neighborhood of Windsor Terrace. The course is nearly halfway through, and I still feel like we just started. Here, we stream onto a larger road that feels more like a highway. This road will take us all the way down to Coney Island. We descend into a tunnel beneath an overpass, and the energy in this cool silent place is positively feral as runners' whoops and hollers and claps bounce off the concrete walls. Holy shit!

When we emerge from the tunnel, it's a straight line down the rest of the way. The crowd has thinned here. The early morning chill has passed, and the air is thickening with humidity. At a crosswalk, a large Hasidic family waits by the race tape for a cop to tell them when they can dash across the course. A young woman cradling a small white dog takes fate into her own hands, ducking under the tape and bobbing across the course like a game of Frogger. A reminder that this may be a big fateful life event for us runners, but for most Brooklynites, it's just a regular Saturday. *Oh holy shit*, perhaps they mutter, inconvenienced, as they notice the race blocking their path.

Around mile 9, I start to feel some tightness in my left knee. Not pain exactly, just a little tension, like someone pulled a string inside me sharply taut. I spool my breath in and concentrate very hard on not panicking. *It's not pain, it's not pain yet.* I try to keep my stride steady, my arms moving. *If it starts to really hurt, then you deal with it. But not yet. Not yet.*

As much as the first part of the race flew by, the second part stretches on without rhythm or landmarks. I trod and trod and feel like I'm not advancing. The scenery around me stops changing all that much. Every block is lined with big apartment complexes, tall trees, parked sedans. The intersections come and go, all looking the same. Am I alive? Is this purgatory? Holy shit, why am I even doing this? This is stupid. The way you felt 40 minutes ago was stupid. Why did you get so sweepingly emotional about a bunch of idiots running in a line? Running sucks!

My brain stews in simple misery—*running sucks, running sucks*, I repeat internally like a drumbeat—but I keep my body moving. Another runner bobs past me, and I think, *where does this bitch think she's going?* She settles in several yards in front of me. I pick up my pace just a smidge to try to keep the back of her head in my line of sight, at first out of stubborn jealousy but then out of a competitive interest in seeing if I can keep up with someone faster than me. I focus on her shiny, swishing black ponytail, her impeccable white sneakers, her waist belt of tiny water bottles, and this focus drags my brain back from the brink. I can finish. I'll just chase this beautiful bitch the whole time. Yes! Thank you, bitch! You go, bitch!

Around mile 11 something incredible happens: The viscous scent of ocean brine enters my nostrils. I realize just how close I am. I can't see the water yet, but I know it's coming up soon. It'll come up soon, and I'll know I've made it. My knee creaks a little more with each step. It's still not actively painful, but the string has tightened more. I ignore it. My heart pounds, and a fresh jolt of adrenaline washes through me. I can get there. I can do it. Holy shit!

Halfway through mile 12 we round onto Surf Avenue, and the loop-de-loops of Luna Park's roller coasters come into view on the skyline ahead. Ponytail is still on my horizon. The crowd has thickened up again, and people hoot and holler, waving their arms and more homemade signs.

Then, a memory comes flying back: Matt and I here, on the 4th of July years ago, watching the Coney Island hot dog eating contest. Matt was a dedicated vegetarian for most of his life, but he always loved a good spectacle, even a meat-oriented one. We drank draft beers out of souvenir plastic cups the size of sand pails, worked our way closer to the stage, and ended up getting stuck in the bowels of the dense crowd, squished among leathery tanned biker dudes wearing ripped jeans and raunchy little vests with no shirts underneath. The crowd of bikers smelled like Hawaiian Tropic and body odor and Marlboro Reds, and they cheered loudly, their wraparound shades obscuring their eyes. We were hot and miserable, but we laughed and laughed.

Finally, the racecourse curves up onto the boardwalk. This is it, the true last bit here. The wooden planks shake beneath hundreds of pounding feet as we ascend. The ocean waves roll lazily in the distance. Seagulls surf the cool breeze.

The finish line is straight ahead now, so I break into a sprint. The crowd cheers loudly. Up-tempo music blares from big rectangular speakers. I look up at the overcast sky and the slow-moving cloud masses and wonder what percentage of the air around us holds particles reappropriated from the people we've loved, how much of them is still here and how much of them is elsewhere, and what will it feel like to become part of that myself. Wherever he is now, whatever he is now, does my brother know I love him and that I'm so sorry?

My feet carry me across the wide black finish line, and then it's over. Holy shit.

16

Peace

AFTER CROSSING THE FINISH LINE, I'M HIGH. TOTALLY AND COM-
pletely. I bask in postrace glory on the boardwalk, and my heightened state makes everything feel so much more textured. I eat a hot
dog with mustard, ketchup, relish, and sauerkraut, and the condiments pop and sizzle and melt on my tongue, tangy, then sweet, then
savory. I drink two enormous beers, their golden crispness almost
overwhelming. I hug my mom, who's come down from Boston to
cheer me on. I hug my friends. And the hugs aren't those quick
little shoulder leans of passive acknowledgment—no, they're deep,
bracing, do-it-like-your-life-depends-on-it hugs. After a couple of
hours of reveling, I ride the subway home, wrapped snugly inside
my tin foil blanket, as if I were the largest, happiest, sweatiest piece
of trash the Q train had ever known.

At home, the buzz wears off, and my body reminds me of
what I just put it through. I slowly peel off my medieval-looking
zero-bounce sports bra, and extracting the fabric from the raw, red
indentations it has worn into my rib cage makes me yelp out loud. I
shuffle around the apartment with a bit of a limp, my IT band having been freshly strained during those last few miles of the race. I'm
a little wind-chapped, a little beaten, a little queasy, but emotionally, I feel incredible. Euphoric. Swimming in the singular pleasure
of having set a challenging goal and then met it. I take a steaming

shower and then a long nap, wearing my medal over my sweats, with Eddie balled up at my feet. My bed somehow feels fluffier and floatier than it had the night before, or possibly ever. I don't need any Xanax to help me reach a deep and dreamless sleep.

Running has changed my understanding of my body. I see now that I'm not a mosaic of parts with clear borders in between, like a Barbie doll with her evenly demarcated hinges, her pop-off-able head. The fact that my body is actually one complete mass has never made more sense to me. I experience this oneness with every jog: Holding tension in my shoulders causes pain in my shins, moving my legs relieves congestion in my sinuses, activating my glutes makes my feet feel lighter. It's so clear all of a sudden. It's like when you're trying to learn a new language and you spend countless hours struggling through conjugations and vocab until one day as if by magic you find yourself watching foreign films with the subtitles turned off.

My body itself has changed, too. Grief had shrunken me down: It used up my fat deposits, softened muscles, took my already-pale skin tone to impressive new shades of translucence. But running has built me up again. My sad, starved thigh gap is gone—now, my rock-hard ham hocks are back to rubbing together with each step I take. Fat deposits have returned, ready to sustain me the next time I need them. Muscles have hardened. I have ridiculous tan lines slashed across my arms, chest, and legs from hours spent training in the springtime sun. The awkward and unattractive bits don't bother me, though, not the way they used to. Because I know what my body can do now, and that makes me much more content with the way my flesh happens to sit upon my bones.

My lifelong aspiration of being a floating brain doesn't feel as urgent with this new understanding. I am starting to appreciate the relationship between my dumb appendages and my intellectual control center, how each carries weight for the other, how they work in concert to help me experience and navigate the world around me.

Still, my brother is dead. Running has not changed this. My grief is still alive in me, hot and throbbing. I still need to tend to it regularly. But at some point after my race, it stopped feeling like the main driving force in my daily life. I can't put my finger on how, or when, or why this shift occurred. But the grief doesn't shrink, I've learned. It doesn't reduce down to a nub or melt away like a seasonal frost. You can't whack it into submission or alter its nature in any serious way. The trick seems to be that you just grow more stuff around it, on top of it and below it, even threading through it.

Lush, protective vines now encase my grief. They hold it close, insulated and contained, as if it were an organ all its own. They prevent it from taking over. They keep its harsher edges from bumping painfully up against my insides.

But all around this vine-covered growth, there's a notable emptiness. One thing I never really understood about grief before experiencing it so intensely is just how consumptive it is. Tending to my grief took up all my time, energy, and resources. It felt like a hot gaping wound. But once it began to scab over, the startling void that had come to fill the space around it became very clear. I could holler into it and hear the echo. I could see all the needs I'd ignored in order to play full-time host to my mourning.

When I holler into the void, I discover that, actually, I'm pretty lonely. I've been living, working, and running all by myself for months now. Solitude felt necessary at first, and overall, it's been fun, even liberating. After years of losing my sense of self to my souring relationship and after those hard final months with my brother, doing whatever I want all the time rules, frankly. Making nachos in the microwave and calling it dinner, deciding on a whim to take a long bike ride to the good thrift stores, staying out late with friends without being grilled about it later—these things will never get old. But at night when things are quiet, I feel a metallic little pang of need. Once I get over the embarrassment of admitting it, I realize what I really want is regular as hell: I want to love and be loved, but not in the shitty way I'm used to.

As a result, I've become cornily interested in romance. I swoon over couples I see laughing in the park, comparing nutrition labels in the supermarket, doing crossword puzzles on the subway. I allow myself to desire what they have without apologizing or feeling the impulse to assign myself a lesser, store-brand version. I try to imagine what I want this sort of happiness to look like for me as vividly as I can—how it'll be shaped, how it'll sound.

When I was at my most disconnected, it was easier to date. I'd control my limbs like a marionette, lifting my wrist or crossing my legs as if from a distance. I'd blink through entire conversations without really registering what was being said. My floating brain could stay unimpacted while my body enjoyed a kiss, a touch, a shiver of anticipation. It was fun for a while. But now, I want to invite my brain back to earth. I want to connect with people in ways that involve all of me.

So, I set my mind to it with the same intensity I'd brought to my race training. I update my dating app profiles with nice-looking pictures instead of stupid-looking ones. I remove the joke-y song lyrics from my bios and instead list actual interests I have, in the hopes of attracting people who share them. I swipe with a little more intention. I try to give the fedora-clad masses of the apps the benefit of the doubt.

I don't feel the need to fake coolness or disinterest any more. Why bother? Grief taught me not to dawdle or pretend. I know now that closed mouths don't get fed. If I was hungry, I needed to pull up to the table brandishing silverware in my shameless fists and say, let's eat.

It's a wet Saturday in late June. The weather is doing that gun-shy thing it does in early summer in the Northeast—after weeks of increasing warmth and sun, the heavens get the jitters and plow down rain for days, chilling the air, making you dig out the sweaters you had joyfully shoved into the back of the closet just weeks ago.

It's a chaste 6 p.m. I'm sitting at a table by the bar's big bay window wearing dark-washed jeans, a shirt with the buttons done all the way up, and a brassiere with wires in it. I hadn't had anything to drink at home before I left, and right now I'm sipping a low-ABV draft beer rather than the double well whiskey I used to compel my marionette body to order on dates.

This approach is all part of my effort to pursue romance with a little more coherence. So far it seems to be working, and here's how I know: I've met several nice people lately, and I have been delighted to discover that I didn't really want to sleep with any of them. I no longer feel the urgent need to meat-puppet myself into a sexual interaction out of boredom or curiosity. Some of the dates, I never speak to again. Perfectly acceptable. But two of the dates have turned into warm Instagram flirtations, double-tapping each other's photos of lattes and neighborhood dogs, DMing each other drag queen memes, commenting all the thirstiest emojis (sweating face, heart eyes face, girl with her arm raised) on selfies. I wonder if things might develop over time within the playpen of social media, but there's no rush to it anymore. This shift feels seismic, like I'm really onto something now.

This evening I'm waiting for Jacob, a 29-year-old software developer from Illinois. I nurse my beer and scan every person who comes through the door, trying to compare the in-the-flesh faces with the photos I'd seen of Jacob on my phone.

App dates aren't quite blind dates. Before you meet up, you've likely already messaged with each other at least a little, sometimes even a lot. Usually, you've looked each other up on the internet. All this percolating pre-date knowledge makes those first moments when you're finally face-to-face feel very high stakes. Together you'll either catch the physical chemistry wave and surf it instantly, smiles and good vibes catapulting you into quippy conversation, or you'll fumble for just a millisecond and end up losing your board, flailing in the seafoam. Soon I'll know which it'll be with Jacob.

Finally, I spot him walking in: moppish brown hair, blue eyes, a slightly crooked nose bridge that looks like it'd once been broken and not properly healed. He's got one of those Brooklyn hipster outfits that is so hipster-y, it's operating in dog-whistle tones. He wears a worn-in baseball cap with an embroidered logo; it seems to promote some kind of hyper-local baseball team or maybe a regional towing company. His jeans are baggy and ill-fitting. He sports an actual windbreaker.

I wave a little, and we make eye contact. He smiles and walks over. But as soon as he reaches me, it's clear: Jacob and I are seafoam-bound.

"It's nice to meet—well, not *meet* I guess, but yeah," he says good naturedly. He extends his arm for a—is this a hug? No, it's happening too slowly, it can't be a, oh God, oh wow yes, it is: a handshake.

Feeling awkward, I really put my elbow into the handshake, exclaiming "how do you do!" with a—No, it couldn't have been, oh God, yes it was—British accent? I shake his hand with violence, but my arm is noodly. I smile with my mouth closed, almost wincing, as if I were passing an acquaintance in a tight hallway. Wow.

Somehow, we don't just turn and run screaming from this interaction. Social norms dictate we sit down and have that drink we've been texting about for two weeks, so we steel ourselves and find two stools at the bar.

Jacob asks what I'm drinking and orders the same, which is a sweet gesture. The bar's music hums low in the background, a 1990s rock playlist, while we talk about the weather ("it sucks!"), what neighborhoods we live in ("I don't know, Bushwick kinda sucks when you're over 25"), what television shows we're watching ("Don Draper sucks, but that's kind of the point, right?").

I think Jacob is a nice person. He probably has nice parents who call him up to chat on Sundays from their midwestern home just to check in, to hear what's new in the city, "the big apple" ha ha, or maybe to share what kind of hijinks the family corgi has gotten into this week. He probably has nice friends with whom he goes to brunch, maybe he even has a best girl friend who helps him pick out ties for special occasions. He seems like he's read good books and has respectable interests, but I'm just not very attracted to him. And by the way he's sitting and smiling at me like a regional bank manager, I'm guessing he's not all that attracted to me either. It feels like this should be something we are allowed to respectfully speak into the ether. I wish there was a button under the table that, once both parties push it, terminates the date instantly and wordlessly. But those social norms keep both of our butts cramping atop these peeling leatherette bar stools a bit longer.

"So what's your family like?" Jacob asks. "Got any siblings?"

As Scooby Doo once said, Rut roh. This is a common date question, but now it's a loaded one for me. How could I possibly respond without bringing up my brother? It's completely unacceptable to not bring him up out of fear that, what, talking about dead loved ones on a first date is a faux pas? I need to talk about him to make sure I still remember him because, sure, it all starts with on a stupid date I'll probably forget about in a day or two, but soon enough I can't remember Matt's golden hair, the gaps in his teeth, his sense of humor, or his favorite brand of frozen vegetarian chicken nugget, and then where are we? In hell, that's where. It's a reflex I can't shake, no matter what the social circumstances. I need to talk about my brother, and I need people to know that he was once alive and now he is dead. This is nonnegotiable to me.

"Well my brother Matt was three years younger than me, but he died." I say flatly. I sip my beer.

"Oh," Jacob says, readjusting his baseball hat, eyes cast down and bulging with discomfort. He chuckles nervously and turns it into a cough.

"Oh, no," he continues. Then he remembers the thing people are supposed to say in moments like this and says it: "I'm so sorry."

"It's okay," I say like I always do. I mean it's clearly not okay, but when you're in a conversation where the discomfort of the other person looms larger than your loss, you'll pretend it is. "What about you?"

Relieved to move on, Jacob tells me all about his sister who's in law school.

We make a little more polite chatter until there's just backwash in our beer glasses. The complete and total lack of connection makes it easy to wrap things up. Jacob asks what subway I need to take, but I tell him to go on ahead because I'm going to use the bathroom. I touch his shoulder lightly and slide off my stool before he does, which excuses us from needing to decide on hugging or handshaking. I go into the single-use stall and huff urinal cake fumes for several minutes. I hold my breath and emerge, and I'm grateful to see Jacob's gone.

I go back to the bar and order a nice bourbon. I toast myself for trying. The bartender brings me a basket of stale popcorn and makes knowing eyebrows at me. I tilt my head and shrug, smiling like, "welp." She laughs. I ask if there's any Teenage Fanclub on this playlist, and she says she doesn't know but she'll put it on if that's what I want to hear, and I say, "Yeah, please."

17

Evidence

BOSTON'S DOWNTOWN CROSSING IS A BIZARRE PLACE. Especially on a weekend, when all the nearby office buildings are mostly empty. The area's main drag, Washington Street, is closed to car traffic. You'd think this thoroughfare would be thick with pedestrians, shoppers, weekend revelers. But all that is eerily absent. A few businesses seem open—a T-Mobile store here, a cobbler there—but they're all closed up tight, without a soul coming or going. I wonder if there's a gun duel scheduled that I somehow don't know about.

The area used to be a busy shopping district, home to the flagship location of Filene's, a popular Boston-area department store chain. The building was designed around 1910 by Daniel Burnham, one of the masterminds of the Chicago World's Fair, and it's a landmark of Beaux Arts architecture in this city. My family used to come here every December to visit the Santa's Village display inside of that iconic Filene's. In the 1990s, the area bustled purposefully: Its 1980s designs still looked sleek and modern, and the streets teemed with shoppers, workers, tourists. My dad would meet my mother and us kids by the exit of the Orange Line station. Matt and I would fight over whose mittened hand got to clasp my father's freckled fist as we shuffled along the salted pavement toward the store.

"Pretend they're alive," my brother would whisper to me, his eyes like saucers, as we walked through the theatrically lit display of animatronic teddy bears working away in Santa's shop. To me, they looked like toys. But to Matt, they looked more like people. He'd laugh in disbelief, watching the bears tick along their mechanical tracks. He'd shout it like it was a revelation only he could understand, with the enthusiasm of a Jehovah's Witness: "They're real!"

Filene's and its iconic discount Basement closed for good in 2007, the heaviest Downtown Crossing domino to topple during the Great Recession. The whole area entered a slump. The streets stopped teeming. Now, nearly 10 years later, the scaffolding that obscures the ornately carved limestone of the Filene's building is plastered with "coming soon" signs advertising million-dollar condos, their architecture stark and anonymous, their future tenants hazy and unimaginable.

Among the bowels of this twisty district sits the Boston Jewelers Exchange Building. It's a 1920s structure that still functions mainly as an indoor bazaar for small, family-owned diamond sellers. But I'm not here looking for bling. I'm here because I'm looking to connect with the other side. The Tremont Tea Room, a place that bills itself as "the nation's oldest psychic establishment," is inexplicably situated in a small suite within this giant structure dedicated to the assessment and sale of sparkling earthly stones.

Boston is a college town, and it's one of the first weekends of the back-to-school season. I had sort of expected the place to be overrun with drunk undergraduates seeking to make contact with the ghost of Jack Daniels, but it's empty. Clinical. A young woman sits at a large iMac in the front of the space. Behind her are four cubicles. If it weren't for all the purple draperies and burning incense, you could mistake the Tremont Tea Room for a regional auto insurance branch.

"Name?" she asks.

I'm tempted to respond with the ultimate dad joke for this scenario: "Shouldn't you know that already?" I restrain myself.

"Keefe. I'm supposed to see Raymond at 12:45?"

The young woman processes my American Express payment and gestures for me to take a seat. I wait. A bead of sweat breaks off from my hairline and rolls down my temple as I try not to eavesdrop on the session occurring in the cubicle to my right.

About 10 minutes later, Raymond shuffles over and greets me with a smile. He's old and looks not so much frail as delicate, like a butterfly. He's mostly bald, except for a few thin clumps of short white hair. His skin is pale and slightly yellowing, with sunspots gathered around his sticky-outy ears. His eyes are legitimately twinkling, and his resting facial expression is a wry smile.

He sits me down in his cubicle space at the back left of the suite. Our knees are just an inch or two apart beneath his cloth-covered table. He situates three different decks of tarot cards on the table, each one featuring a different color, pattern, and shape. All the decks look ancient, with the card edges softened and peeling, backs cracked.

Raymond is talking in a low voice, hurrying the syllables together. I can't tell if he's talking to me, or just ... talking. He occasionally giggles a little. He shuffles the cards from the first deck over and over. He maneuvers them with precision, occasionally issuing commands to me, telling me to pick three cards, or gesturing for me to cut the deck.

"Many spirits are around you all the time," Raymond says, finally making a flicker of eye contact to indicate he's talking directly to me. I roll my eyes internally.

"Oh. Um. Ohhh," I say. I tilt my head and nod a little, attempting to broadcast earnestness while I panic internally that I perhaps just spent $70 to watch a Miss Cleo infomercial play out.

Raymond is amused. He laughs a little at the obvious discomfort I'm trying to conceal.

"Is there someone in particular you're interested in hearing from?" he follows up. Raymond is so seamlessly cutting and shuffling his deck of cards, they seem to glide around the tabletop as if commanded by cosmic force.

My eyes start to well up immediately. I'm annoyed to be getting this emotional so quickly, so I focus on holding the tears in the bottom rung of my lash line, refusing to let them roll downward, knowing once I really start crying, I won't be able to stop.

"Yes," Raymond says, answering his own question. "The veil is very thin with him. 'M' name?"

My heart jumps and starts to beat fast, ramming against my rib cage. I try not to be alarmed by the immediate, casual precision.

Raymond keeps shuffling. His demeanor barely changes. With his resting perma-smile, he says, "How did he die? He feels like he let his family down."

Psychics and palm readers have long been omnipresent in American city life. And lately, they're very trendy. Vague millennial spirituality, coupled with a post-Trump desire to curse the patriarchy, has led to a semi-ironical rise of witchiness: geodes, astrology, tarot, hexes. My Instagram feed is peppered with incantations for self-love and memes portraying Rihanna as a classic Pisces. Tarot readers have started popping up at happy hours and office parties, right alongside the bespoke cocktails and the vegan snacks. Spooky consumer products are no longer relegated to specialty stores on the seedy side of town—I can purchase a set of "healing crystals" at my local Urban Outfitters for $25.

I'd never considered seeing a psychic in a serious capacity until Matt died. That's when the neon signs started to stick out to me a little bit more, beckoning to my grief-stricken brain like a fragrant pie on a windowsill beckons to a cartoon nose. My gaze lingered on the storefronts of Linda the Pure Energy Healer and Jasmine Essence. I started talking about the idea of seeing a psychic more and more, testing the waters with my friends and family. Always half joking, hyperaware that it's probably all just bullshit, right, haha. I waited for them to tell me the idea was ridiculous, but their reactions were impressively neutral. They're kind people. They would let me say all sorts of nutbag things to them during the apex of my grief.

Once I started talking about the idea more directly and without my customary irony shield, I was surprised to receive some enthusiastic recommendations from several people I knew. My friend Emily, who had suffered a great loss during her teen years, recommended the Tremont Tea Room. She told me uncanny stories of her visits with a psychic named Raymond, who picked up on all manner of oddly specific details about her dear departed friend, offering wisps of inside jokes that seemed impossible to know or guess. This story sucked me in completely, and I trusted Emily on this topic for two main reasons. One, her loss was adequately horrific, like mine. (No offense to those trying to connect with Mimaw and Pawpaw or whatever, but losing a peer at a young age is just its own kind of thing.) And two, she's from Rhode Island, which automatically gives a person several extra punches on the Dunkin Donuts Rewards Card my mind uses to evaluate a person's legitimacy.

Raymond, I told myself. Raymond at the Tremont Tea Room.

Raymond's shuffling his tarot deck, waiting for my answer.

"He overdosed. Heroin, mainly," I say quickly. Every time I admit what happened to my brother out loud, it feels like an incantation, a curse.

"Mhm," Raymond nods. He mumbles a little, but not to me. He finally stops shuffling the cards around and throws one down faceup. It features an illustration of a man hunched over, struggling under the weight of a load of sticks.

"Boy, do you like to make yourself suffer!" Raymond giggles like a muppet. His eyes are twinkling especially now. He's acting like he just told me a very funny joke.

I laugh, too. It actually is funny, in that moment, the way he's calling me out without saying much at all. "I know. I can't stop," I say, wiping a tear from my cheek—the force of my surprised chuckling launched it out of my eye and set it rolling down my face. I think about my brother, about how he's gone and it's my fault, how I didn't help Matt the way that he really needed, how I always just assumed everything would be okay again one day but then it never was and now it's too late.

"It's not your fault, though. What happened." Raymond states it simply, plucking the thought from my head with a blandness, like he's reading from a recipe for banana bread. It's not your fault, then fold in the melted butter.

"I know," I say, suddenly aware of my guilt-wracked face, forcing my brows into an unconvincing furrow.

Raymond takes one look at me and laughs again.

Proper spiritualism, which became popular in America in the late 1800s, is a lot more literal than your run-of-the-mill Judeo-Christian religions. An essential tenet of most traditional religions is faith in the unknown: acknowledging that you'll never really understand heaven until you are there, submitting yourself to God's mystery and accepting His plan without question. Spiritualism, however, removes the metaphor. It asserts that spirits continue to exist, in a realm not all that far removed from our own. Spirits are available to us right here in real time and are able to communicate with us. They can teach us things about our lives and our realities, if we just reach out and ask.

Spiritualism is also about cold hard proof. Séances, asking for "signs." Shadows and orbs in the corners of photographs. Temperature changes. Knocking once for yes, twice for no. The wacky ghost-hunting gadgets of our modern day—thermonuclear whatevers, hunting for streams of "spirit" that actually look more like infrared farts—follow this proof-oriented standard to its logical techy conclusion.

Bible-fearing America started taking a shine to the supernatural in the period right after the Civil War. With the mud of so many American green spaces still thick with the blood of local teenagers, spiritualism was on the rise. There was squalor on a mass scale. Families torn apart. For the first time, the white population of the United States was experiencing some version of the mass suffering that the country had been inflicting on Native Americans and Black Americans for generations. And it left a mark.

It's easy to understand the appeal of a movement like spiritualism after a cultural moment of large-scale loss because it offers specifics that traditional religion doesn't. Spiritualism doesn't just believe in life after death—it believes there is no death. According to spiritualists, bodies mangled by war would be reconstructed, returned to their former glory, once they'd moved on to the other side. Those who'd suffered would be happy living forever in the spirit realm, yet simultaneously, they'd never leave the side of their living loved ones. It's the best of both worlds. Average citizens witnessed such horrors, lost family in such unfathomable numbers, they needed the comfort of knowing that their loved ones were okay in the afterlife. Calm, free, maybe even better off than they were as flesh and blood. They needed the proof.

The Civil War killed more Americans than any other U.S.-involved conflict by hundreds of thousands. The only official wars we've waged on American soil since the Civil War have been metaphorical in nature: the War on Poverty, the War on Drugs. But civilians have paid for them dearly with flesh and blood just the same.

The opioid crisis has continued to mutate over the past several years. With a sharp rise in stimulant use, combined with powerful fentanyl widely contaminating the illegal drug supply, it's really become more of an overdose crisis, a mass poisoning event. Its impact is similar to that of the Civil War in some ways. It affects every state, every community. Many of us have lost more than one loved one to it. Militarized police units stage drug bust raids on regular homes, often at the wrong home entirely, leaving carnage in their wake. Families desperate for resources wait at treatment facilities for days on end, hoping a bed will open up. They try to get their loved ones out of prisons and jails, swearing that their sons and daughters are good people caught up in a battle they aren't responsible for. The daily capacity for trauma feels endless, fluid, unknowable.

Overdoses are wiping Americans out in numbers we've never seen before. They're now the #1 cause of accidental death in America, killing more of us than gun violence or car crashes. At this point in the overdose crisis, it incurs a death toll on the scale of 9/11 every week and a half. Unlike a bayonet wound to the heart, though, drug use doesn't have to be a death sentence. But our warlike approach to it is fueling the fatalities.

Like the Civil War, the drug war pits family members against each other. It thrives on confusion, panic, nativism, our cavemen senses of who owns what, who's bad and who's good. When your loved one dies from drugs, the grief becomes about so much more than simple loss. It's about the concept of right and wrong. Did I do enough to help? Was my loved one a criminal? My brother died from an overdose involving illicit heroin, not clean round prescription pills—am I allowed to grieve this shameful death? Survivors of the drug war are often scrambled up inside. The scramble leads to the searching.

"What about a pink sash?" Raymond offers. "I'm getting pink. Feathers and things. He's trying to figure out which dress to wear."

I feel my throat tighten. I hadn't mentioned anything about Matt's fashion sense, or his even queerness, to Raymond. My mind's eye displays a slideshow of Matt: here, in a silver bodycon dress and purple tights, and now here, in orange David Bowie makeup and ripped jeans, and also here, in an everyday outfit, a collared shirt and black trousers accessorized for after-work beers with a long, pink feather boa.

I open my mouth a crack, but nothing comes out. I'm stunned. I catch myself thinking: *Here it is. The proof.*

"You should look for the sash," Raymond says to the table, shuffling the cards around rhythmically while I start to finally, really, actually cry.

Not two hours after I leave the Tremont Tea Room, I'm back on the Amtrak to New York. I've cut my visit home short because a friend nabbed some tickets to a coveted party, a series thrown by a group of cool kids and artists in the warehouses of Bushwick every other month or so. The parties always have a theme; this one's is *Stranger Things*. The show had just come out, and the zeitgeist was very focused on the character of Eleven, her penchant for Eggo waffles, and the concept of secret government psychic experiments. I just couldn't say no to that.

By the time we arrive at the warehouse, it's about 10 p.m., and the party is kicking off. The whole space has been transformed into an arts-and-crafts version of the Upside Down, all spindly gray tendrils of crepe paper and ethereal smoke. There's a cool DJ. There are hot young people. There's an extremely muscular man in sexy Demogorgon drag, sashaying through the shadows around the strobe lights, sneaking up on people in his six-inch patent leather heels. There's a house cocktail with cannabis oil in it. There's a magician in one corner and a psychic in another.

Another psychic? Right in front of me? Today of all days? I loiter nervously by her table, trying to decide if it's possible to overdose on woo-woo comforts. This psychic is the polar opposite of Raymond: She's young, blond, and bubbly. She's dressed to the theme, wearing a hot pink 1980s-style bodycon dress, topped with a shoulder-padded blazer that has little mirrored plastic shapes hotglued all over the lapels. She catches my eye and raises her eyebrows invitingly, sweeping her hands over her tabletop like a magician's assistant would.

"Oh, I don't have any cash," I stammer.

"I take Venmo!" she chirps, tapping a little card on her table spelling out her username.

Are you really going to see another psychic? The prospect seems both insane but also perfectly correct. I'd be stupid not to, I think. So I sit down. I scan her Venmo QR code with my phone and send over the relatively cheap $25 payment. She starts shuffling her single deck of crisp, new tarot cards and asks if there's a question I'd like answered.

"I, um. Well, I lost someone recently, and I just want to know if he's okay," I manage to articulate without crying or wincing, finally realizing what I wanted from Raymond but was unable to really ask for.

She nods once and takes to the cards. Shuffle, flip, stack, twist. Stylish illustrations of women draped in bright colors, holding cups and swords, dance across the table. She stops and cocks her head.

"I'm getting . . . bubbles. All these pink bubbles. Like, bright pink. You know, like—you know in cartoons, when Bugs Bunny takes a bath, and he kinda does this silly backstroke?" She mimes it for me. "He's showing me that."

Pink, again. So much for not crying. Tears roll down my face without me realizing it, and I swipe them away quickly. The psychic isn't looking at me. Her gaze is fixed at a corner of the ceiling.

"There was a lot he couldn't figure out when he was here," she says with a genuine sadness. "He didn't really get it. He says he's sorry. He says he understands now." She pauses. "He's okay. I can tell."

She offers me a smile and I reciprocate. She gets a dreamy look in her eye and again averts her gaze to the same corner of the ceiling.

"He says he tries to show you things. Flowers that grow in the cracks in the pavement. Do you ever notice the flowers that grow in the cracks in the pavement?"

I laugh. I say I do notice them. She laughs too. We're both laughing and smiling, and she keeps chatting about the good feeling she's getting. It feels like this odd, invisible balloon of warmth inflates and inflates between us. After a few moments, there's something like a release. The shape between us is gone, but the warmth remains. Our laughs turn into contented, closed-mouth smiles.

"That was really nice," she says to me genuinely. "It's not always like that. He made it really nice. So, thank you. Can I give you a hug?"

In the late 1800s and early 1900s, many high-profile figures were seduced by spiritualism. Mary Todd Lincoln, grieving the deaths of not just her husband but her cherished sons, sought out famed "spirit photographer" William H. Mumler to take her portrait around 1869. Sure enough, the developed photo astonished all: It showed Mary seated normally, hands folded in her lap, while a tall, bearded, ghostly apparition loomed behind her, hands lovingly placed on her shoulders. (Mumler was later taken to court on fraud charges. He was acquitted, but few customers sought his services after the trial.) Around this time, even impressively mathematical people found themselves drawn to supernatural ideas, including Daniel Burnham, the famed architect who designed Boston's old Filene's building. In *The Devil in the White City*, Erik Larson quotes Burnham as waxing one evening, "If I were able to take the time, I believe that I could prove the continuation of life beyond the grave."

Emotional trauma can put a person at odds with traditional religion. Because that kind of faith requires letting go, trusting the higher power, finding comfort within your own heart. But when you're traumatized, the last thing you want to do is sink into whatever the hell this is that you're feeling. The hot confusion of your pain is too urgent. Trauma slashes up your torso like a well-trained samurai, leaving you with these gaping wounds, fleshy holes that you have to hold closed yourself all the time, folding your skin over itself with your grubby palms while you go about your day, performing wholeness for the comfort of others. And when you feel like your guts are actively pouring out of your body and you'll soon perish from the exposure, it's hard to take people seriously when they tell you to . . . you know, sip some tea and soul search. You need bandages. You need the tinctures, the sutures. You need proof that your loved one is okay.

And then, eventually, as time passes and the proof gets digested and it fertilizes the protective vines that have begun to grow around your grief, you'll realize that your gaping wounds have closed. Your pain has transformed. It shouldn't have been bearable, but it turns out it was, in its way. It just wasn't exactly you who bore it. A new-ish you did. A twisted, sparkling, beautiful, hideous new you who grew out of the old one like a holy spore. As this new you, you'll become like the oracle yourself. People will look at you with queasy awe when they learn of your loss, their faces all screwed up in half pity half fear, and they'll ask, "How are you holding up?" But they'll mean, "How can I avoid suffering like yours?" And you'll say brightly, contentedly, "Fine, hanging in there." But you'll mean, "You can't. You'll see."

I understand the skeptical explanations for spiritualistic revelations. Psychics are empaths; they pick up on our demeanor, they guide the conversation based on the clear-as-day nonverbal cues we all broadcast, always thinking we're hiding them so well. They hold a mirror up to us, and we can choose how to interpret what we see. During the Civil War era, the skeptics were nearly as ubiquitous as the spiritualists. They'd work to expose frauds, to debunk the elaborate touring séance acts, to shut down those who took advantage of vulnerable, often grieving people. Today, skeptics can use technology to facilitate their gotcha moments, setting up bogus social media accounts and seeing if the psychic they booked brings up any of the phony information. There's plenty of videos like this on YouTube. For as long as this country has known spiritualism, it has also known fame-hungry fakers.

But when it comes to the simple act of visiting your local psychic, getting too caught up in what is or is not real is a waste of time. Because what does "real" even *mean*, man? For me, at the end of all this, there's just one thing I understand as real. It's the full feeling of peace that washes over me occasionally. This feeling was unavailable to me before, and it has replaced the panic attacks and most of the nightmares. And I can access this feeling almost exclusively when I notice the flowers that grow in the cracks in the pavement.

18

Transcendence

Somewhere west of Newark we lost the yacht rock radio station we'd been enjoying since we left Brooklyn. Jane starts jabbing at the car's computer-screen radio interface, surfing over talk shows discussing the upcoming 2016 presidential election, past classical music and scratchy top 40 until we arrive at a station in the midst of a lunchtime DJ set of 1990s hip-hop. JAMN 94.5, Boston's hip-hop station, used to do this every day at lunchtime—they called it the Back in the Day Buffet. All three of us whoop appreciatively, and Jane rolls down her window.

Jane is sitting shotgun, and Corey is driving. The car is a black, petite SUV, one of those new breeds of American automobiles that manage to take up a ton of space externally while still feeling cramped and uncomfortable internally. Eddie is sitting in the backseat with me, slobbering on the window as he looks out at the trees which go by in flashes. Most are still covered in vibrant foliage, but some have already started shedding their leaves, their spindly branches embarrassed and bare.

Corey and I have been dating for a few months now. He has red hair, like me, and a relaxed temperament, unlike me. When something's very funny, he does this two-syllable laugh like a honking goose. When something's very annoying, he doesn't take it out on the people around him; instead, he says things like "oh, shit on my dick." Before our first date, I looked him up on the internet of course, and I found his Rate My Professors page from years ago, when he taught community college after graduate school. His page featured the chili pepper icon, an indication reserved for teachers deemed sexually attractive. All the reviews were glowingly positive. "I learned a lot and he'll give you extra help if you ask," one student said. "Chill, fair, knows what he's talking about," another wrote. "He looks really sad when nobody answers questions in class," one noted sorrowfully.

On a humid summer evening in the gravelly backyard of a South Brooklyn bar slash flower shop, we had that first date. Eventually, Corey asked about my family. I told him that I had had a brother, an amazing brother actually, a very funny and warm and wonderful brother, but that he had died not too long ago. Corey's eye contact didn't waver as I stumbled through my reply. His face did not show pity, discomfort, or disgust. He just softened his brow, leaned in a bit, and said the thing that people say: "I'm so sorry." Hearing it felt bizarre this time—not because it was bad but because he really meant it. Like he'd said it in a totally different language. It was the first time I'd told a new person about my brother and then felt them stop to really make space for that information.

The early days of our relationship felt just like city summer itself: warm, gloriously unhurried, full of possibility. Our lives came together slowly and easily. We met each other's friends and often hung out with each other's crowds. When we mentioned to Jane, a good buddy of Corey's from DC who now lived in Greenpoint, that we were planning to spend a long weekend doing magic mushrooms in the Poconos, she was keen on the idea as well. So we all chipped in for a Zipcar and a dog-friendly rental cabin and headed out together.

Indigenous peoples have understood the power of psychedelic plants for thousands of years. But for the United States, the path toward knowledge in this area has been a winding one. When European colonists first came to this continent, in addition to their contagious diseases they brought along their puritanical disinterest in having a nice time. But in 1938, Swiss chemist Albert Hoffman first synthesized lysergic acid diethylamide—LSD. He was the first person to drop it, too. This kicked off a global, scholarly interest in psychedelic compounds, and the United States is nothing if not competitive. So in the 1950s and 1960s, our own research institutions got on board, exploring the effects and therapeutic potential of psychedelics. But in the decades that followed, the hippie-era hangover combined with panicky Drug War energy put an abrupt end to much of that research.

Now, we're in a period of renaissance. Johns Hopkins University has established the Center for Psychedelic and Consciousness Research, dedicated to the study of "how psychedelics affect behavior, mood, cognition, brain function, and biological markers of health." Their work is led by Dr. Roland Griffiths, a pioneer in the space whose research has shown the potential of psychedelics to treat posttraumatic stress disorder, Alzheimer's, depression, anxiety—even addiction. Harvard University, one of the most high-profile institutions to initially support and then squash this kind of research in the 1960s, has recently launched the Project on Psychedelics Law and Regulation, a policy hub within the law school dedicated to shaping protocols for safety and equity in the uncharted territory ahead.

Still, all this innovation in academia has yet to trickle down to the masses meaningfully yet. And on our adventure in 2016, psilocybin was still criminalized in every state. So we didn't get our mushrooms from a pharmacy or a legitimate distributor as perhaps future generations will. We just got them from some guy.

There's no denying that there's a certain upper-crust acceptability to the casual use of psychedelics that does not apply to other drugs. This kind of branding is an "attempt to dissociate middle-class psychedelic users from users of drugs such as crack and heroin, who are disapprovingly called 'crackheads' or 'dope fiends,'" neuroscientist and Columbia University professor Dr. Carl Hart writes in *Drug Use for Grown-Ups*. As a Black man himself, Dr. Hart is acutely aware of these sorts of prejudices. His book features several harrowing accounts of the death threats he received and racist caricatures he was made subject of while communicating his research and expertise around the world. One struggles to imagine a white, turtleneck-wearing type of intellectual receiving the same vitriol for saying the same sorts of things as a Dr. Hart.

"Consumption of psychoactive substances is a normal human pastime, as old as humankind itself," Dr. Hart posits. "It would be foolish to expect our species not to use drugs." This statement flies in the face of so much of our "drug free" American programming. Instead of the status quo—which for the United States means hemorrhaging billions of tax dollars playing futile games of whack-a-mole, trying to outlaw every new drug formulation that comes along while punishing people who partake—Dr. Hart suggests that "the task of responsible governments is to balance the natural human desire to alert one's mood with the public's health and safety."

The puritanical roots of America's approach to drug regulation are squarely noted in *Drug Use for Grown-Ups*. "I think H. L. Mencken put it best," Dr. Hart says, "when he defined puritanism as 'the haunting fear that someone, somewhere, may be happy.'"

This is going to be my first time doing mushrooms. I never really had the interest before. After my high school prom, I split a particularly potent pot brownie with my date, and it made me feel like I couldn't listen to people and look at their faces at the same time. Sitting around a beach house living room after-party in my sweatpants and my crusty updo and pearl earrings, I spent most of the evening feeling my contact lenses dry out and fuse with my eyeballs, locked in a blinkless stare-down with the carpet, while a skinny friend-of-a-friend named Zach waxed philosophic about how pot brownies offer "a whole 'nother kind of euphoria." That experience put me off the whole idea of hallucinogens, and even crappy weed, for a good long while. I'd struggled to imagine myself feeling comfortable being so out of my own mind. That started to change after Matt died. Because my stone-sober grief often made me feel like I was tripping, whether I liked it or not.

It's like you're a little radio sitting on a side table. When something like grief comes along, it bumps you hard and scrambles your receptors. It jumps the frequency from a prim news broadcast to a grainy samba station. You start picking up foreign, groovy tunes that you can't quite place. Most of the people around you, they're still tuned in to the news. But you're perceiving things differently from them, hearing totally different sounds.

Grief also rips the veil off the way most of us live most of the time. It forces you to realize, down deep to your core, how close we all are to departure from this realm. How it's the only certain thing any of us can count on. You ache for the person you've lost and know that someday you will lose more people, and then some day some people will lose you, *you'll* lose you. Understanding this so fundamentally while watching people scurry around, parallel parking and shopping for plastics and arguing about zoning regulations as if this is all there is and ever will be—it's jarring on a level I can't explain. It's a real trip. It can be scary, but if you can try to lean into it, things get pretty interesting.

As horrific as that initial stage of grief was, once it passed, I started to miss it in a strange way. I missed feeling a multidimensional awareness of the world. I missed not sweating the small stuff because I understood, deeply and truly and simply, that it did not matter. I missed feeling broader connection, even if it came by way of loss and sadness. I missed poking at the soap bubble around me, seeing the rainbow reflections within its translucence, feeling its walls bend around my touch. So when Corey told me about the positive experiences he'd had with mushrooms, how they'd helped boost his mood and alleviate depression symptoms and quell existential angst, I was more receptive to the idea than I'd expected. I started asking when we could try it together.

When it comes to drug use, set and setting are important. Dr. Hart explains that "set" refers to "the user's mind-set, their preconceived notions about the substance, their expectations of its effects, and their mood and physiology." The concept of setting is just as straightforward. It's "the environment: the social, cultural, and physical 'place' in which the drug use occurs." The process of a drug attaching to the brain, releasing dopamine, and all the subsequent effects described in most scientific overviews of drug use and addiction can only tell us so much. "It is biology *and* the environment that determine our drug experiences." Addiction doesn't just happen, it unfolds.

My set today is complicated. I'm excited but also a little afraid. Still, it's easier to get used to the idea of doing mushrooms because when I look at them, they don't seem scary. They look just like the sort of vegetable you'd simmer in a nice arrabiata. Though, I guess the pot brownie's approachable bake-sale-iness didn't necessarily spare me a bad time. I try to focus my mind on positive thoughts.

I steady my breathing. I root myself in my physical body; running has helped me understand the benefits of this, wiggling my fingers and toes, stretching my neck.

I ask Corey what I should do if I start to feel not-so-good. He thinks for a moment and then says, carefully articulating each word in an attempt to emphasize his hard-to-explain conceptual meaning, "Just try to remember: You *chose* to do this." He laughs a little and continues in a breezy tone, "You know? Like, you chose it. It's all okay. Your body is just reacting to something you chose to do. And it's all temporary! Try to think about those things, if you can."

I also feel secure doing mushrooms because you can't overdose on them in the traditional sense. This drug isn't going to potentially depress my breathing until I die. If I take too large a dose, that could be unpleasant, but my biological health isn't as at risk as it would be with, say, a bunch of OxyContin pills.

In terms of setting, it was Corey's idea to leave the city and surround ourselves with calming greenery and seclusion. But "setting" is also more general than our immediate surroundings. It refers to a broader environment that encompasses the social order, the relationships I'm in, the places and services I have access to. Generally speaking, my setting is content and secure. True, I live within the crushing parameters of our capitalist hellscape, but I have a house to live in and food to eat, I have supportive loved ones and access to health care, I'm not a victim of violence or discrimination or any real social hardship, my mental illness is decently managed. Overall, I'm good—and I'm terribly lucky to be so. This big-picture setting will factor into what sort of experience I'll have while using psilocybin.

Corey mixes the mushroom stems into some Greek yogurt, and we chew the unholy mixture up like cows, mouths open and frowning, gagging a little on the ripe, pungent flavors. It tastes like armpits. Once we've all swallowed, we look to each other approvingly. Then we sit down on the living room couch and wait.

When I realize that the thing I chose to do is about to get to doing, I panic a little. My senses start to tingle, and my heart rate increases. It feels like the cabin's wooden walls are adopting a texture I didn't know was possible: swirling, mealy. I looked at my hands, and they seemed foreign. I started to breathe more quickly.

Corey had advised us to put electronic devices away before we started. I had not taken that advice seriously—my iPhone sat on the coffee table. I touch its screen, just wanting to know the time. But as soon as it illuminates, it's like a whole band of jazz musicians start warming up in my mind, their cacophony blasting. The colors on the phone screen hiss and clash. The light is violent, shooting up at my face like an assault. I look at the numbers but do not understand their meaning. I flip the thing over and winced back from it like Gollum. I feel myself on the precipice of a panic. I close my eyes and think, *I chose this.*

"We should go outside," Corey says in an intentionally calm voice.

The cabin has a small bit of private yard and a quaint stone pathway that leads down to a larger meadow area, to which all the nearby properties have access. But we're the only people outside, and none of the other cabins show any signs of life. Everything is damp and lush and safe. The sky is overcast, and the clouds feel so low. It's like we're inside a snowless snow globe. I sit on a paving stone, looking down at a mossy bit of earth. The green fibers throb, gently, beautifully, incredibly beautifully. As I observe the leaves and the moss and rocks and the dirt, all throbbing ever so slightly, I sort of feel like I'm looking at my own insides. But it doesn't gross me out. It makes me laugh.

I look at my hands. They still look foreign, but instead of that being terrifying, it feels interesting. I stare into each crevice and wrinkle. I examine the outline of each freckle. I take note of the ridges of my knuckles, the half-moons of my nail beds. It feels utterly incredible that any of this is even here and looking this way, that I'm even here and feeling this way. That I'm me but also not me, not really, because clearly, I'm also everyone. I'm not even trying to meditate or be corny, but the beautiful corniness just flows through me organically. I remember how afraid I felt of these kinds of feelings, when I was 13 and looking at my hands and feeling so separate from reality. I want to go back and pull that version of me into a tight hug, tell her, "It's okay. Don't be afraid. This is temporary."

I think about Matt as I watch the leaves rustle, explosively purple, radiantly purple, purple, and then deep red and then purple again. I realize he's probably everywhere and nowhere, and this feels completely acceptable. I feel certain that he's all right. It's like Alan Watts observes in *The Way of Zen*: "The anxiety-laden problem of what will happen to me when I die is, after all, like asking what happens to my fist when I open my hand, or where my lap goes when I stand up."

I wish Matt were here to experience this with me. But then again, isn't he here? It feels obvious and unremarkable to me that he is. I close my eyes and angle my head up to the canopy of trees above me and say in a plain voice, "hello."

"There has never been a drug-free society," Dr. Hart says. "It is unlikely that there will ever be one, and almost no one wants to live in such an uninteresting place."

Most of us use substances. Caffeine, prescription medication, Mai Tais. The line that's been drawn in the sand between legal and illegal ones is not super coherent, and the arbitrary distinction has a cost.

Unlike most of the bored teenagers and big Irish American families of our hometown, Matt wasn't a big drinker. His substance of choice was pot. Now, I'm under no auspices that weed is harmless. But on its face, his preference for smoking grainy spliffs instead of pounding 12-packs of Natty Ice wasn't more risky or less moral. But he was punished for his preferences in ways that the Natty Ice drinkers were not. Whenever cops broke up our high school or college parties, the underage drinking most often evoked tongue clucks of winking semi-disapproval, rarely resulting in actual arrests or legal problems. The presence of pot, however, was a serious criminal matter every time. And when you're already using one illegal, stigmatized substance, the idea of using others, the ones with bigger and less understood risks, doesn't seem so far out.

What if that—any of it—were not the case? What if we could clearly perceive all substances for what they are, alcohol included: an arrangement of molecules with no inherent morality, which can have certain benefits and certain risks, certain positive effects and certain negative effects. What if we could regulate substances rationally, without the whack-a-mole crackdowns on "illicit" drugs, or the zealous commercialism of alcohol, or the unmitigated corporate malfeasance of pharmaceuticals? What if we could educate about the real risks of substances with a clear head and useful information, without the undulating mascots and the melodrama and the scare tactics? What if we could help those people who do develop substance use disorders by using proven scientific methods, without the bludgeon of permanent abstinence or a higher power or a criminal record?

"There is no such thing as being completely safe," Dr. Hart says. "Any life worth living is not without risk. So I would suggest you live your life as you see fit. At least you will be living."

My afternoon trip is not all deep thoughts and spiritual peace, though. It's still just drugs. So it's silly, too. For example, at one point Jane and I cannot stop laughing, hysterically laughing, about the cabin's living room. Corey doesn't understand what's so funny, but Jane and I do, even though we can't even come close to articulating it. We're on the exact same page about it somehow.

"This *room!*" I shout, choking it out between guffaws.

"It's *wrong!*" Jane chokes back, tears streaming down her flushed cheeks.

"What *is* this!" I exclaim, gesturing to the room's perfectly normal couch, as if it were some kind of proof of whatever kind of point we were trying to communicate. We both scream in recognition, clapping our hands together, shaking our heads "no" at the vibe of the couch specifically and of the room in general.

Corey stands off to the side with his mouth slack, chuckling along but completely confused. Eddie snores while snuggled up in a quilt in the bedroom, unbothered.

And then later, after a few hours, the intensity of the experience starts to wane. We sit together in the shared meadow space, talking still about the grass and the sky, occasionally chuckling as we recall the wrongness of the living room. Then, something novel happens: A car pulls into the driveway of the house directly adjacent to the meadow. It parks. Its ignition switches off. Doors open and close, and two people come into view.

The absolute shock of the fact that there were other humans out in the world today rings in my head like a gong. I press my palm into the grass and take a deep breath. Incredible. Amazing. Here, with us, more people. Who would've ever thought?

It's a young mom with short hair, dyed purple, and glasses. She has a young girl with her, aged maybe five or six. They carry a few tote bags up to the porch from the car and then look over at us, smiling. We smile back. Noticing our smiles, their smiles intensify, and then they turn from their house's back door and begin to, oh God, walk over in our direction.

"Hi there!" the mother chirps.

Oh God. Oh no. No no no no no no. Jane and I looked at Corey, panicked. He steels himself and says in such a normal tone of voice, "hello!" Taking one for the team, he stands up and engages the mother in conversation. The little girl comes straight over to Jane and me and sits between us on the grass.

"And then next after snacks it was time to paint the magic wands," the little girl says, starting her stream of consciousness right in the middle, talking while pulling up clumps of grass with her little fists. Jane and I sit rapt before her. The little girl's chestnut brown hair is cut into quite a chic bob, with bangs, all stick-straight and shining, freshly shampooed. Her eyes are as perfectly round as globes, wet like a salamander's, blue as lakes. Her skin is so pale, almost translucent, I feel like I can see her blue veins underneath. She's wearing a pink t-shirt, overall shorts, and tennis shoes.

"Everybody got to pick a spell, and I picked *wingardium leviosa*. And we practiced doing the spell in our outdoor voices, we had to do it really loud in order to get it to work, the witch said."

I stare at her transfixed. Spells! It came as no surprise to my addled brain that this translucent blue fairy child spent her afternoon doing spells. Of course she did. That's only right! The most perfect child in the world, so small and perfect, her nose utterly poreless, her bangs flat and shining, like Matt's did when he was young.

"Then we got to have snacks. I had a chocolate frog."

My eyes widen. I register the information like an alien anthropologist might. She consumed a frog, dipped in chocolate? I look at the grass around us, then at the mossy hill behind us. Frogs certainly loomed somewhere nearby. Are they in danger? Was the translucent blue fairy child going to hunt them down and turn them into delicacies? I feel a hot need to excuse myself to warn the frogs, but I don't want to be rude to the translucent blue fairy child, so instead I lean in and say, "Ooh."

"And then, pretty much, after that, that was all!" The child hops up to her feet as she speaks, extending her arms out at her low sides, palms facing forward, like a "ta da." She smiles a small smile at us, then runs over to her parent and becomes one with the side of the mom's leg, wrapping her translucent little arms around and burying her face in the mom's hip.

I had forgotten about the mom and Corey in the rapture of the little girl's story. Now, I register their presence anew. The mom chuckles and rubs her daughter's back.

The mom says to the translucent child, "Okay honey, ready for dinner now?" Then she turns to us. "They had a Harry Potter party down at the library today. Lots of excitement—and *candy*." She looks down at the girl and gives her a little noogie. "We're gonna have our vegetables tonight, right?"

A Harry Potter party. She had been describing a Harry Potter party. A party of make-believe, of pretend, doubtlessly presided over by a kind librarian in a witch's hat. I feel a little disappointment that the spell wasn't real but am instantaneously relieved about the fate of the local frogs. We all smile at each other like old friends. The mom and child bob back to their house, and we retreat to ours too. The sun is starting to set, turning the sky to watercolor.

After a little nap, we avail ourselves of the cabin's hot tub. (Another thing I like about Corey is that he insists that every vacation rental we ever book has a hot tub.) I sit in the warm water and watch the bubbles rush to the surface. I don't feel stoned anymore, but so many of the other feelings I developed during my trip are still urgently present. I feel so grateful for Corey, Jane, Eddie, the little girl, her mom, and every human, plant, and creature that may be within our vicinity. I feel soothed by the presence of the trees and leaves, the grass and gravel. I feel certain and secure, held and holding. I feel so happy to be alive and yet totally divorced from the fear-driven preciousness of my individual life.

All my years I've been anxious, afraid of some unnameable bad thing happening, vigilantly trying to protect myself and the people around me from imagined harms. And yet, all that startled energy did nothing to tangibly protect me and mine from certifiable bad things. So many bad things. It didn't empower me to engage with and address actual threats in down-to-earth ways, it just snow-balled, making me more and more afraid as life went on. Here in the hot tub, I can really see this clearly. I feel knots that I didn't even realize I harbored begin to loosen within me. I sense this is the start of something interesting.

The next day, we drive back to the city. For almost a whole week after my first psilocybin dose, when I look at the foliage in Prospect Park and Bryant Park and all along regular city blocks, it still appears to throb and sparkle, gently, beautifully.

19

Resilience

THERE'S A TIME THAT COMES AFTER A GREAT LOSS WHEN SMALL moments become thick with meaning. Daily events feel like cotton balls sopping with liquid, and if you poke at one, meaning oozes out. Songs come on at just the right moment, blue jays swoop into your line of sight and hold eye contact for just a bit too long, little totems appear before you as if placed there by someone on high. One day on the couch, watching a documentary program about native birds in China, I was struck by just such a soggy, meaningful moment.

The narrator was discussing a certain type of rare bird. I don't remember exactly what kind. I'd been using this calming nature show as zone-out fodder, but my attention was drawn back to the television by the B-roll footage showing these gorgeous birds soaring through the sky—healthy, effortless, regal. The narrator explained that this species has just barely escaped extinction thanks to focused and dedicated Chinese preservation efforts.

As the narrator elaborated on the rare birds' flight patterns, diet, and mating preferences, I started to poke the cotton ball. These birds could have *died*, I thought to myself. All of them. They could have been erased from the earth, and no one would have ever known about their auburn under-feathers, their delicate beaks, their impressive inner radar system that helps them follow weather patterns. But look at them now. Someone, somewhere in China noticed the collateral damage our human habits were inflicting upon these birds. They found out what these birds needed to survive and then delivered it to them. Set them up for success. Now they're not dead—they're glorious, flourishing. Beautiful! These birds! Look at these beautiful fucking birds!

As I admired the beautiful fucking birds, feeling teary wetness begin to glaze over my eyes, the narrator intoned, "Given the right help, even the rarest creatures can return from the brink."

According to the National Center for Health Statistics, nearly 1 million Americans died from overdoses between 1999 and 2020. And in the past couple of years, things have gotten even worse. Fueled by the COVID-19 pandemic, 2021 saw more overdose deaths than any previous year on record—over 100,000. Once the CDC has more recent data available, it will likely be even grimmer because the official response of the United States to this situation so far has mostly amounted to an occasional press conference and a shrug.

Matt was one of those 1 million. Every single one of them was born of the same stardust as you and me. They were once somebody's baby, small and fragile and precious, photographed in swaddling clothes and dressed in tiny booties. Then they grew up to touch even more lives as somebody's best friend, somebody's first kiss, somebody's favorite coworker who would do the biggest exaggerated eye rolls that made the whole shift team crack up. They were somebody's somebody, and they were their own somebody. Maybe they loved photographing street signs with their grandmother's old Nikon, or collecting ceramic figurines of farm animals, or crocheting potholders with swear words on them, or playing the French horn so loudly that their downstairs neighbor would whack the ceiling with a broom handle. They probably weren't all perfect, and they probably weren't all that exceptional, but they were all people just the same. None of us needs to be some incredible specimen in order to deserve the life we're given.

Addiction doesn't just happen, it unfolds. By truly understanding the risk factors, many addictions can be prevented from unfolding in the first place. Cop lectures and pantless mascots won't do it. According to the CDC, the best ways to prevent the types of life experiences that can lead to health problems like addiction is more big-picture than that. Safe and stable housing, strong economic policies that support working families, affirming communities for all young people (especially queer ones). Simple things can go a very long way, like having enough food to eat, clean water to drink, strong education systems, engaging job prospects and after-school activities, and more compassionate support for kids who experience mental illness, trauma, neurodiversity, or behavioral struggles.

Addiction doesn't just happen, it unfolds. The pills aren't the problem; the people who profit off of them are. The Sacklers and Purdue are often held up as exceptional, and in their cool and blatant cruelty, perhaps they were. But the basics of their business model are quite common. Pharmaceutical companies lobby Congress and government bodies, swaying policy in their favor every day. They take taxpayer-funded innovation and turn it into proprietary, marketable widgets. They put simple medicines out of reach through pricing schemes that would make King Midas blush. When people express suspicion of medications, it's rarely the molecules themselves that they don't like—it's the machine that creates them. This can be stopped less through limits on prescribing or outlawing certain chemicals and more through a serious rethinking of how the sausage is made.

Addiction doesn't just happen, it unfolds. But treatment works. There's loads of research showing that substance use disorders can be managed with the same efficacy as other chronic conditions, like diabetes and hypertension. Effective, high-quality treatment does exist—it's just much harder to access than the bad kind. The good news is that more and more health care professionals are getting certified in addiction medicine. These doctors are less likely to shove a pamphlet at a family and more likely to guide them toward appropriate services, ones that are less focused on pottery or horse therapy and more on individualized care, with access to medications and holistic wraparound services. AA and NA can even factor in, too. They just don't have to be the only card in the deck anymore.

Addiction doesn't just happen, it unfolds. Criminalization pours lighter fluid all over the creased paper and sets it ablaze. As long as people who use drugs are viewed and treated as criminal deviants, the stigma against them will persist, high-quality treatment will remain elusive, and lives that could otherwise be repaired will remain permanently and harmfully entangled in our legal systems. Especially Black and brown lives.

Criminalization is also largely responsible for making the illegal drug supply into what it is today: frighteningly potent, deadly, and chaotic. Overdoses are at record levels in no small part because people just don't know what they're taking anymore. The street-level people selling the drugs rarely do, either. In drug policy research, there's this phenomenon known as the Iron Law of Prohibition. It says that government crackdowns don't tangibly reduce supply, they simply create perverse new incentives for illegal manufacturers to adapt and intensify their product. This makes sense when you think of alcohol prohibition. Those old-timey smuggling trucks were filled with moonshine that'd make you hallucinate rather than beer that'd make you giggle, for a reason. More potent, less volume, easier to transport and sell while staying under the radar. Some experts describe this effect like a party clown's balloon: When you squeeze one end, the air doesn't disappear. It simply rushes to the other end, latex bulging perilously under the pressure. The intensely powerful opioids like fentanyl that now contaminate the illegal drug market can be easily synthesized in a lab. Technicians can keep remixing the molecules to dodge criminalization efforts, creating endless new analogues for us to whack our stick at and just miss.

If you've ever played a game of whack-a-mole in your local arcade, you know that pounding down on the mole's head isn't the only way to get it to go away. If it sits there long enough, it retreats back down into its hole eventually. You don't get any make-believe points, but the outcome is the same: a level field devoid of moles. What if we focused on reducing demand for once instead of supply? What if we poured our billions into measurably improving people's lives instead of into militarized drug busts and crackdowns? If the moles of fentanyl analogues were made to sit there with their plastic asses out for long enough, maybe they'd retreat.

What if we prioritized keeping people alive and safe first and foremost? Harm reduction measures like syringe exchanges, safe smoking equipment, fentanyl testing strips, and more are time-tested and research-backed ways of reducing death, illness, and injury while also connecting people to treatment services when they need or want them. The idea of providing a safe drug supply, a radical concept long championed by unions of drug users, is gaining mainstream steam as well. A 2020 article in the *International Journal of Drug Policy* by Leo Beletsky and others notes that providing pharmaceutical opioids in known dosages is "urgently needed" at this point in the crisis "to disrupt the toxic drug supply and make safer opioids widely available to people at high risk of fatal over-dose." This might sound extreme or even ironic at first, given the Sackler-y roots of this mess, but think about it for an extra minute or two. You can't recover if you're dead.

For people with addiction, a seed of healing can be planted through services like these and given the time and attention it needs to bloom. The distribution approach can range from dedicated facilities filled with caring professional staff, to quick-and-easy naloxone vending machines, like the ones New York City has just installed around town. Maybe if I'd walked by something like that in Boston in 2015, I would have stopped and picked up a dose. Maybe it would've worked. Maybe Matt would still be here, and I wouldn't even be writing this book. We'd be on a beach in Cabo, and you'd have your afternoon back.

It's human nature to want to help each other until we're taught otherwise. Our instincts are encouraged at first: In kindergarten we learn about the importance of sharing and caring, in Sunday school we learn about the importance of loving others as Jesus did. But somewhere along the way the tone changes. We're told to get real and grow up. These early lessons are replaced with a cultural notion that wanting others to have their basic needs met is for impractical softies, that actually it's much more reasonable to protect some dignities, maybe 1 in 5 or 3 in 10, but only when people meet certain obligations and terms, when they are adequately humbled and grateful. It becomes more important to like how something sounds than to understand how it actually is. We're told of the unimpeachable good of compromise, even when one hand holds dark chocolate and the other holds dog shit. Don't just pick one; that's not fair. Clap them together and call it progress.

One of the best things my brother taught me was that you don't have to fall for this. You simply don't. You get to choose your ideals, goals, values, and morals. You can seek to hold leaders and systems accountable to them just as they are. You don't have to compromise in these cynical ways. You shouldn't.

When it comes to drug and addiction policy, a lot of difficult thinking is required to untangle our internalized biases and bad impulses. A compassionate, public health approach to drug use and addiction is our only way out. It's an approach that is measurably proven to save and restore lives. But it also does something that can't be tangibly measured. It broadcasts love, care, and acceptance. It shows people in need that we get it, or at least want to get it. That we will ask them what they'd like, what they need, and that we will listen to their answers. That the goal is to help, not to hurt. If you spend your whole life marinating in a system that wants to support you instead of punishing you, I'd bet that it's a whole lot easier to reach out for a hand when you need one. With the right help, even the rarest of creatures can return from the brink.

My only pair of high heels have been collecting dust in the back of my hallway closet for God knows how long. I notice that the grooves in the pebbled brown leather of the spiked-heel booties are filled in with fine gray powder, microscopic particles, evidence of neglect. I blow on them dramatically like people do in the movies, but no dust flies cinematically forth. It stays stubbornly stuck on the leather.

After wiping the boots down lovingly with a damp paper towel, I sit on the edge of my bed and yank them on. Their heavy brass zippers make an industrial crunch as I pull them closed, a satisfying click signifying when I've reached the top. Like a newborn giraffe, I stand up, all of a sudden 5'11", knees knocked together and ankles twisted outward. I haven't worn these boots in years, and I'm afraid

I don't know how to get away with heels this skyscraping anymore. Nervous, I shuffle carefully over to the hallway mirror and take it in.

Oh! This is why people wear heels: The boots make my legs look a million miles long. My thick running calves look more svelte, my ham-hock thighs look more rounded. Instantly, without thinking, I pop my left knee and shift my weight to one side, sticking my ass out a little. My unusual level of self-confidence must have an odor—Eddie cocks his head and lifts an ear with confusion.

I bend down from what feels like the heavens to give Eddie a single good-bye pat, then I head out to begin my two-bus journey from south Brooklyn up to the Knockdown Center, a venue so far out in East-East-Bushwick that it's technically Queens. I'm headed to Bushwig, Brooklyn's premier DIY drag queen festival.

Bushwig was founded years ago by Horrorchata, an iconic scene queen and queer community organizer. The festival has evolved into a two-day glitterbomb of performance artists, DJs, food trucks, craft vendors, and, of course, drag queens and kings of every stripe. Some are tightly tucked and padded in shimmering bodysuits, while others adorn their natural silhouettes with sequined thongs or leather chaps. Some wear electric-colored wigs so volumized and fake breasts so enormous they'd both give Dolly Parton back problems, while others rock their natural chests and hair, simply styled with a cool-girl center part. There are men in full female illusions, tucked and padded and painted for the gods. There are fluid people with full faces of makeup surrounding their beards and jacked masc folks with armpit hair jutting out from the sides of their pink slip dresses. The drag on display is a little edgier than what you might see on VH1.

We're just a few weeks out from the anniversary of Matt's death, and I'm getting that squirrelly feeling, the antsy need to go out and exist on his behalf. So I step off the B57 and sashay past the rusted industrial buildings and abandoned scaffolding toward the Knock-down Center, joining the growing stream of fluorescent queer hipsters heading for the entrance.

Inside, I weave through the scattered masses as the opener queens perform to clusters of people gathered around the main-stage. The late afternoon sun streams through the tall windows, adding a warm glow to the artificial lights on the stage. The Knockdown Center has a pavilion-like interior, with the sort of well-worn wooden beams you'd expect to see in a summer camp mess hall. Oversized, multicolored balloons gather in clusters up by the ceiling and in bunches tied to the beams. Thin Party City tablecloths cover the particleboard tables that line the edges of the space, cold metal folding chairs littered around them. Plastic party cups and strings of tinsel are strewn across the floor. The disco ball glistens as it lazily rotates. It's like the high school dance we all really wanted and never had. It feels freeing for a second: remembering that once you're an adult, you can make your own reality. With enough glitter and good vibes, you can even reinvent your own childhood.

I'm not nervous or self-conscious here, the way I used to feel in queer spaces, even with Matt as my chaperone. I finally feel at home, unselfconscious. Clutching a sports-stadium–sized vodka Red Bull, I make my way up to the second or third row from the stage. The performers have become more well known as the sun has set. People have filled in behind me—patchily at first but steadily progressing into a tightly packed crowd. I kind of want another drink, and my heels are starting to hurt, but I don't want to give up my prime standing-space real estate. So I knuckle down, shifting my weight back and forth, slackening one ankle for a minute, then the other, trying makeshift relief methods, thinking through some of the running stretches I can do if I start to get really desperate.

I forget my foot pain when Mini Horrorwitz emerges on stage in a blue wig, overdrawn purple lips, and spiked-heel boots that make mine look like sensible church shoes. She's dressed as a schoolgirl, clutching books to her chest, blinking with big, exaggerated movements as the crowd hollers. She lip-syncs along with "Dear Diary" by Britney Spears with dreamy sweetness and darts around the stage avoiding the wrath of her backup performer, a severe-looking teacher character sporting a topknot and, well, a Hitler mask. After one too many ruler thwacks from Hitler Teacher, the music switches to a more upbeat Britney song, "Overprotected." Little cheers roll forward from the crowd. Mini twirls out of her schoolgirl outfit for a dramatic reveal: a blue and gold Superwoman-style leotard, emblazoned with a giant Star of David at the chest. She stomps down the catwalk so that the crowd can feast upon her look, before returning to the Hitler Teacher for a dance-fight. It culminates with Mini thwacking the teacher to the ground, mounting her as the music drops, and the mix focuses on Brad Pitt's voice from *Inglorious Basterds*: "We're gonna be doing one thing, and one thing only," Pitt's voice booms from the speakers. The crowd catches on and joins the voice for its grand finale. The whole room vibrates together to shout it: "Killin' Nazis!" Mini snaps the Hitler Teacher's neck, and the crowd loses it, the light cheering morphing into a more cathartic thumping howl.

I look around the crowd and take in the demographics. A lot of gay men of course, but there are also a good number of butch lesbians and genderqueer people. There are plenty of femme women too, and they're dressed in rave-tastic outfits, smiling, dancing, hugging their friends and snapping selfies. They're wearing hot pink lipstick and false eyelashes, spiked stilettos and fishnets. Their cheekbones: contoured. Their hair: teased. Their ass cheeks: peeking out from beneath the edges of their short-shorts, like chicken cutlets. They're relaxed in a way that can only be felt in a space like this, totally absent from the traditional male gaze.

Many women of all stripes love drag. I think that's because the art form takes all the conventionally feminine things that we've been taught to perceive as simultaneously de rigueur and frivolous—hair and makeup, frills and fashion, bright girly colors and sparkles—and glorifies them. Worships them. Actively chooses them. Makes them big, bigger than average, Amazonian and otherworldly, almost godly. These attributes become so exaggerated when crafted by a drag queen that all who behold them are forced to engage with them. See now, look and don't flinch: Here is the shimmering pinkness of my lips, the height of my long, flowing hair. Behold! The contours of my intentionally engineered fat ass!

This flies directly in the well-lit face of the loudest message that the patriarchy delivers to women about everyday beauty. The message that above all, you should aspire toward effortlessness. A natural look. A loveliness that you just woke up possessing and merely enhanced with simple and modest tools. Radiant yet humble. And when you eschew one of those conflicting ideals, that makes you either a homely troll or a shallow bitch.

But drag queens labor for hours to beat their faces into exaggeratedly feminine shapes, they wriggle into rubber shapewear and suffocating panty hose, they work *hard* to carefully craft an illusion of womanhood. And above all, they take great pleasure in the exercise. This pleasure alone is countercultural, and women especially can appreciate it. Because one of the loudest social messages that American girls receive growing up is this: labor constantly to look conventionally beautiful—but don't you dare enjoy the process. Be quiet about it. Suffer through your waxes and dye jobs with dignity, breathe slowly in your tight skirts, dab on your anti-aging night cream with the bathroom door firmly closed. Drag bucks back at this whole idea with the full force of two double-wide buttocks. Drag creates a beauty that is loud, dramatic, and which exists for its own glorious and simple purpose. It's no wonder that many women look upon the boldness of drag queens and, rightly, exalt in joyful worship.

It's easy to assume that drag queens, in their lace and glitter and mile-wide painted grins, are exclusively cheery and light. But the duality, the multiplicity of queendom runs deep. When rocks and bottles started flying at the Stonewall Inn, legend has it that one of those first flings came from iconic New York City queen Marsha P. Johnson. She was celebrating her 25th birthday on the night of the famed police raid on Stonewall on June 28, 1969. Almost exactly 20 years before Matt was born, queens like Marsha had had enough of the brutal, regular abuses of law enforcement, so they picked up what was available—in some tellings it's bricks, in some it's bottles or shot glasses—and threw it cop-ward. The story of the uprising has reached mythic proportions, so much so that people online joke that Nicholas Cage or certain snack foods "threw the first brick." But the mythic proportions of the tale are a testament to that night's lasting impact. Out of the ashes of Stonewall, the Gay Liberation Front was formed, and their bold activism forced the powerful to make way for many of the queer rights we enjoy today. If Marsha did throw a bottle at any point that night, here's hoping it was a classic American Budweiser.

Matt would've been a big-time bottle-thrower if he'd lived to see our current political climate. When we were younger, I'd sometimes read Matt's contrarianism as petty. He was so often using it to be a bit of a pill, to feel bad for himself, to excuse bad behavior. But he also used his powers for good. He regularly put his ass out on the front lines to holler for justice, and he didn't expect any praise for it. Matt didn't have a Twitter account—he just went out in the real world and did what was right as if it were routine, expected, and the bare minimum. He knew justice doesn't come from sitting around making construction paper cards for people and asking very, very nicely for basic dignities. Matt knew sometimes you had to get a little loud, a little elbow-y, a little discomfort-inducing to get it.

I know that Matt would be at every protest if he were still here. He'd be organizing. He'd be supporting. Maybe he'd even be finding new meaning in this era of mainstream activism and resistance. If he had had the chance to really recover, he could've been happy. *Jesus*, I realize quietly standing in the crowd, *he really could have been.*

Bushwig's main stage is thumping. Chris of Hur is in the midst of an elaborate number, taking layers of her chunky costume off and placing them on a maypole, creating a sort of master beast penis-person, complete with giant felted balls. Dolly Parton's campy cover of "Lay Your Hands on Me" blares from the speakers while a tank-top–clad gaggle of guys up front raise their arms up in faux worship. Once the penis-person is finished, Chris of Hur picks it up and starts jousting it toward the crowd. Pieces are falling off, flopping onto the stage or into the crowd, but everyone's eating it up.

I think about how soft and cushiony those balls look and how nice it'd feel to be standing on them. I don't want to admit it to myself, but these fabulous shoes of mine are really starting to hurt. The heels are putting a foreign-feeling pressure on the balls of my feet. Things are starting to tingle and not in a fun half-drunk way.

Just stick it out. Alyssa Edwards will be on soon, then you can go sit down, I pep-talk to myself like I learned to do in my half marathon, feeling a little pathetic.

The performances are getting increasingly elaborate. Club kid dance moves, dips and splits, outfit changes, caged heels and black leotards on broad-shouldered backup dancers. After a few heavily choreographed performances, the next queen emerges in a dance-unfriendly fitted floor length gown. She's cheekily nicknamed "The Mouth," and once she starts her number, I understand why. It's not about choreography for her. She's serving pure face: quivering her lips perfectly to match the vocal ornamentation of the pop star who sings the dramatic ballad that's blasting from the speakers.

My spiked heels feel like they're painfully merging with my heels, like a scene from a David Cronenberg movie, twisted gooey special FX showing the shoes becoming an unwelcome extension of my fibula. I'm also crying, all of a sudden, watching The Mouth manipulate her painted lips. There's a stabbing sensation in the left side of my rib cage as I realize, viscerally, not just that my brother is dead but that my brother's gone and he's not coming back. He's missing all of this, and he'll miss everything that comes after it, too.

Well, this was bound to happen. Weeping to the top 40, surrounded by grown adults wearing rubber false cleavage.

I flick tears off my cheeks in a hurry, embarrassed, feeling exposed. The crowd fills in tighter behind me, and I avoid eye contact with groups of people as they weave their way forward. The crowd churns and I teeter to the side to accommodate the movement. My ankles throb. I want to rip my fucking feet off.

There's a tap on my shoulder. I brush my damp face one last time, then turn around with the sort of total relaxation a woman feels when she's certain she's not about to be hit on by a straight man.

It's the guy directly behind me doing the tapping. He's got large round eyes emphasized with heavy black kohl liner, and his closely cropped textured hair is dyed lavender. He's wearing a sailor striped tank top and silvery body glitter on his bony shoulders. He extends his hand toward me, a small bag perched in his palm, like he's passing the collection dish at Mass. I look at the bag, and it's filled with something frilly and pink. He smiles and jerks his hand slightly, making it clear that he's offering the bag to me. I take it and inspect it. It's filled with rose petals, smelling like they were just plucked. I pull one out and run it between my thumb and forefinger, admiring the smooth velvety flesh. I still don't quite understand what I'm supposed to be doing with these petals. They're certainly not being passed around just so strange women in uncomfortable shoes can enjoy a moment of sensory indulgence. I look back to the man for guidance. He notes my confusion and with only the slightest eye roll at my ignorance—he mimics a fancy jump-shot movement with his hand, like an Alvin Ailey interpretation of the NBA.

"To *throw*," he mouths exaggeratedly so that I can understand him despite the pulsating Ke$ha.

Oh, joy! I feel a little thrill in that moment of comprehension. I get it! I get it now! I look ahead at the crowd, and just then, someone up front throws a handful of rose petals at the stage. The petals catapult upward, surrounding Horrorchata in a sweet cloud as she struts on the catwalk. Then a split second later, the explosion is over—every petal falls back down and lands on the stage, on the floor, in people's hair, and on their shoulders. I look back at lavender hair guy, and he's still smiling, this time closer to laughing at me, I think. I roll my eyes at myself, make a sort of "duh" palm-to-forehead gesture, and nod "thank you." He laughs a little, shakes his head, and turns his focus back to the stage.

I turn back too, dipping my hand into the bag and filling my palm with flowers. My shoes don't hurt anymore because my feet are numb—but finally it's that half-drunk, pleasant numbness. The petals are warm in my hand. My throat is full and pulsating. My eyes are filling up with tears again, but I don't mind anymore. I'm smiling. The crowd is dancing, churning as a single warm entity, and no one is looking at me. I'll wait for just the right moment to throw my handful skyward and watch the velvety petals rain back down, a little explosion of carefully executed beauty that will follow the rules of physics and eventually stop all on its own, exactly when it's supposed to.

Acknowledgments

To my intrepid agent, Priya Doraswamy, and my sure-footed editor, Jake Bonar: Thank you for your faith in this book and in the value of difficult stories. Thank you to my friends and early readers, especially Lindsay Berrigan, Erin Calligan Mooney, Colleen Dinn, Kristen Everman, Madeline Felix, Ellen Haun, Emily Kunkel, and Devon Tarby. Thank you to Matt's loved ones who shared memories with me, especially Brian Biciocchi, Annie Fallon, and Taylor Swyter. Thank you to Caroline Davidson for answering my random questions about dense scientific research with generosity and genius. Thank you to my dog, Eddie, who cannot read but deserves my formal gratitude regardless.

Thank you to Casey Scieszka and Steven Weinberg of the Spruceton Inn, at whose artists' residency this book first began to take shape. Thank you to the fine folks at the outlets that first published my writing about my brother, especially *Brooklyn Magazine*, *Filter* magazine, and *HuffPost*.

To my brother, Matt: I wrote a whole book about you but still can't really describe what you meant to me and countless others. I miss you. See you around.

To my parents, Mike and Janet: Thank you for your love and support and for accepting my burning need to tell this story. And to this project's first editor and most spirited cheerleader, Corey Beasley: Thank you. I love you.